The Gospel of John
and the Religious Quest

The Gospel of John and the Religious Quest

Historical and Contemporary Perspectives

JOHANNES NISSEN

PICKWICK *Publications* • Eugene, Oregon

THE GOSPEL OF JOHN AND THE RELIGIOUS QUEST
Historical and Contemporary Perspectives

Copyright © 2013 Johannes Nissen. All rights reserved. Except for brief quotations in critical publications or reviews, no part of this book may be reproduced in any manner without prior written permission from the publisher. Write: Permissions, Wipf and Stock Publishers, 199 W. 8th Ave., Suite 3, Eugene, OR 97401.

Pickwick Publications
An Imprint of Wipf and Stock Publishers
199 W. 8th Ave., Suite 3
Eugene, OR 97401

www.wipfandstock.com

ISBN 13: 978-1-62032-466-0

Cataloging-in-Publication data:

Nissen, Johannes.

    The gospel of John and the religious quest : historical and contemporary perspectives / Johannes Nissen.

    viii + 210 pp. ; 23 cm—Includes bibliographical references.

    ISBN 13: 978-1-62032-466-0

    1. Bible. John—Criticism, interpretation, etc. 2. Religiousness. 3. Religion. I. Title.

BS2615 N45 2013

Manufactured in the USA

Based on the Danish book: *Vejen, sandheden og livet: Johannesevangeliet og den religiøse søgen* (Aarhus: Forlaget Univers, 2010).

Contents

Preface vii

1 Introduction: Aim and Method of This Study 1

Part One: Images of a Greater Reality—Interpretation of Selected Texts

2 The Distinctive Character of the Fourth Gospel 17

3 The Word 25

4 Rebirth 43

5 Water 59

6 Bread 78

7 Light 89

8 Truth 104

9 Love 120

10 Way 134

11 Tree 151

Part Two: The Gospel of John and the Religious Dialogue

12 The Fourth Gospel, Incarnation, and Inculturation 159

13 Models for Dialogue with Other Religions 167

14 Images of Christ 173

15 The Truth and the Love—On Criteria for Religious Dialogue 185

16 The Johannine Experience of Faith 194

Bibliography 201

Preface

In 2010 I published a book in Danish on the Gospel of John and the religious quest that forms the basis of the present volume. Although the content and outline are essentially the same, the English version is not a direct translation. Some minor changes and additions have been made for the following reasons:

In the first place the present book is aimed at an international circle of readers. In consequence, more literature is surveyed and the number of references to the scholarly debate has increased.

Second, I have taken into consideration new books and articles published since the Danish original. The debate on the character of mission and religious dialogue is an ongoing process. It is my hope that this publication will make a contribution to this discussion.

My purpose with this publication is not to present a new commentary on the Fourth Gospel, but rather to interpret selected parts of the Gospel with a specific view to the religious quest and the encounter of religions. The title of the book has a twofold meaning. On the one hand it reflects the understanding that the Gospel in its origin was part of a dialogue with people of various religious traditions. On the other hand it indicates how the Gospel is used today—by Christians and non-Christians in a vivid dialogue with those who live in non-Christian religious traditions.

Biblical quotations are from the New Revised Standard Version (NRSV) unless otherwise stated. Translations of quotations that I myself have made are marked with an asterisk.

Special thanks are due to Edward Broadbridge, who read and corrected the English text. I am also grateful to Aarhus University Research Foundation for financial support for the linguistic revision. Finally, I would like to thank Pickwick Publications for their readiness to publish this book.

Johannes Nissen
Aarhus, February 2013

1

Introduction

Aim and Method of This Study

The Religious Quest and the Religious Encounter

Individualism and Religious Diversity as a Challenge

IN RECENT YEARS CHURCH and Christianity have faced a number of challenges, including two crucial questions: How should the church respond to the religious quest in our time? And how should the church be involved in the issues raised by the religious encounter and religious dialogues? The two questions are closely related, since people are searching not only for Christianity but also for other religions and philosophies.

My concern here is to consider how from a Christian perspective, and in particular via the Fourth Gospel, we may be engaged in a dialogue with the religious diversity of our time. Throughout the book I employ the terms "religious quest" and "religious encounter," but with an emphasis on the former. This is due to two considerations. First, the term "religious quest" is conceived of as being more comprehensive than "religious encounter." Second, while "religious quest" is primarily linked to the personal aspect, "religious encounter" may point to an understanding of faith *systems*.

The Gospel of John and the Religious Quest

In other words: the first term is about faith meeting faith, while the second is more about the encounter *between* religions.

The religious landscape today is undergoing a fundamental change, characterized in particular by two trends: individualization and religious diversity. The religious scene is dominated by globalization and pluralism, and when the world is "one world," the religious encounter occurs everywhere. No longer do the different religions live in splendid isolation in diverse places, now they are potentially everywhere.

In such a situation we have all become autonomous, and can choose a creative approach to the religious diversity by pursuing our own personal religiosity. The outcome is a kind of patchwork, with many people finding inspiration in various religious traditions and choosing a multi-religious identity in consequence: in such a free-for-all the incarnate can even become the reincarnated. This religious change has been described as a transition *from classical Christian faith to "new spirituality,"* and is marked by a number of traits. It is a change from the transcendent God to the God within, from God as lord and master to God as friend and helper, from "understanding" to "experience," from "faith as truth" to "faith as trust," from a philosophical truth to a psychological truth, from hierarchical relations to reciprocal relations.[1]

Such individualism is a challenge to the church as the *body* of Christ. Is this self-centeredness compatible with Christian faith? Does it reflect a personal responsibility in a new and significant way? By way of answer we can begin by asserting that it is an important function of the church and the Gospel to be present in the individual life and to take part in forming it.[2] At the same time, the insistence on the church as community and the individual as self-focused must not be seen as mutually exclusive. They may well be mutually interactive and even mutual correctives of each other. In the years to come this relationship between communal worship and personal spirituality will be decisive for the church.[3]

The present situation is not unlike that in the first century AD.[4] The Graeco-Roman world was dominated by a common culture, usually called

---

1. For a full list of the characteristics of the classical Christian faith and new spirituality respectively, see Mortensen, "For All God's people," 476.

2. Ibid., 476.

3. Bollmann, *Kirke til tiden*, 90–92.

4. There is a risk of using an analogical model which is too simple. To avoid such a risk, one must argue that patterns and paradigms exercise a normative role through analogical imagination, which seeks to act in new situations in ways that are faithful

Aim and Method of This Study

Hellenism.[5] But at the same time Hellenism was marked by a great variety of religions and philosophies, and Christianity was just one among many.[6] So what was the specific character of Christianity compared to other religious movements in the first century?

The most immediate way of answering this question is to study the New Testament writings, in particular those books addressed to a Hellenistic audience. The Gospel of John is one of these. The presupposition for this claim is that the readers of this Gospel are living in different religious and cultural settings. At the same time the Gospel of John points unambiguously to the unique salvation in Jesus Christ. It is precisely these two features—the wide spectrum of the audience and salvation in Christ alone—that make John's Gospel particularly relevant to the encounter of contemporary Christians with other religious traditions. The crucial questions then as now are: How can we maintain genuine Christian integrity while at the same time being open to people of other faiths? And how is it possible to combine the two dimensions of openness to religious diversity, yet belief that salvation is exclusively bound to Christ?

The Gospel of John and the Encounter with Modern Religiosity and Spirituality

My purpose here is not to present a new commentary on the Gospel of John but rather to interpret selected parts of the Gospel with a specific view to the religious quest and the encounter of religions. The title of the book, "The Gospel of John and the Religious Quest," has a twofold meaning. On the one hand it reflects the understanding that the Gospel in its origin was part of a dialogue with people from a variety of religious traditions. On the other hand it indicates how the Gospel is used today—by Christians and non-Christians—in vivid dialogue with those who live in other religious

---

to the original pattern. In order to be both free and faithful, modern believers reason by analogy from the earlier interaction that is witnessed in the biblical text to a similar response to the challenge of their own time. Analogical thinking relies on imagination and the ability to discern similarities and differences between one situation and another (Spohn, *What Are They Saying about Scripture and Ethics?*). On analogical imagination, see also Nissen, "Bible and Ethics," 86–87.

5. On characteristics of Hellenistic culture, see Stambaugh and Balch, *The Social World of the First Christians*.

6. This reminds us of the modern phenomenon of globalization. For further characteristics of globalization in early Christianity and today, see Nissen, "Mission and Globalization in a New Testament Perspective."

traditions than the Christian.[7] Three ways of using the Gospel should be considered.

First, the Gospel is used by Christian theologians who wish to dialogue with representatives of other religions, such as Buddhists, Hindus, and Muslims. Examples are given in the first part of this book. It is interesting to note that the Fourth Gospel has played a special role in India. An Indian bishop is reported as having said that while the Catholic Church is primarily Petrine, i.e., inspired by the pope as the follower of Peter; and while the Protestant Church is primarily Pauline due to its doctrine of justification by faith, the Indian Church is first and foremost Johannine. It is no coincidence that one of the great theologians of the last century, A.J. Appasamy, published several books on Indian mysticism and the Gospel of John.[8]

Second, it is clear that the Fourth Gospel enjoys a certain popularity among representatives of non-Christian world religions, and among those who are active in the New Age milieu and new spirituality. To support the first observation we can cite the various attempts to combine Christianity and Buddhism, or to prove that John's Gospel is rooted in Buddhist ideas. Some argue for "the Christian Buddha," others for a "Buddhist Jesus."[9] An example of the second observation is the work of Rudolf Steiner, who wrote several commentaries on the Gospel of John.[10] Sections of his work will be discussed in the first part of this book. Interest in the Fourth Gospel among new religious movements is probably linked to the disputed claim that it is related to Gnosticism. Some New Testament scholars assert its gnostic character while others argue the opposite, albeit accepting that its vocabulary has certain similarities with the gnostic worldview. The Gospel's relation to Gnosticism will be discussed in Part Two under the heading: "As a Gnostic to the Gnostics"?

---

7. The present investigation only sporadically touches upon the relation between the Fourth Gospel and Judaism. From a historical point of view this relation is important (see also chapter 4 of this book). Biblical scholars have produced a number of analyses. For instance, there has been much discussion as to whether the Gospel has some anti-Semitic dimensions, a question that has also relevance for the present dialogue between Christianity and Judaism.

8. E.g., Appasamy, *Christianity as Bhakti Marga*.

9. Borup, *Dansk Dharma*, 22–24. Notto Thelle (*Buddha og Kristus*, 89–102) gives a review and critical evaluation of some recent books.

10. Steiner, *The Gospel of St. John*; and Steiner, *The Gospel of St. John and Its Relation to the Other Gospels*.

Aim and Method of This Study

Finally, in recent years the Gospel of John has proved to be a great inspiration to those working with Christian spirituality. Its metaphorical language and meditative form appeal to people engaged in spiritual guidance and theology of pilgrimage. An example of this is Lene Højholt's *Vejen: Meditativ fordybelse in Johannesevangeliet* ("The Way: A meditative immersion in the Gospel of John") from 2006, see also the survey and comment on this work in chapter 10 of this study.

All these examples of contemporary readings of the Fourth Gospel raise the question of whether it is possible to establish any criteria for a religious dialogue. Or to put it in another way: How far can Christians go in dialogue without betraying the essence of the Christian gospel? The question will be addressed throughout the book and discussed in greater detail in Part Two.

Methodological Reflections

Bible Readings—Academic and Experiential Approaches

For the past few centuries the study of biblical texts has been dominated by an academic approach, aiming at objective, even "neutral," analyses of the texts. It has often been taken for granted that this approach was in opposition to an immediate and more popular reading. Today, many scholars try to combine the two ways of reading, an approach that is characteristic also of this book. However, in combining both approaches we must be aware of the strengths and weaknesses of both.

The academic approach covers a variety of different readings. The most widespread method is historical criticism which is at one and the same time both necessary yet insufficient. It is *necessary* because it takes seriously the human side of the revelation; the incarnation is the theological basis for the historical analysis of texts.

1. It insists on the text in its "otherness"; in this way it protects the text against subjective wishes and ideological exploitation.
2. It investigates the historical and linguistic peculiarity of the text and thereby points to its message.
3. It is actually self-critical; the interpreters should be prepared to abandon what they know in order to learn something new.

4. It contributes to an open dialogue about the Bible; the results can be tested in a public, inter-subjective discussion.

However, historical criticism also has a number of *weaknesses*. Firstly, by concentrating on discovering the historical meaning of the texts it can easily create a distance to present time. If the research is content with this, the biblical text will never have a chance to show its actual relevance. Second, this approach is strongly dominated by the professionals. They often disagree on the interpretation, or their interpretations are difficult to take in at a glance. All this creates the feeling of alienation. Third, historical criticism is oriented towards a cognitive apprehension. Yet reality is not just that which we can comprehend with our reason; it also includes existential questions and experiences. The historical method therefore needs to be supplemented with other methods that are open to the inclusion of contemporary experiences in the interpretation of biblical texts.

It is here that experiential readings become interesting, comprising as they do a wide variety of approaches that include psychological readings, liberation theology, interactive Bible reading, and didactics of symbols.[11] The latter, in particular, is of special interest in this book; cf. the paragraph "The language of symbols and metaphors" in chapter 2 of this book. As an alternative to describing these readings as "experiential" we may also call them *creative Bible studies*. The term "Bible study" is a child of a literary culture in which the capacity for meditation often remains underdeveloped. Likewise, "the tendency to individualism and the focus on privacy can be fostered by the printed book. Each person has his or her own Bible to read and explain as one wishes."[12] It is therefore a challenge to liberate the Bible from being captured by a one-sided literary culture.

Academic Bible studies tend to focus only on rational thinking and intellectual activity. But according to the love commandment in Mark 12:29–30 we must love God with all our heart, soul, mind, and strength—and not just our reason. The command to love insists that the *whole person* has to be taken into consideration, including the emotions, experiences, intuition, and the body.

Creative Bible study places a special emphasis on ordinary people, who themselves are encouraged to work creatively with the texts. Both the

---

11. A survey of the strengths and weaknesses of the different methods is given in Nissen, "Mødet mellem Bibelen og nutidens mennesker," 73–89.

12. Weber, *Experiments with Bible Study*, 10–11.

"insight of the feelings" and the "knowledge of the brain" are important. The Bible can be studied in a creative way by everyone—professionals and amateurs, scholars and students, clergy and laity, male and female alike. All kinds of experiences count. The only presupposition is that we accept the methods employed as valid. Creative Bible study is based on the conviction that Scripture is not reserved for theologians or church leaders and that the Holy Spirit is present and active in the life of ordinary people. The meaning of the Bible is not restricted to what was said by its authors to its first readers; it is relevant to God's people at any time in history, including the present.

The Christian community interprets its life in the light of the biblical texts, in particular those concerning Jesus Christ. While constituting the decisive framework of interpretation for the community, they nevertheless depend on the context in which they are heard and read. It is the context that gives the foundation a present interpretation. Hence, in any Bible study we must take into consideration the twin poles of text and context, the latter being the life we are living and the experiences we have. There is an essential interaction between the biblical text and the present experience. There is no unambiguous answer to the question: "What comes first: the text or our life?" since the text interprets our life; and our life interprets the text.[13]

The Cut and Thrust of Question and Answer

The encounter between biblical text and modern man is characterized by a double movement. We bring our questions and our own situation to the text and the text brings its questions and its statements to us. We read the text and the text "reads" us. But how can this encounter between the text and our life become an authentic dialogue? Here we must see the reciprocal interaction between question and answer. In principle there are three possibilities:

(a) *The church provides the answer—but it is not an answer to people's questions.* This is the one-way model: The church proclaims its message but without listening to the real questions posed by today's people. We meet this form of communication when for instance we see emblems with statements like: "Christ is the answer, God's answer." In such cases we have to find out

---

13. Hammar, *Det som hörs*, 21–24; Nissen, "Mødet mellem Bibelen og nutidens mennesker," 49.

to whom the answer is given. What is the benefit of answering if no one is putting a question? It is in fact a problem if the church has the ultimate and final answers, while at the same time the religious and theological questions are situated in different contexts and are asked in a different language and in conditions that differ from the answer.

(b) The Bible does not answer. The Bible in many cases is a strange text. It deals with a number of issues that do not seem relevant in our part of the world, nor does it address issues that we would like to know about, such as abortion, gene technology, and nuclear weapons. We are asking too much of the Bible here; it cannot answer such questions directly. But it does answer the *first* Christians directly, so we can gain a better understanding of *them*—and then we shall discover that they often struggled with the basic problems that we face—and even from our presuppositions.

From a methodological point of view we have to go into reverse. We must start with the answers in the text and work backwards through them to find the questions. Using the methods of biblical research we can clarify the meaning of the text with a certain assurance, that is a *historical reading*, and afterwards we may ask what the text means for us today, that is an *actual reading*.

Here a distinction is made between a text's *meaning* ("Sinn") and its *significance* ("Bedeutung").[14] A given text has only one meaning, which is the author's meaning (what the author intended to say), but it can have many significances. The significance is the result of the *application* and *appropriation* of the text in a *new* situation. From this it follows that it is as important to establish what the text *means* today (its significance) as it is to find out what it *meant* in the first century.

To conclude, the interplay between question and answer cannot allow Christians to deliver their answers without knowing the questions, nor can it turn to the Bible alone for a simplified solving of a problem.

(c) The authentic dialogue. Here the starting-point is an analysis of the concrete questions of our times with the intention of coming to a better understanding of these questions and finding the Christian answer.[15] According

---

14. Nissen, *New Testament and Mission*, 15.

15. Traditionally theologians have defined the sources of theology as Scripture, Tradition, Experience and Reason. The Indian theologian Thomas Thangaraj has suggested the addition of a fifth source, namely dialogue: "Dialogue as a source brings new knowledge and opens our minds into newer ways of thinking and knowing" (Thangaraj, "What Are the Implications of My Experience of Interfaith Dialogue for the Understanding of Christology?," 11).

to Johannes Aagaard, the Christian answer is given as a reply to the ancient search of humanity: "This means that we learn more about the answer of the Christian faith by having a fuller understanding of man's religious request. For instance, we do not understand the cosmic significance of the resurrection, if we do not know the concept of *samsara* (transmigration of souls) as a cosmic theory. We do not understand the essence of grace if we do not know the idea of *karma*. Likewise we do not understand the necessity of the theology of creation if we do not see the result of seeing the world as *maya*. And last, but not least we do not perceive who Jesus was and is, before we have realized that he refused to be a guru for the people."[16]

Mutual Critical Correlation

In recent times biblical studies have been marked by a shift of attention from the relationship between author and text to the interaction between text and reader.[17] A new model of interpretation has emerged, based on the belief that deep insight and relevance lie neither in the original meaning of the Bible alone nor in the contemporary context, but in the cut and thrust of question and answer between them. This model is that of a conversation.

The relation between text and context can be seen as a *fusion between two horizons*.[18] The text represents the first horizon, and the context of its readers is the second horizon. The ultimate goal of this model of "interpretation as conversation" is to fuse these horizons in a way that is true to the past and relevant to the present. In the fusion of the readers' world with the world of the text both are transformed. When readers enter the world of the text it transforms them by providing a new way of seeing and being; it offers them new possibilities. When the readers' world is brought to the text it transforms the text by allowing a plurality of possible meanings not perceived in the past to be appropriated by them in the present; it offers the text a new way of speaking.[19]

Any reading of the Bible will start with certain specific questions. We cannot take up some privileged place of neutrality or complete objectivity; it is from within our "life-worlds" that we engage in the reading task. This raises certain questions, however.[20] If our own life-worlds are the starting

---

16. Aagaard, "Den religiøse dimension," 19.*
17. Nissen, "Matthew, Mission and Method," 74–75.
18. Gadamer, *Truth and Method*, 101–21 and 293–326.
19. West, *Contextual Bible Study*, 44.
20. Green, "The Practice of Reading the New Testament," 415.

point for reading the Bible, will we not find in its pages only what we are looking for? Can we as readers be open to the *challenge* of the biblical text? Any use of Scripture must face the risk that the text becomes no more than a mirror reflecting what we want it to say. Some way of reading must be employed which allows the text to *speak* to us, and to serve as a window through which we see something besides our own thoughts.[21] This relation between the biblical text and our actual request may also be explained by means of the *concept of "correlation."* To understand this, reference is often made to Paul Tillich's "method of correlation," that is, the ideal of an interaction between God and humankind. Theology provides analyses of the human situation that provoke existential questions, and it demonstrates how the symbols in the Christian message answer these questions.

The work of theology can be compared to an ellipse with two foci: the existential question, and the Christian answer. For we have a double starting point: on the one hand an analysis of our present condition, on the other the statement of the biblical text. This question-answer correlation may of course result in a simplification, as there is a latent risk we will try to find opportune answers to our questions. Instead the relationship between the text and the interpreter should be seen as a mutual challenge. Sandra Schneiders notes that "for the dialogue between text and reader to be genuine, the text must maintain its identity, its 'strangeness', which both gifts and challenges the reader. It must be allowed to say what it says, regardless of whether this is comfortable or assimilable to the reader."[22]

What is the theological basis for this method of correlation? Any correlation presupposes that the biblical texts deal with the same basic questions asked by contemporary readers—about blessings, good fortune, sorrow, anxiety, hope, suffering etc. But the relation is not just that we ask the questions and the Bible provides the answers. The simple scheme of question and answer is rightly corrected by Eduard Schillebeeckx, who instead speaks of a mutual *critical* correlation between text and experience. Our experiences have a hermeneutical, critical productive force vis á vis the Christian tradition. And conversely, the Bible and the Christian tradition have an original, critical, and renewing effect on our human experiences. The biblical texts ask questions of us, and we are forced to transcend our own self-understanding.[23]

---

21. Cf. Nissen, *New Testament and Mission*, 15. On the problem of self-asserting Bible reading, see my remarks on Luke 4:16–30 (ibid., 68–69).

22. Schneiders, *The Revelatory Text*, 171.

23. Schillebeeckx, "Erfahrung und Glaube."

Aim and Method of This Study

The Gospel of John provides several examples of this interaction between question and answer, such as the concrete dialogues in John 3:1–21 and John 4:1–42; it is also illustrated by the use of the "I am" statements and the basic symbols, as we shall see in chapter 6 of this book.

The Five Languages of Religion

Some years ago Martin Lönnebo argued that there are five different languages in the world of religion, each language with its own specific mark. All these languages are known in Christianity.[24] The first is that of *experience*, which includes mysticism and prophecy and emphasizes the importance of the guidance of the Holy Spirit; in its foreground stands the subjective affirmation of what may be seen as objective in Scripture and tradition. The second language is that of *cult*, that is the worship of the church, its gospel, its prayers, and its sacraments. The third language is that of *action* which includes love and the ethical dimension. The fourth language is that of *doctrine*, the teaching of the church that gives knowledge and transmits the tradition. In this language the focus is on the objective aspect of Christianity. This mode of speaking is often despised but it is indispensable for authentic Christianity. Each of these languages is important, and they are united in a fifth language called the language of *unity*, which reflects a holistic view of humankind and the world. Unfortunately, the church often expresses itself in the language of *dis*unity. Spirit is dissociated from matter, love is separated from justice, fear of God is separated from love of our fellow beings, care for people is separated from responsibility for the created world, faith is separated from knowledge, the individual is separated from the structure, and science is separated from devotion.

The order of the five languages is not random. Nor is the space allotted to their various descriptions. The language of experience is mentioned first. In his preface to a book on Christianity and new spirituality Lönnebo claims that no one is short of spiritual experiences but they often lack the language to describe them. The experience of life as being more than the material and visible world is true for all people—from small children to the elderly, from the intellectually gifted to the mentally disabled. The language of experience is the most important language of all, and it therefore has to be developed and delineated. If this occurs, a liberating and mature spirituality may be created, which in turn can make us more human and lead

---

24. Lönnebo, *Religionens fem språk*.

us to a sense of community, to peaceful co-existence, and to taking great pleasure in all things in nature. The most important method is an open and respectful dialogue—both within Christianity and between Christians and representatives of other faiths. The more we open ourselves toward others, the greater is God. We will discover new well-springs in our own Christian tradition.[25]

Experience and Theological Reflection

In his description of experience Lönnebo highlights individual experience and mysticism. By contrast I wish to underline collective experience, as well as point out the interaction between practice and theory. This interaction is seen in many New Testament texts, two of which deserve our attention.

The first is the Emmaus story (Luke 24:13–35), which has three phases: (a) The *experience* of the disciples saddened at the events of Passover week. (b) The emergence of a stranger who shares his *reflection* on biblical texts with the disciples, and (c) The *turning-point* of reflection into the new practice of fellowship at the Eucharistic meal. It is essential that this experience be shared with others, and so the disciples return to Jerusalem and from this city the Christian mission takes its start (Luke 24:44–47).

Reading the Emmaus story we learn that understanding the Bible is more than just an intellectual exercise. Gesture and action have a similar importance, with the real *change* occurring at the breaking of the bread. Here Jesus discloses his identity, the eyes of the disciples are opened, and they recognize him. There is a problem, however, when it comes to transmittance and communication; it has to do with the relation between the experiences of the first communities and what is experienced in later generations. We cannot just repeat the first followers' experience of faith. This problem is reflected already in the New Testament, and it brings us to the second text.

The passage of 1 John 1:1–4 has four aspects that are expressed in various ways. The first aspect is *the experience of the disciples*: "what we have heard," "what we have seen with our eyes"; "what we have looked at and touched with our hands." The second aspect is *the Christ event*: "what was from the beginning"; "the word of life"; "the eternal life." The third aspect is *the communication*: "we have seen it and testify to it"; "and declare to you." And finally the fourth aspect which is *the goal*: "so that you also may have

---

25. Lönnebo, "Trons språk," 11–12.

fellowship with us"; "and truly our fellowship is with the Father and with his Son Jesus Christ."

This introduction to the First Epistle of John gives expression to the foundation of all Christianity, namely the concrete experience of Jesus, the Word that was incarnated. It is a new experience of what life is. At the same time the text poses a specific problem of the relationship between such alien experiences and our own. The experiences of Jesus in the flesh came at a specific time and cannot be repeated. But they can be proclaimed for another group of people who in their specific situation can enjoy fellowship with Christ and other Christians. Here we see how the text must be transmitted in a double sense. It has to be a bridge over the distance in time, and it has to create a new fellowship.

Experience undoubtedly plays a significant role in reading and understanding biblical texts—in particular the Fourth Gospel (see also the paragraph "Come and see!" in Part Two). But it is also important that we do not overlook the interplay between experience and reflection, for there is a risk here of overemphasizing the role of the experience.[26]

In a comment on the document *Tro i lære* Niels Henrik Gregersen rightly warns against the risk of what he calls the "fundamentalism of experience." We each have all kinds of experiences in many different contexts, yet we are all responsible for considering which of them are the most important. When encountering spiritual currents we may be tempted to reduce Christianity to a religion of experience or to say along with one of the conversation partners in the book who says: "[W]hat is real Christianity is the experience of what has an effect on us. People have a claim on experiences. Christianity is a religion of experience."[27] However, according to Gregersen, Christianity cannot be defined as a religion based on experiences, for "if that were the case, it would have become a backward-looking religion, based on experiences from the past—instead of being open to the present time in the hope of a new future."[28]

---

26. The relation between the experience of the first Christians and our own experiences is discussed in an important article by Sauter ("Wie kann Theologie aus Erfarhrung entstehen"). He asks if we are able to formulate authentic experiences without just repeating previous experiences. The dilemma can be put as follows: On the one hand stand the biblical texts, which came about in a very unique historical situation; hence, they reflect specific experiences. They are seen as a sort of "primordial" (original) experience and it is presupposed that we should try to imitate them. On the other hand the biblical texts belong to a concrete historical situation which is impossible to imitate or copy.
27. *Tro i lære*, 23.*
28. Gregersen, "Kirkens grænsegængere," 38.*

There is a need for a balance between experience and theological reflection. The dialectic between "the text" of life (experience) and the text of the Bible is the kernel of the interpretative enterprise.[29] Without the interaction between the two entities we have either a theology from above which neglects the present context, or a theology from below which uses the Bible to illustrate and validate a predetermined activity. There is a need for a perspective that involves a view from above and below simultaneously.

---

29. For further reflections on this issue, see Nissen, "Scripture and Experience as the Double Source of Mission," 182–86.

Part One

Images of a Greater Reality—
Interpretation of Selected Texts

2

The Distinctive Character of the Fourth Gospel

The Category of Space and the Formation of Images

READING JOHN'S GOSPEL IS like looking at a Chinese print.[1] In the foreground we see an everyday scene drawn very realistically—a water-carrier crossing a bridge or a sage meditating under a tree. Similarly, John paints only a few scenes from Jesus' life, drawing them out with many realistic details so that they often fill a whole chapter: for instance, the night conversation with Nicodemus or the meeting with the Samaritan woman at the well. Behind this foreground Chinese prints usually show a landscape with trees, mountains, a lake or other natural scenery, but through a haze as it were. Often a third dimension can be discerned, a horizon vaguely visible where heaven and earth meet. It is just so with John's Gospel. There are deeper levels of meaning within and behind the scenes and sayings from Jesus' life which he reports.

John's Gospel invites prayer and meditation rather than intellectual analysis. It is a *vision* of Jesus rather than a story or explanation of him. When the Greeks approached a disciple they did not ask, "Sir, tell us about Jesus and explain him to us." According to John's testimony they said:

---

1. Weber, *Experiments with Bible Study*, 213–14.

Part One: Images of a Greater Reality

"Sir, we wish to *see* Jesus" (12:21). As with a Chinese print, John's Gospel invites us to "see" Jesus.

Traditional research in the Gospel of John has placed a strong emphasis on the category of time. This is especially characteristic of the existential analysis by Rudolf Bultmann. The focus is on realized eschatology. It is argued that elements concerned with the future have been added by a later redactor of the Gospel. However, recent research points to a combination of both the realized and the final eschatology. Present and future elements are united in the figure of Christ.[2]

This emphasis on the category of time seems too strong. Inspired by social anthropology a number of scholars claim that the categories of *place and space* are actually of greater significance. Thus, Halvor Moxnes underlines how changes in identity are connected with removal from one place to another—and to a new experience of space. Meaning and identity are connected to *place* rather than time.[3] According to traditional theories it is the locality that creates the person and their character: "Can anything good come out of Nazareth?" (John 1:46). The concept behind this kind of statement is that those who know the place also know the character of the person coming from it.[4]

These observations have relevance for the Fourth Gospel. The incarnation means that Jesus is connected to a specific place. In addition, it is interesting to note that the Gospel in fact contains several characteristics that reveal the importance of locality. The first half of the Gospel depicts Jesus moving *from place to place*, and there is various topographical information that presumably reflects primitive tradition. As an example we can cite the well at Sykar in John 4.

The religious significance of space is underlined by Mircea Eliade in *The Sacred and the Profane*, in which he analyses how "sacred space" is established in the profane world. Crucial to his thinking is the concept of hierophany. In all traditions there are examples of sacred places, centers where a primeval hierophany sanctifies undifferentiated, profane space, and ensures that sacredness will continue there: "For it is the break effected

---

2. Nissen, "Sted og rum i Johannesevangeliet," 24.
3. Moxnes, "Jesu galilæiske kontekst," 106.
4. See also Moxnes's book, *Putting Jesus in his Place*, which is a study of Jesus in his environment. The goal of the book is to study the spatial dimensions of the historical Jesus and uncover identities that were "located, developed and sustained in place" (ibid., 2). Place, according to Moxnes, is not only geographical but also social, cultural, and ideological (ibid., 4).

in space that allows the world to be constituted, because it reveals the fixed point, the central axis for all future orientation. The manifestation of the sacred ontologically founds the world."[5] If the world is to be lived in, it must be founded: "The discovery or projection of a fixed point—the center—is equivalent to the creation of the world."[6] The threshold is the boundary or frontier that differentiates between two opposing worlds—and at the same time the paradoxical place where those worlds communicate, where passage from the profane to the sacred world becomes possible. Sacred spaces, such as temples, constitute an opening in the upward direction.[7]

A threshold and a door are symbols of the transition between the profane and the divine world. In the Fourth Gospel Jesus himself is considered to be the new temple (John 2: 21), the meeting-point of eternity and time (1:51). In him divine reality is revealed to humankind, and as its center he bestows the meaning from which all other meanings derive.[8]

The Language of Symbols and Metaphors

While the first three gospels write and think in metaphors drawn from social and political life (kingdom, justice, servants, masters, etc.), the Gospel of John uses a "biological" language, speaking much of birth and life and growth. Thus Jesus came that we should have life, and that abundantly (10:10). In John it is all about life and the process of life.[9] Various metaphors link this experience and process of life fundamentally to the story of Jesus. These metaphors are often universal, since they address all human conditions of life. We are born into the world, and one day we must leave it. We encounter forces that promote life, and forces that destroy it. At the same time the way in which these metaphors are stamped depends on a number of historical and sociological factors. By connecting these metaphors and symbols with the story of Jesus John shows that eternity may be experienced in historical time, that Jesus gives us life in its authentic meaning, and that fellowship with him gives us a share in eternal life.[10]

5. Eliade, *The Sacred and the Profane*, 21.
6. Ibid., 22.
7. Ibid., 26.
8. Cahill, "The Johannine *Logos* as Center."
9. Stendahl, *Energy for Life*, 28.
10. Mogensen, *Således elskede Gud verden*, 51–52; cf. Stendahl, *Energy for Life*, 28: "The life of faith is the eternal life, it is a life called eternal since it is in communion and

Part One: Images of a Greater Reality

Most importantly in our context these symbols and metaphors are accessible to readers from a variety of cultural settings. They can be heard and understood by both Jews and Greeks. The Gospel is not written for insiders alone; rather it aims at a wide spectrum of readers.[11] In other words, the symbols are polyvalent—although there are limits to their potential of meaning.[12]

The Fourth Gospel has a great variety of symbols, such as life, light, water, bread, vine, and way. However, these symbols do not carry the same weight in the Gospel. Following R. Alan Culpepper we may distinguish between core symbols and peripheral symbols. Core symbols are those whose centrality is demonstrated by their higher frequency and their appearance in more important contexts. The three core symbols of the Gospel are light, water, and bread. Each of these points to Jesus' revelatory role and carries a heavy thematic load. To these are related several coordinate symbols, metaphors, and concepts in different passages, such as darkness, life, wine, flesh. Subordinate symbols can also be gathered around a core symbol. For example, among the subordinate symbols for light are lamps, fires, torches, lanterns, day (and night), morning, seeing, and healing the blind.[13] As mentioned, these symbols convey general and universal experiences about the meaning of life, in particular the three core symbols.

The fundamental meaning of the symbol of *light* is demonstrated in the Prologue that "links *logos*, life, and light so powerfully that the cluster dominates the symbolic system of the entire narrative."[14] The Word incarnate in Jesus is the exclusive source of life to humankind (1:4).

---

continuity with the eternal One. To John 'eternal' does not refer to the quantity of time, but to the quality of life (cf. 5:24)."

11. Cf. Koester, *Symbolism in the Fourth Gospel*; and MacRae, "The Fourth Gospel and *Religionsgeschichte*." Other scholars think that the Gospel has a sectarian character. According to Meeks ("The Man from Heaven in Johannine Sectarianism") the Gospel reflects a docetic tendency in Christology and ecclesiology.

12. See also Vellanickal, "The Gospel of John in the Indian Context," 149: "John's language has a distinctive and strongly universalistic character. This is particularly evident in his practice of employing words which have a double—Jewish and Hellenist—background. John's ideas and terminology may have developed within the Palestine heterodox Judaism under the influence of pressing Hellenism. But the very choice of such heterodox Judaistic language shows that John is deliberatively moving towards a wider world which seems approachable to him only through the kind of 'open-ended' language we find in John."

13. Culpepper, *Anatomy of the Fourth Gospel*, 189.

14. Ibid., 190.

The Distinctive Character of the Fourth Gospel

The symbolism of light is applied a number of times in the Gospel, e.g., 3:19–21. Of special importance is 8:12, where Jesus is called "the light of the world." For a more detailed analysis of the symbol of light see chapter 7 of this book.

The symbol of *water* appears frequently and with the most varied associations of any of John's symbols. We meet stories about being baptized with water, about water changed into wine, about being born by water and Spirit (rebirth), about the living water (the Samaritan woman), about the healing pool (Bethesda), about thirst, about streams of living water, about foot washing, and about water and blood coming from the side of the crucified Jesus. The use of the water symbol is so broad and varied that it may be difficult to find an overall pattern. In general, while water is a dominant motif and expanding core symbol in John, it is less unified than either light or bread. For a more detailed analysis of the symbol of water see chapter 5 of this book.

In contrast to the scattered and varied use of water, the symbol of *bread* is used in a more uniform way. The reason may be that in the Christian tradition bread is linked directly to the Eucharist. Attention is drawn in particular to John 6. In the "economy" of the Fourth Gospel true bread cannot be bought, it can only be given and received, cf. Philip's remark in 6:5. Furthermore, in the terminology of the Gospel, the one who provides the bread is himself the bread (6:35). Bread has a greater interpretive role than water in defining Jesus' identity.[15] More reflections on the importance of the image of bread may be found in chapter 6 of this study.

The uniqueness of the Fourth Gospel is that Jesus is introduced as the principal symbol in the Prologue. Jesus is *the Word* that became flesh and lived among us. He is the divine power of creation that is made concrete in the form of a man. The incarnation may be characterized as the most sublime form of symbolization. Indeed, in a sense we may speak of a twofold symbolization: "God's creative power is symbolized by a Word that again is symbolized by a human person in flesh and blood. In this symbol the spiritual and invisible is united with the bodily and visible to such a degree that the believing community can confess that it *has seen* his glory (John 1:14)."[16]

---

15. Ibid., 196.
16. Mogensen, "Symboler og symboldidaktik," 247.*

Part One: Images of a Greater Reality

The "I am"—sayings

John's symbolism is often combined with the so-called "I am" sayings. Here we can distinguish between two categories: (1) The absolute use with no predicate, for instance 8:58: "Before Abraham even was, I AM"; other examples are 8:24; 8:28 and 13:19. And (2) The more common use with a predicate nominative. In seven instances Jesus speaks of himself figuratively:

- I am the bread of life (6:35, 48)
- I am the light of the world (8:12)
- I am the gate (10:7, 9)
- I am the good shepherd (10:11, 14)
- I am the resurrection and the life (11:25)
- I am the way, the truth, and the life (14:6)
- I am the (true) vine (15:1, 5)

It is disputed whether these statements should be seen in the light of the Old Testament or of gnostic traditions. My response is that it is probably not an "either—or," but rather a "both—and." And yet, the main emphasis must be placed on the Old Testament statements of revelation, in particular Exod 3:14: "I am who I am." In this passage God declares that he will be present among his people as the one who protects, liberates, and holds faith with them. It is noteworthy that the "I am" words point to God's faithfulness as well as his exclusivism.

The "I am"—sayings are structured in the following way: (1) A self-presentation consisting of two elements: (a) "I am," and (b) a metaphor or a concept of salvation. Then follows (2) a call for decision consisting of: (a) an invitation and (b) a promise of salvation. In a few cases the promise is accompanied by, or replaced by, a warning or a threat (see 14:6 and 15:6).

The Human Quest

"What are you searching for?" (1:38; NRSV: "looking for"). These are the first words of Jesus in the Fourth Gospel. The question is addressed to the first two disciples who are together with John the Baptist near the Jordan river. As Jesus is coming towards him, John declares: "Here is the Lamb of

God who takes away the sin of the world." The disciples hear him say this and follow Jesus.

The question "What are you searching for?" is crucial in John's Gospel. In fact, the Gospel seems to be written with the purpose of showing that Jesus brings what people are looking for. The problem is that people do not always know what this is, as can be illustrated by the exchange of words between Jesus and his first disciples. Their response to Jesus' question in 1:38 is "Rabbi, where are you staying?" He answers with an invitation, "Come and see!" In consequence they go along to see where he is staying, and they remain with him that day (1:39). Something similar occurs in the calling of the other disciples. The words of Jesus are concise but full of overtones, and the disciples do not fully understand him. Yet in their encounter with Jesus they become aware of what they are lacking and they understand where they can find it.

Throughout the Fourth Gospel there are people searching for something—for fellowship with God and with other people, for the meaning of life, for a place to belong.[17] In 1:35–51 this search is undertaken by the first disciples, but elsewhere in the Gospel there are others coming from various religious and cultural traditions. Three passages are of particular importance. In chapter 3 Jesus is approached by Nicodemus, a representative of the *Jewish* leaders. In chapter 4 he meets a representative of the *Samaritans*. And in chapter 12 some *Greeks* wish to see him (12:20ff.)

Seeing Two Realities Simultaneously

In the chapters to follow a number of texts from the Fourth Gospel will be analyzed for two reasons: their special relevance in the religious quest and the religious encounter of today and their great importance for the theology of John's Gospel. For my purpose I am excluding certain central Johannine texts, such as most of the healing stories and the passion narrative.

The heading to Part One of the present book is "Images of a greater reality," since I am primarily concerned with images of life such as water, bread, light, the way, and the true vine. Yet in three cases the focus is on concepts rather than images, namely Word, Truth, and Love.

---

17. To be noticed is the parallel of the Areopagus speech in Acts 17:17–34. The Athenians are described as being very religious people (17:22) and it is said that "they would search for God and perhaps grope for him and find him" (17:27); see also Nissen, *New Testament and Mission*, 61–65.

Part One: Images of a Greater Reality

John takes as his starting-point material reality, while pointing simultaneously to a greater reality beyond. In the last verses of chapter 1 Jesus says to Nathanael: "You will see greater things than these" (v. 50). And immediately after this he uses an image: "Very truly: I tell you, you will see heaven opened and the angels of God ascending and descending upon the Son of Man" (v. 51). The remainder of the gospel is the story of *how* Jesus opens heaven for his disciples so that they *see* who he truly is.[18]

To speak of a "greater reality" does not necessitate a flight from our material reality. On the contrary, the Gospel witnesses to eternity becoming reality here and now. Indeed, we can only discover the meaning of life, and this encounter occurs precisely where we are. The point is that we see the invisible *in* the visible, the eternal *in* the ephemeral. The challenge is to see two realities at the same time (cf. my reflections on "bread" in chapter 6).[19] John is telling his audience that heaven meets earth in Christ.

---

18. Mogensen, *Således elskede Gud verden*, 120.
19. Bjerg, *Øjnenes faste*, 124.

3

The Word

HISTORICAL PERSPECTIVES

The Structure of the Prologue

THE PROLOGUE SETS THE tone for the rest of the Gospel.[1] It is the conceptual center from which all other dimensions radiate.[2] From this center light is thrown on other parts of the book and on all its important issues. These include an understanding of both the human quest for the meaning of life and the relation between the universal and the particular elements in Christianity. The relation between the universal and the specific Christian elements is crucial to understanding the structure of the Prologue. This text has a twofold character: on the one hand its structure is concentric; on the other it reflects a progress from the universal to the specific Christian. Both these aspects have relevance for contemporary interpretations of the Gospel.

The first approach may be characterized as literary; it reflects a *spacious* understanding. The structure of the Prologue is *concentric*, as is seen from the following scheme:

---

1. Barrett, *The Gospel According to John*, 130, rightly comments on v. 1: "John intends that the whole of his gospel shall be read in the light of this verse."

2. Cahill, "The Johannine *Logos* as Center," 65; Senior and Stuhlmueller, *The Biblical Foundations for Mission*, 284.

Part One: Images of a Greater Reality

    A. The Word was with God (vv.1–2)
      B. All things were made through the Word (v. 3)
        C. The Word was life and light for human beings (vv. 4–5)
          D. John witnessed to the light (vv. 6–8)
            E. The true light came to the world (vv. 9–10)
              F. He came to his own (people)—they received him not (v.11)
              F. Whoever received him . . . he gave power to become children of God (vv.12–13)
            E. The Word was made flesh (v. 14)
          D. John witnessed to the Word, who was before him (v. 15)
        C. From his fullness we have received grace (v.16)
      B. Grace and truth came through Jesus Christ (v. 17)
    A. The only Begotten Son—himself God—has interpreted God for us (v. 18).

In this structure a special emphasis is placed on the beginning (A) and the end (A), which correspond to each other, with the center at F-F, where it is underlined that those who have received Jesus have become God's children (vv.12–13). The Prologue is about the Word, but in the last two verses it is clarified that Christ is the only Begotten Son, himself God. In this way the Prologue describes a movement from God to God with the incarnation of the Word as a turning-point. The aim is that all those who receive the Word become part of this divine movement.[3] According to this understanding the main emphasis is on *soteriology*, the understanding of salvation.

The structure reflects John's understanding of God. In a number of passages God is presented as the ground of all being and the source of all life (cf. the paragraph "Witness" in Part Two). In this sense God is greater than anything else.[4] This observation is relevant to how we nowadays can be engaged in a dialogue of religions, since the transcendence of God is underlined by other religions than Christianity, e.g., Islam. But the Gospel of John does not stop there of course. The book not only says that the Son is subordinated to the Father, but it also insists on the unity between Father

---

3. Kieffer, *Johannesevangeliet*, 19.

4. Cf. Olsson, "*Deus semper major?*" This point is underlined by John's mission theology. There are four types of sending in the Fourth Gospel (John the Baptist, Jesus himself, the Paraclete, and the disciples). All of them revolve around Jesus: John the Baptist announces his coming; the Paraclete confirms his presence; and the disciples proclaim his Word to the world. But the endpoint of John's mission is not Jesus but the Father. The Father, alone is *not* sent. He is the origin and goal of all the testimony of the Gospel, cf. John 1:1–18 and 17:20–23 (Nissen, *New Testament and Mission*, 76).

and Son. And the crucial point in the last verse of the Prologue is that the Father has revealed himself in the Son. This may be interpreted as a critical concern for other religions, including Islam.

The second approach is the traditional historical-critical analysis, which is based on a *temporal* conception: a chronological axis, where v. 1 and v. 18 constitute the frame, and the climax is v. 14. The emphasis here is on *Christology*:

<u>v. 1   v. 14   v. 18</u>

According to this understanding the Prologue reflects *a course or a progress*. It has two major parts and a transitional passage. In the first half of the Prologue John uses general terms like Logos, God, all things, life, light, darkness, world etc. In the second half he uses specific Christian terms such as the only begotten Son, Father, grace, truth, Jesus, Christ, glory etc. John's attempt to express his experience of Christ in a language that would raise echoes in a non-Christian world around him should remain an inspiration and model for us to continue the same process in our own times.[5] The transition between the two halves is fluid. In the Greek text it is not quite clear when the author passes from the impersonal "it" to the personal "he." Some modern translations choose the personal pronoun already in verse 2 ("He was in the beginning with God"), while others have it later in the text, e.g., verse 10.[6] The latter alternative is to be preferred, since this is in line with the context.

The Word in the World

It is beyond dispute that the Word (the Logos) has a unique position in John's theology. Scholars have sought the origins of Logos in many different contexts. Some argue that the concept is rooted in the creative Word of the Old Testament and/or the Wisdom literature (e.g., Prov 8), while others point to the Hellenistic world, e.g., Hermetic and gnostic literature or Stoicism and Philo.

---

5. The first half of the Prologue gives the divine-human encounter in general terms, the second half gives it in a specific Christian language (Vellanickal, "The Gospel of John in the Indian Context," 150).

6. The New Revised Standard Version is an example of the first option, as is the New Danish authorized translation from 1992 (over against the Danish authorized translation from 1948).

Again it is probably not an either-or question; Logos has to be seen in both contexts. It seems that the author deliberately uses a language that is "semantically" open.[7] The value of modern research is that by way of comparison or contrast, it brings out the manifold aspects of John's thought. Jesus is seen as the fulfillment of all this but in a specific way. As Kysar puts it: "Yes, Christ is all of this—Stoic Logos, Old Testament Word, and Jewish Wisdom—rolled into one person. And that is the thrust of the prologue, I believe. Logos for the Christians is a *person*. The Logos is not an abstract philosophical concept. It is not a category of religious experience. Nor is it speculative religious mythology. It is a person, infleshed, living, historical person."[8]

From the beginning the Prologue points to a Christology that is inclusive and cosmic. The focus is on the universal Word that is active in all places. First comes a description of the divinity of the Word (vv.1–2); then the Word is conceived of as the source of all life (v.3) and as the light of humankind (v. 4). Hence, there is no doubt whatsoever that the Word plays a crucial role in God's creation, cf. also the Christ hymn in Col 1:15–20.

Two aspects of the Prologue point to the cosmic significance of the Word. First, the Greek words *en archē* in verse 1 are usually translated by the phrase "in the beginning." This is a reference to the creation story in Gen 1. But the meaning of the words is probably broader than that. In Greek philosophy the term *archē* is often connected to the doctrine of the elements. A Hellenistic audience might have heard this as well when reading the beginning of John's Gospel. Accordingly, the author of the gospel wanted to stress that the Word (Logos) is the crucial and most important element, transcending all others, but at the same time encompassing them all.[9] In other words, Logos is the elementary grounding of life.

Secondly, it should be noted that the concepts of life and light are of great importance in the Gospel. Of specific interest is the concept of life, since this term is usually connected to the fundamental salvific concept of eternal life (e.g., 5:40; 10:10). Some scholars therefore argue that this must also be the case in the beginning of the Prologue. This interpretation would give a Jesus-centered understanding of v. 4. On the other hand, to others it appears that the jump from *Logos* in all creation to the specific mission of Jesus is far too abrupt. They also think that if vv. 4–5 refer to Jesus, then the

---

7. Berger, *Exegese des Neuen Testaments*, 230–31.
8. Kysar, *John the Maverick Gospel*, 25.
9. Aagaard, "Findes der en elementær kosmologi?," 179; Aagaard, "Tao," 3.

explicit references to the coming of Jesus would seem tautological.[10] In fact, it is more natural to understand "life" in vv. 3-4 in a broader sense than eternal life—as being about the life of creation, life as a *pre*-supposition for everything else in our existence.

The first part of the Prologue, then, reflects an inclusive and cosmological Christology which is of great importance for the religious dialogue. This is in line with the insight of the early church fathers, such as Justin Martyr, Clement of Alexandria, and Origen. They developed the idea of *Logos Spermatikos*, of the Spirit of Christ being present like seeds in non-Christian cultures and religions.[11] The Spirit of Christ is sprouting forth, sometimes undetected but sometimes in real beauty and splendor, in poetry, rituals, holy scriptures, and so on; cf. Acts 17:23-28. God has manifested "Godself" in Logos in all cultures and religions in preparation for the decisive, definitive manifestation in the God-man of Jesus Christ. Consequently, what seems to be true, good, and noble in the different peoples, cultures, and religions has its origin in him.

This Logos Christology makes sense as a means of describing God's working in all human lives. On the other hand the Fourth Gospel also affirms that religion as a human phenomenon is deeply ambiguous: "The light shines in darkness, and the darkness did not overcome it" (1:5).

The Incarnated Word as the Interpretation of God

The response to this fundamental ambiguity in the human being may be found in the second part of the Prologue, which in a confessional form expresses the unique character of the Christian message. The climax is the incarnation in v. 14: "The word became flesh and lived among us." After the incarnation the Word is not just present in the world as that which shines in the darkness—cf. the concept of *Logos Spermatikos*. Now God has revealed himself in his fullness in the only begotten Son. In him is grace and truth. No one is comparable with him, not even Moses. The law *was given through* Moses, grace and truth *came through* Jesus Christ, that is in his person (1:17). The uniqueness of Jesus is underlined even in the concluding verse 18. No one has ever seen God—but the only Son, the incarnated

---

10. Cracknell, *Towards a New Relationship*, 99.

11. Cf. Reichelt, "The Johannine Approach," 94; Nørgaard-Højen, "Kristendommens absoluthedskrav," 234. Various nuances differentiate the thought of these three church fathers. Yet, in the main lines their Logos-Theology shows a remarkable consistency, see Dupuis, *Toward a Christian Theology*, 70.

Word, has interpreted him to all mankind. The linguistic form of the verb (in Greek: aorist) is a clear indication that the verse refers to the historical and personal life of Jesus. God's real nature is expressed in his encompassing love and power.

There is a yearning among human beings to see God. John does not deny this, but he insists that it is merely through the incarnated Word that man is able to know who God is. It is in believing in Jesus, the incarnated Word, that people can see God, cf. 1:18 and 14:9: "Whoever has seen me has seen the Father." In the middle of the Prologue (vv.11–13) the emphasis is on human decision. Jesus came to his own (i.e., all people or perhaps just the Jewish people), but his own did not accept him. However, to all those who did receive him was given the power to become the children of God. These words remind us of the thrust of the entire gospel: that those who believe that Jesus is the Messiah, the Son of God, may have life in his name (20:31); the point is that they are born of God.

Particularity and Universality in the Interpretation of Christ

This analysis of the Prologue shows that from its very beginning the Gospel is cosmic and universal in perspective. The issues are all ultimate: the origin and meaning of creation, the attainment of authentic life, and the search for God. These are elements common to all religious systems. But a Christian interpretation cannot remain here; and so *John moves from these universal elements to the earthly, historical Jesus.* The movement is from the universal to the particular, from the global to the local, from eternity to history, from the impersonal to the personal. Men and women are called to follow that movement, and thereby realize that Jesus Christ is the unique revealer of the living God (1:18).

The Gospel as a whole also reflects a movement in the opposite direction: from the historical and concrete to the universal and cosmic. A salient feature is the emphasis on the *universality* of Christ. One of many examples is the cross of Jesus with its inscription: "Jesus of Nazareth, the King of the Jews," written not only in Hebrew, but also in Latin and Greek (19:20), that is, the major languages of that time. Towards the end of his public work Jesus is found by some Greeks wishing to see him (12:20ff.). He answers their request by speaking of his suffering, death, and glorification, and says that he will draw *all people* to himself when he is lifted up from the earth (12:32). The universal importance of Jesus is also underlined by the use of many different titles of Christ; this is particularly evident in 1:35–51, cf. "Images of Christ" in Part Two.

The tendency to move from the more particular to the universal is characteristic of many religious systems of that time, since their location in the Eastern Mediterranean area brought them under the influence of Greek culture. A similar development might well have taken place within the Johannine tradition. A growing number of scholars have noticed that the Johannine community was in dialogue with a wide spectrum of groups and ideologies in the first century.[12] The gospel in its present form may represent an attempt to communicate with a great variety of dialogue partners. Nevertheless, John's insistence on the universal dimension is not due simply to the impact of a more cosmopolitan culture. Rather, the universalism of the message flowed from the universal significance of Christ himself. Jesus revealed God, and only faith in this Jesus was an adequate response.[13]

The Gospel, then, is not the end-product of a succession of encounters with other groups and viewpoints that have influenced John's theology. On the other hand, the author seems to be quite sensitive to movements and currents of his time. John's attempt to express his Christian experience in a language that would awaken echoes in a non-Christian world around him should always remain an inspiration and model for us to continue the same process in our own times.[14] In what follows we shall see examples of how contemporary religious dialogue has been inspired by the Prologue and the Logos Christology.

---

12. Several scholars argue that the Johannine community has undergone a development before it reached its present Christology and its special ecclesiological form. Brown (*The Community of the Beloved Disciple*) points out that the Johannine community originated among Jews who believed that Jesus had fulfilled well-known Jewish expectations, e.g., of a messiah or of a prophet-like-Moses. At a later stage there developed within the Johannine community a higher Christology that went beyond Jewish expectations by describing Jesus as a pre-existent divine savior who had lived with God in heaven before he became man.

13. Senior and Stuhlmueller, *The Biblical Foundations for Mission*, 280.

14. Vellanickal, "The Gospel of John in the Indian Context," 150–51.

Part One: Images of a Greater Reality

CONTEMPORARY PERSPECTIVES

Syncretism and accommodation

The first example is the Norwegian theologian and missionary Karl Ludvig Reichelt who in his mission to Buddhism did not hesitate to translate Logos with the Chinese term *Tao*.[15] Reichelt rejects the charge that this implies syncretism. On the contrary he argues that "Tao has found its full realization in Christ."[16]

According to Filip Riisager, a specialist in Reichelt's theology of mission, two reasons can be given for this identification of Logos and Tao. First, Reichelt's Christology has a platonic tendency; and his Logos is interpreted more in a Hellenistic way as a transcendent-cosmic principle than straight from its biblical and Old Testament background. This implies a weakening of the incarnation and the historical dimension; the cosmic dimension in Christology becomes more important than the historical dimension. Second, Reichelt's approach to the issue of Logos-Tao comes through a mystical experience that includes a search for the foundation of existence; and as a mystical experience it also has a sense of the encompassing, divine power behind everything. According to Riisager, Reichelt did what is justifiable and natural when his premises are taken into consideration, that is, he did what we always have to do when the Christian gospel is translated or interpreted into a new cultural situation: we employ words and concepts from that culture and give them a new content. In the time before Reichelt Protestant Christians in China did the same as him, using the term Tao to render the Johannine "Logos."[17]

Yet, in other contexts Reichelt underlines the importance of the incarnation. In an article from 1939 (originally presented as a lecture at the mission conference in Tambaram in 1938) Reichelt observes that from the hour of incarnation "we have not only the Logos as a grain of seed or as small beams of light flashing out from the religious systems, but now we have God revealed in His fullness."[18] The uniqueness of the incarnation

---

15. Reference is made to searchers for the truth among Buddhists, Taoists, Confucianists and others. "They style themselves spontaneously '*Tao-Yu*', i.e., 'Friends of Tao' (Logos). Christ is for them the full realization and incarnation of the wonderfully rich Tao-idea which holds the supreme sway in all three religions in China (Buddhism included)." (Reichelt, "The Johannine Approach," 99).

16. Reichelt, *Fra Kristuslivets helligdom*, 53.*

17. Riisager, *Lotusblomsten og korset*, 163–64.

18. Reichelt, "The Johannine Approach," 95.

is given in the closing sentence in 1:18. Here it is said that God the One and Only "has made him known (i.e., the Father)." As Reichelt puts it, he "declared him, not only by giving one side of the godhead, like an Indian *Avatara*, not only by giving the essence of an inner pattern, as the Buddhists have it in their idea of the *Bhuta-ta-tha-ta* and the *Tatha-ga-ta*, but giving in a historical and personal life in all-embracing love and power, the full expression of the heart of God."[19]

Many Indian theologians have likewise argued that Logos may be compared with *atman* and *Brahman* or similar notions. Matthew Vellanickal considers John's presentation of Jesus as Logos very interesting in the Indian context. The corresponding Vedic term for Logos is *Vac* or *Vak* which means word or wisdom, and is the first-born of *Rta* (direction/destiny). "The similarity between the 'Word' in John's Gospel and the *Vak* of Hindu scriptures seems to show that the Incarnation was the answer to the age-long prayer of the pre-Christian religions."[20] The Logos in the thought of John seems to be in the last resort the very principle of all that is and all that lives. It is connected to the concept of *atman* and *Brahman*, self and absolute. This principle is in the depths of God and is itself God. These attempts to combine Logos with central concepts like *Tao* or *atman* and *Brahman* are sometimes seen as an expression of syncretism. It is therefore relevant to ask: What is the difference between syncretism and a necessary accommodation?

This question is addressed by the Japanese theologian Kosuke Koyama in the book *Theology in Contact* (1975). According to Koyama we *must* differentiate between syncretism and accommodation. In the new translation of the Thai New Testament, John 1:1 is translated as "In the beginning was *tamma*" (*dharma*). Koyama sees this as the insight of an accommodating and not a syncretistic mind. "The word *tamma* in Buddhist Thailand is as rich as logos in the Hellenistic world of the New Testament times."[21] In the light of this we may ask: Can the purity of Christian doctrine be maintained with the introduction of such a central Buddhist word? Would it not be possible to find a more neutral word? Koyama has three observations in relation to these questions.

---

19. Ibid., 95. The terms *tathata* or *bhutataka* mean the Absolute, conditioned by nothing, which is in itself that which is; cf. Raguin, *The Depth of God*, 111–12.

20. Vellanickal, "The Gospel of John in the Indian Context," 151.

21. Koyama, *Theology in Contact*, 60.

Part One: Images of a Greater Reality

First, if *tamma* is too strong a word and a danger to the purity of the Gospel (and thus expressive of an encroaching syncretism), we must remember that so it was with the word that John himself chose. In both cases it was a dangerous situation. When the Bible was translated in 1967 *tamma* was used out of the conviction that the power of the living Christ can capture it and baptize it with new meaning (2 Cor 10:5). It is the context of Christ which can baptize such strong words as *tamma* and Logos. The context is that of grace. It speaks of God's initiative in coming to the world in the ultimate event of the incarnation of the Son. "How profoundly in the incarnation God accommodated himself to realize his love in the world (cf. Joh 3,16)."[22] It is this love which is the substance of God's method of accommodation.

Second, Koyama asks: How do we maintain the purity of the Gospel in the process of accommodation? He is not alarmed at "In the beginning was the *tamma*." But if Jesus the Buddha rather than Jesus the Christ is proposed in the present-day religious context of Thailand, he would be alarmed. Yet he does not immediately condemn Jesus the Buddha as dangerous syncretism. First he must find out whether this suggestion is contextualization or syncretism. Is the concept of "the Buddha" here baptized into the new Christian context? Will Jesus the Buddha mean Jesus the Light in the Johannine sense: "the true light, which enlightens everyone, was coming into the world" (John 1:9)? If so, it is an accommodation, and is too great a risk to take. This line of thought may make sense to a small group of theologically sophisticated people, but it will cause only immense and unnecessary confusion in the minds of both Christians and Buddhists.[23]

When "Jesus the Buddha" is said with the understanding that "here is no unique revelation in history, that there are many different ways to reach the divine reality," then it is a straightforward syncretistic affirmation. What is meant is that Jesus of Nazareth *plus* Gautama will constitute greater universal religious truth than just Jesus or Gautama in separation. The "plus" here is fundamentally different from contextualization, which is a creative way of maintaining purity in the process of accommodation. But Jesus *plus* Gautama will distort the truth they proclaim respectively.[24]

---

22. Ibid., 61.

23. Ibid., 62–63.

24. On the problem in general see also the paragraph "Transcending Categories—Toward a 'More Than' Christology" in Part Two below.

Third, in our present discussion *indigenization* means a theologically informed endeavor to root the contents and expression of Christian theology in a community of different cultural localities.[25] Speaking concretely, it means the total process for the emergence of a Thai Christian community, who speak the Thai-language, serve their neighbors in Thai fashion, and who own a Thai Christian theology. Indigenization means "rooting." The event and message of Jesus Christ, which was brought by the missionaries, must be rooted in India, Thailand, Indonesia, Hong Kong.[26]

Logos—Christ Impulse or Incarnated Man

Other attempts to demonstrate the relevance of the Prologue are to be found in various new gnostic interpretations of the Gospel of John. One outstanding example is by Rudolf Steiner who gave twelve lectures on the Fourth Gospel in 1908, originally published in German, and later translated into English. Steiner argues that the very first words in the Gospel "permit of no other interpretation than that in Jesus of Nazareth, who lived at the beginning of our Christian era, a being of very high spiritual order was incarnated."[27] However, Logos as *being* is seen first and foremost as a principle ("Christ Principle"), or a Force-Impulse. "When Logos became flesh and appeared among men, then it became a Force-Impulse which is not only a teaching and a concept, but exists in the world as a Force-Impulse in which humanity can participate."[28]

Christ as a Force-Impulse is closely connected to the understanding of human beings as possessing a free "I-am" consciousness. An "I-am" statement is not limited to Jesus Christ; it is characteristic of all mankind. The words of Jesus in John 8:58 play a special role: "Very truly, I tell you, before Abraham was, I am."[29] Steiner comments: "My primal ego mounts not only to the Father-Principle that reaches back to Abraham, but my ego is one with all that pulses through the entire cosmos, and to this my

---

25. Indigenization "is not the transplantation of a grown tree, say from Amsterdam to Djakarta. Actually, indigenization is a critical antithesis to this whole process of big-tree-transplantation. The shift from transplantation to rooting is a difficult and painstaking process" (Koyama *Theology in Contact*, 67–68).

26. Ibid., 67.

27. Steiner, *The Gospel of St. John*, 19.

28. Ibid., 118.

29. Steiner's own translation of John 8:58: "Before Father Abraham was, was the I AM."

spiritual nature soars aloft. I and the Father are one! These are important words which one should experience, then will one feel the forward bound made by mankind, a bound which advanced human evolution further in consequence of that impulse given by the advent of Christ. Christ was the mighty quickener of the 'I AM.'"[30]

According to Steiner, the incarnation of the Christ-Impulse in the human person of Jesus did not take place at one event only. Rather it was a process that began at Jesus' baptism and after three years ended at the cross. The baptism is of particular importance: "All four Gospels stress this moment when the Christ was incorporated in a personality of this earth. However much they may differ in other respects, they all point to this event of Christ slipping into the great initiate, as it were: by baptism by John. In that moment, so clearly defined by the author of the John Gospel when he says that the Spirit descended in the form of a dove and united with Jesus of Nazareth, in that moment occurred the birth of Christ; as a new and higher Ego the Christ is born in the soul of Jesus of Nazareth. Until then, another ego, that of a great initiate had developed to the lofty plane on which it was ripe for the event."[31] The one who descended and incarnated in Jesus of Nazareth was the Logos.

Essentially, Steiner represents a modern gnostic worldview. He operates with two Jesus'es who were simultaneously born in Bethlehem as reincarnations of Zarathustra and Buddha. The two were united into one twelve-year old person and because the abode of Christ, the sun-spirit, at the baptism in Jordan, which was an initiation in the Essene community. Christ, the macrocosmic sun-spirit, dwelt in this special man named Jesus for the three years between his baptism and his crucifixion. This Christ-Impulse is unique, and turned the development of humankind from a devolution after the fall to an evolution towards godhood. Jesus *prototypically* realized the divinity of all human beings.[32]

The Christ-Impulse describes the path that every human being has to tread. The goal is for our ego to control our bodies: the astral body, the etheric body, and the physical body. Regarding the astral body this means that our ego and our will have to be masters in the house of our own consciousness and our feelings, passions, and desires. Regarding the etheric body it means that we control our forces of life, our capacities, and our

---

30. Steiner, *The Gospel of St. John*, 57.
31. Steiner, *The Gospel of St. John and Its Relation to the Other Gospels*, 33–34.
32. Romarheim, "Various views of Jesus Christ," 95.

temperament. Regarding our physical body it means that we control all the organic processes from within. Steiner asserts that Christ had reached all this within three years, and he supports his assertion primarily on the Gospel of John.[33] "Jesus increased in wisdom (in his astral body), in maturity of disposition (in his etheric body), and in gracious beauty (in his physical body) in a way manifest to God and man."[34]

There are at least two objections to this interpretation of the Fourth Gospel. The idea of a macrocosmic "I" (The Christ Principle) living ever more deeply in the body of Jesus of Nazareth is speculative. The Gospel itself does not support such an idea. The decisive feature of the Prologue is the movement from pre-existence to incarnation, from the impersonal to the personal. In this passage the principle of life (Logos) is identified with the name "Jesus Christ." In the Fourth Gospel the center of life has a clear and unambiguous name. He is understood as a concrete, historical person and not as a spiritual principle. Another objection is that the Gospel clearly differentiates between the person of Jesus and the believers. This point is illustrated by the I-am sayings. It is not about the emanation of a Force-Impulse.

From the Impersonal to the Personal Image of God

Images of God are crucial in the encounter between Christianity and religious seekers. In a publication from 2008 entitled *Tro i tiden* three representatives from the organisations, Folkekirke og religionsmøde (The Danish Lutheran Church and the Meeting of Religions) and Areopagos presented a report on their conversations with Danish representatives of those who are inspired by Eastern religiosity and spirituality. According to the report there are many different ideas about God and the divine. Some people use pantheistic terms to indicate that the divine is something immanent: a consciousness, a divine aspect within us, the innermost part of the human being. Others speak of the divine as a reality transcending that

---

33. Damm, *Kristendommen i antroposofiens lys*, 16–20.

34. Steiner, *The Gospel of St. John and Its Relation to the Other Gospels*, 38. Steiner argues that the writer of John's Gospel strongly emphasizes the existence of something divine in humankind, as well as the fact that this appeared in its most grandiose form as God and the Logos itself. "In the individual human being a great and mighty event can take place that can be called the rebirth of the higher ego" (ibid., 9). "Then, when the human principle had reached its height in Jesus of Nazareth, his human body having become an expression of his spirit, he was ripe to receive within Himself the Christ at the Baptism of John" (ibid., 18).

Part One: Images of a Greater Reality

which can be found in ourselves: as a power of life, as intelligence, or just as "something" which we nevertheless are closely related to, or perhaps are a part of. At the risk of simplification we may speak of three understandings of the divine here: as insight, as energy, and as relation.[35] 1) As *insight*, we may speak of a divine reality in humankind rather than of a personal God. 2) As *energy*, the divine is seen as an impersonal force or a spirit. 3) As *relation*, the word 'God' is used of something that is both within and outside humankind. The ultimate goal is the merging of the human soul into God.

It is characteristic that the different names for the divine do not include the idea of God as creature, master, or judge,[36] so the concept of God is impersonal. Modern Christians are facing the same challenge as the author of John's Prologue: how to move from an impersonal to a personal conception of God; in other words how can we demonstrate that the cosmic Christ has been incarnated in the person of Jesus?

Tro i tiden was followed by another report that year, *Tro i lære*, which contains conversations with 10 persons who as Christians are engaged in the religious encounter. These persons (clergy and laity) may have various motivations for their engagement, but they all seem to think that "to be in Christ makes it possible to be open-minded (and spacious)."[37] The report underlines how Christology is developed in the concrete encounter with people from the new spiritual milieu. One of the respondents says that "we should not demonize others; instead we should see Christ in our neighbor." Another states that "Christ as Logos also has an effect outside Church and Christianity and goes on to refer to the concept of '*logoi spermatikoi*'—which might be taken as a point of contact for the proclamation of Christ."[38]

One of the interviewees is Ole Skjerbæk Madsen, founder of a number of Christian communities called "I Mesterens Lys" (In the Master's Light).[39] He has explained the theological idea behind this movement in a number of publications, including an article from 2003 focusing on John's Prologue. Madsen insists that the whole understanding of the order of the universe was personalized in the creative Word of God who was made

---

35. *Tro i tiden*, 18–19; Thelle, *Buddha og Kristus*, 142–52.

36. *Tro i tiden*, 17.

37. *Tro i lære*, 25. This is a free translation from the Danish text: "Kristus-forankring gør det muligt at være rummelig."

38. Ibid., 25.*

39. See also the paragraph "In the Master's Light" in chapter 7 of this book.

flesh. The Logos of the world was not an abstract law or principle, but a self-communication of God calling his creatures into a relationship of love with Godself.[40]

Furthermore, it is pointed out that speaking of the Logos/logos is especially relevant in communicating with theosophy, which, however, operates with a much more complex understanding of the term. Theosophy thus speaks of the Solar Logos, the God of the Sun System, the planetary Logos, the God of the planet Earth, a Logos-being on each different plane of consciousness, in a hierarchy of beings. Against this, the Christian understanding has as its focus on the incarnate Logos of God in Jesus Christ and recognizes through the work of Christ how God created the universe through Logos and how creative love orders creation according to the Logos.

The concept of Logos as known, manifested, and revealed in the logos of the created world may be combined with a Christianized use of the concept of Tao. This is relevant to the neo-spiritual movements, perhaps even more than using the logos terminology, since the concept of Tao pervades much New Age thinking and practice. Tao signifies the eternal order or the foundation and basic principle of life. Tao is the cause of all foundation, but in this sense is incomprehensible, unspeakable, and transcendent. Nevertheless, the term "Tao" is used because the unspeakable Tao is also immanent in the created world. In this second meaning, Tao is the mother of creation, power and norm of existence. Skjerbæk Madsen points to the fact that in the Chinese Gospel of John, "Logos" is translated as "Tao." John 1:14 thus means that the eternal foundation and basic principle of life is not impersonal, but is met in person in a human life.[41]

The Cosmic Christ—in the Midst of Human Beings

The importance of the Prologue is also underlined by Harry Månsus, the founder of the Bromma-dialogue, a Swedish movement which highlights the dialogue between Christian faith and new spirituality. According to Månsus many Christians see spiritual currents of our time as a threat or even a sign of our living at the end of time. This situation is not new, however. Early Christianity was itself an "alternative spiritual movement" to the established order. It was born in a world that is as religious complex as

---

40. Madsen, "Theology in Dialogue," 267.
41. Ibid., 269.

Part One: Images of a Greater Reality

our own.[42] In Hellenistic culture many people distanced themselves from the ancient gods and the public religion. The void after the traditional religions was filled with alternative spiritual movements—including mystery religions, astrology, various forms of healing, and Christianity. Stoic philosophy is of particular importance in this context. It is said that Logos as the "cosmic world reason" permeates everything. In this way it may be said that God was present in the cosmic cathedral.[43]

Månsus is convinced that God uses many different means in his attempt to reach man. If the church proves unsuitable he will employ other means. Today the new religiosity and the new spirituality may be seen as a quest for sincere spiritual experience and a wish for a personal encounter with the cosmic Christ. Hence, the church should not isolate itself inside the walls of churches and chapels, but follow the example of the first Christians and meet people in public places, following Paul's dialogue with the Athenians at the Areopagus in Acts 17:17–34.

The Prologue in John's Gospel is another example of this open, dialogical approach. The text has the form of a hymn which was probably written in a Hellenistic environment with gnostic tendencies. The similarity with the new spirituality is striking. After all, we might have expected the author of the hymn to take steps to avoid any alternative spirituality, but in fact, he does the opposite. According to Månsus, John takes over the winged words from the spiritual circles of his time, "baptizes" them, and uses them in his presentation of the cosmic Christ. In his hymn John appropriates the concept of Logos from Stoic popular philosophy and the gnostic "terminology of light," as well as including cosmic perspectives from the Old Testament story of the creation, cf. John 1:1–5.[44]

John's theological intention is obvious: The cosmic Christ should not be isolated in churches, in false piety, or in religious dogma. God is not withdrawing himself from the earth into a religious reservation. On the contrary, in the gospel we meet the Creator himself as the cosmic Christ who descended into the fallen creature in order to liberate and heal creation from below. The cosmic Christ—"the true light, which enlightens everyone"—has incarnated himself in the world (John 1:9).

In Månsus's view, John's message to the new spirituality of the first century is: If you are searching for the light, you will find it embodied in

42. Månsus, *Vägen hem och resan vidare*, 108–14.
43. Ibid., 255–56.
44. Ibid., 111.

a dark world! His message to seekers with a popular philosophy is: Logos—the wisdom that permeates everything—has revealed its glory, and we ourselves have seen it! His message to Judaism is: The Wisdom that is referred to in the Old Testament, has become man and lives in our midst![45]

The Role of Incarnation in the Encounter with Other Religions

All religions operate with a center where eternity and time, divine and human, sacred and profane meet. The center signifies the irruption of divine reality into human reality. Hence, centering is the bestowal of some meaning from which all other meaning derives. The old reality is replaced by a new reality. The Fourth Gospel describes the Logos as this center, the axis of life. Everything else in the Gospel emanates from the central affirmation made in verse 1 and verse 14. In v. 1 the reader is brought into a primal, archetypal time in which the *Logos* existed and was God. It is this *Logos* that v. 14 affirms to have become flesh.[46] Through the structure of the Prologue John seeks to express the experience of Christ first in a language that echoes his non-Christian environment, and then in a Christian language.[47] It is a double movement, from pre-existence to incarnation, from the impersonal to the personal.[48] John insists that the Word that became flesh has become the new center, the new reality that irrupts into the old world and has replaced the old centers. Thus, the center of Judaism, the temple, is replaced by Jesus who is the "place" where God tabernacles among us (1:14).[49]

The preceding examples of modern interpretations of the Prologue raise the question of how far Christians should go in communicating with non-Christian religions. A similar question was addressed by John. The Fourth Gospel is the classic example of the challenges and risks that are posed by translating the Christian message into the languages and perceptions of other cultures. Some would say that in order to win over the

---

45. Ibid., 113.
46. Cahill, "The Johannine *Logos* as Center," 65.
47. According to Dupuis (*Toward a Christian Theology*, 328) there are several manifestations of the Word in history. But not all of them have the same significance. Incarnation, as compared to enlightenment, has a historical density of its own. In other words, there is a clear distinction between the Word's "incarnation" in Jesus Christ and the "enlightenment" by the divine Logos of other saving figures.
48. Dunn, *Christology in the Making*, 243.
49. Note also Jesus' conversation with the Samaritan woman in John 4. See chapter 5 in this book.

Gnostics John almost became a Gnostic himself (cf. Part Two). Yet he differed from his audience on two decisive points: his insistence on the historicity of Jesus and on his human nature.

It is essential for any dialogue today that Christians take the same movement as the Prologue: from the impersonal to the personal and from pre-existence to incarnation. In other words, we must do the same as the Gospel of John did: identify the Logos, the principle of life, with the person Jesus Christ. He is not just the core of life, but also life in all its fullness (1:16), for he gives life in abundance (10:10).

4

Rebirth

Historical Perspectives

THE PATTERN WHICH IS recognizable in the Prologue—a movement from the universal to the specifically Christian—reappears in a number of other episodes throughout the Gospel.[1] An obvious example is the conversation between Jesus and Nicodemus (3:1–21). The figure of Nicodemus can be interpreted in two ways: On the one hand he symbolizes "man as he is"; cf. the use of "man" (Greek: *anthrōpos*) in v. 1. On the other hand he is a communal symbolic figure representing those Jews who have some sympathy for Jesus but who nevertheless hesitate to join him.[2]

The Figure of Nicodemus

a. Nicodemus—a symbol of "man as he is." The first of these interpretations puts the emphasis on the existential and individual aspect. Nicodemus is described as the thoughtful seeker of truth. He symbolizes "man as he is," in need of an entirely new origin for his salvation and yet unable to see the

---

1. The identity of Jesus is gradually revealed. At some stage it is accepted or rejected. See the stories of Nicodemus, the Samaritan woman, and the lame man; cf. Culpepper, *Anatomy of the Fourth Gospel*, 88–89.
2. Cf. Nissen, "Rebirth and Community."

possibility of it.³ In this view, Nicodemus' need, and the transformation that is offered to him, is essentially an inner and individual one.

Two things are characteristic for religious seekers. First, they are living "*at night,*" a term that has a double meaning. It has a literal aspect denoting the fearfulness and insecurity of Nicodemus, and it has a symbolic aspect denoting his lack of understanding. The discourse in John 3 is held together by an inclusion, beginning with Nicodemus coming to Jesus at night and ending on the theme that people have to leave the darkness and come into the light (vv. 19–21)—probably a reference to 1:5. The note that Nicodemus comes "at night" is repeated in 19:39. This suggests that he does not walk in the light.

Second, a religious seeker will often be content with a "*teacher.*" In v. 2 Nicodemus addresses Jesus as follows: "Rabbi, we know that you are a teacher who has come from God." A teacher is a person who helps us to a better understanding of our existence and guides us to the way we should follow.

b. Nicodemus as representing a group. Recent studies have opened up the possibility of seeing in Nicodemus something more than just "man as he is." Various aspects of the text support the interpretation that he occupies the role of a *communal* symbolic figure. First, Nicodemus speaks to Jesus in the plural, and Jesus likewise addresses him in the plural, e.g., "*We* know . . ." (3:2), "You *people* must be born again . . ." (3:7; NRSV: "You must . . ."). In vv.11–12 there is an abrupt switching from the dialogue between Nicodemus and Jesus to the writer/reader relationship. Here it is even more evident that the Johannine community is speaking to its opponents, e.g., "*We* speak of what *we* know and testify to what *we* have sent and *you* do not receive *our* testimony" (3:11).

Second, most scholars agree that Nicodemus also stands for a specific group, though they disagree on its character. Nicodemus is known from two other scenes: 7:45–52 and 19:38–42. But there are contradictory signals in John's description. Some interpreters emphasize his characterization as one who comes to Jesus "at night" (3:2 and 19:39). "Nicodemus appears as a man of inadequate faith and inadequate courage, and as such represents a group that the author wishes to characterize in this way."⁴

---

3. E.g., Bultmann, *Das Evangelium des Johannes*, 95.
4. Rensberger, *Overcoming the World*, 40.

Others think that Nicodemus develops as a character. When he first meets Jesus he is afraid and does not understand at all (3:11), but later we see him speaking up indirectly for Jesus to the Pharisees (7:50). His final appearance might be seen as an illustration of the words of Jesus in 12:33–34: "And I, when I am lifted up from the earth, will draw all people to myself . . ." Nicodemus comes forward publicly after the crucifixion to bury Jesus (19:39). He is linked to Joseph of Arimathea, who has been a secret disciple of Jesus "for fear of the Jews," but who in asking for the body of Jesus, is now making his faith public, 19:38.[5]

Whether or not Nicodemus represents the "secret Christian Jews" or the "Crypto-Christians," there is little doubt that we are dealing here with a borderline group. And it is interesting to notice that the stories in John 2:14—4:42 are all about just such socially important groups in the Johannine community: first the unbelieving Jews (2:14-22), then Jews who had some sympathy for Jesus or "secret Christian Jews" (2:23—3:21), then followers of John the Baptist (3:22-26) and finally the Samaritans (4:1-42).

The Dialogue between Jesus and Nicodemus

The conversation between Jesus and Nicodemus illustrates the interplay between the human religious quest and the response of the Gospel. The dialogue focuses on the meaning of "begetting" from on high, as can be seen from the context. Here we must look at the structure of 3:1–21, which may be divided in two parts.

In the *first part* it is argued that begetting from above through the Spirit is *necessary* for entrance into the Kingdom of God—natural birth is insufficient (vv. 2–8). In vv. 2–3 the *fact* of begetting is illustrated. In the *second part* the point is that the begetting is made possible *only* when the Son has ascended to the Father—and it is offered only to those who *believe* in Jesus (vv. 9–21). This is another way of saying that begetting through the Spirit can come about only as a result of Jesus' crucifixion, resurrection, and ascension.[6] The structure of the text is as follows:

---

5. Brown, *The Community of the Beloved Disciple*, 72.
6. Brown, *The Gospel According to John*, 136, 145.

Part One: Images of a Greater Reality

1. Introduction (v. 1)
2. The first question and answer: *the fact* of begetting (vv. 2–3)
3. The second question and answer: the *how* of begetting (vv. 4–8)
4. The third question and answer: Rebirth is *only possible* due to the ascension of Christ on the cross—which at the same is the sacrifice of love (vv. 9–21).

Nicodemus' opening statement looks like an assertion: "Rabbi, we know that you are a teacher who has come from God; for no one can do these signs that you do apart from the presence of God" (v. 2). But it is more than this; it is Nicodemus' quest for salvation. The following dialogue indicates that Jesus takes Nicodemus seriously in his honest search for the truth, even when he is correcting him at certain decisive points.

In his first response Jesus states the conditions for entering into the Kingdom of God: "No one can see the kingdom of God without being born from above" (v. 3). This statement shows that Jesus does not settle for merely fulfilling Nicodemus' expectations. He is not like any other rabbi; he is the teacher who reveals the true character of God. And his message, the good news about the Kingdom of God, is not just a fulfilling of the religious quest. God's kingdom is not a prolongation of human longings, it is about a totally new beginning.

Understandably, Nicodemus is unable to make sense of how "man can be born again," so Jesus elaborates his response by using metaphors. His point is that an existence based on that which belongs to this world—"what is born of the flesh is flesh. . . ."—is fundamentally alien to itself and is contrasted with an existence that has its origin in God and his word: "What is born of the Spirit is spirit" (v. 6). Flesh and spirit are contrasted in v.6, just as begetting in an earthly sense is contrasted with begetting from above. But the contrast between flesh and spirit has nothing to do with a contrast between material and spiritual, as presupposed in the gnostic distrust of the material world as such. "Flesh refers to man as he is born into the world, and in this state he has something both of the material and of the spiritual, as Gen ii 7 insists. The contrast between flesh and Spirit is that . . . between man as he is and man as Jesus can make him by giving him a holy Spirit."[7]

According to John 3 participation in God's new order is not possible through ancestry and circumcision; it is made possible only through the Spirit. In v. 8 John uses an analogy which involves a play on words. Both

---

7. Ibid., 141.

in Aramaic and Greek the same word means "spirit," "breath," and "wind." And who can control the wind or say whence it comes and whither it goes? The breath of life is sovereign and supremely free. Spirit moves among us like the wind, entirely free of human control.

On Nicodemus' third question, "How can these things be?" (v. 9), Jesus explains that the new situation has come about because of the arrival of the Son of Man. Thus from v. 10 onwards there is a reference to the event that is the precondition for the rebirth. The language in v. 13 may sound gnostic, but the following verse makes it evident that the focus is on the Crucified (v. 14) and the real answer to Nicodemus' question about the Kingdom of God is found in v. 16: This verse underlines that God manifested his love to the world by sending his Son. Life in the Kingdom of God is a boundless love. The divine glory is the sacrifice of that love, and this is realized through the death of Jesus on the cross.

Continuity and Discontinuity—on the Relation to Judaism and Hellenism

In John 3 we have an example of the longings and aspirations uttered by a representative from one of the religious traditions (Judaism). However, the concept of rebirth itself conveys such a longing. It is the longing for a totally new being, a longing to transcend oneself. In New Testament times many people dreamed of such things, indeed the dream seems as old as the human race.[8] In Hellenistic literature rebirth means a process of divinization.[9] In their new being the reborn are in fact the All in All, made up of all powers, cf. Corpus Hermeticum, the tractate "On Rebirth" (XIII, 2). Some trends within modern psychotherapy and new religious movements point in the same direction.[10] This idea of divinization is not found in John 3. By contrast, the main emphasis is on the element of discontinuity. Rebirth means a radical transformation and it is not something that can be attained through human effort.

Thus, there is an innovation in John's thought when compared with both Judaism and Hellenism. The Jewish religion which Nicodemus represents cannot move forward continuously into the Kingdom of God.

8. Rebell, *Gemeinde als Gegenwelt*, 151.

9. The Hermetic literature denotes a number of Hellenistic writings mainly of gnostic or mystical character. For a more detailed account on Corpus Hermeticum XIII and John 3, see Nissen, "Rebirth and Community," 124–26.

10. See the references in Nissen, "Rebirth and Community," 137n53.

A moment of *discontinuity*, comparable with physical birth, is essential. Humankind as such, even the Jew, is not by nature able to enter into God's Kingdom. John also differs from Judaism by saying that the Kingdom has already been manifested in the person and work of Jesus. The language of rebirth borrowed from Hellenism helps John to express his realized eschatology: Eternity is now! But John also differs from Hellenism by insisting on the incarnation and the historical character of Jesus Christ (vv.14–16). He does not just take over the concept of rebirth; he incorporates it into his proclamation of Christ without subscribing to the Hellenistic idea of divinization.

In addition, it has often been argued that v.13 reflects the redeemer-myth in Gnosticism—cf. the verbs for ascending and descending—but the similarity with Hellenistic ideas should not be overemphasized, since at the most crucial points John differs from the redeemer-myth. He insists that Jesus is a *historical* person. The description of Jesus as the "one who descended from heaven, the Son of Man" refers to the incarnation. The crucial point in v. 13 is the same as in 14:6 and 1:51. *No one* has ascended into heaven but the Son of Man. Christ *alone* is the link between God and men (cf. 1:51). There is no access to God independent of him (14:6).

This understanding of v.13 is supported by the fact that v.16 refers to Jesus as "the only begotten" Son of God. The importance of these words can be seen by a comparison. The famous Hindu Swami Vivekananada has argued that there is no "only begotten" son of God. There is a plurality of avatars, i.e., there are many "sons of God." God has incarnated himself a number of times. This is a pivotal point in the encounter of Eastern and Western spirituality, as Vivekananda takes issue with Christians, who maintain that the "Lord can manifest himself only once; there lies the whole mistake."[11] Vivekananda's position resembles that of early Gnosticism, but it differs substantially from that of John, in whose understanding the uniqueness of Jesus Christ is beyond question.

"Seeing" the Kingdom of God

In John 3 the author makes use of an unusual phrase: "to see the Kingdom of God" (3:5). This reflects the centrality of the word "seeing" in the Fourth Gospel, as can be noted in "we have seen his glory" (1:14) or "come and see!" (1:38–39; 4:29; cf. the paragraph "Come and see!" in Part Two.

---

11. Vivekananda, *The Yogas and Other Works*, 270.

Right to the end the Gospel emphasizes the importance of seeing—as with Thomas: "Unless I see the mark of the nails in his hands, and put my finger in the mark of the nails and my hand in his side, I will not believe" (20:25). In general we may speak of three ways of using the term "seeing":

(a) seeing in a literal sense (i.e., 1:38; 6:2; 9:8; 20:25)

(b) seeing with the eyes of faith—in a figurative sense (1:39.50–51; 19:34)

(c) seeing God whom no one has ever seen (1:18; 6:46); whoever sees Jesus, sees the Father (12:45; 14:7).

The transition between the two last meanings is fluid. To interpret what Jesus says and does is to "see" the revelation of the Father "full of grace and truth" (1:14). The literal and the figurative meanings of "seeing" should *not* be contrasted. Robert Kysar correctly speaks of John's "sensory theology," the suggestion that faith grows out of immediate, everyday physical experiences; it is precisely why the sacraments are central to Christian thought.[12]

What, then, are we "seeing" in Jesus? The answer is a new and different reality that is revealed in the midst of the old reality. From the analogy between the wind and the Spirit we learn that they are both realities that are perceived only in their *effects*. In the Gospel of John these effects are clearly visible in the new way of life in the community of the disciples, who being born of the spirit are free as the wind. They are not dependent on others' ideas, criticism, and approval, but are moved solely by the Spirit to love each other. This is their *new identity*.

Entering into God's New Order

The Gospel of John calls for a public transfer of allegiance. Those who refuse to believe in Jesus constitute themselves as "the world," the realm of darkness, untruth, and death. Passing from that world to the new identity is only possible through a reorientation so profound as to constitute a new birth (3:5–8). By physical birth one is born into the world and has to accept its order. To be born again "from above" means to "see" God's kingdom and the new order. To see, then, is to experience, to encounter, to participate in.[13] Moreover, John uniquely relates this rebirth to the Kingdom of God *not* as a replacement for life in this world but as a new world *within* this world,

---

12. Kysar, *John the Maverick Gospel*, 108.
13. Brown, *The Gospel According to John*, 130.

Part One: Images of a Greater Reality

the most natural explanation being that John sought to underline the *social* components of salvation.

Thus the Kingdom of God is a social category. The goal of rebirth is entrance into the Kingdom, and the confession of Jesus as Messiah means that the disciple *already* lives in the Kingdom under the kingship of Jesus—a kingship that is not of this world, and whose unworldly character is expressed precisely in his servants' refusal to take up arms in defense of Jesus: "My kingdom is not from this world. If my kingdom were from this world, my followers would be fighting to keep me from being handed over to the Jews. But, as it is, my kingdom is not from here" (18:36). This kingship, which is neither established nor defended by acts of violence, is the kingship under which the messianic community lives out its love for one another; cf. 13:34–35.

The close relationship between rebirth and the Kingdom of God underlines its communitarian character.[14] The rebirth implies not only personal faith, but a change of social location as well. To be born "from above" is to be part of a new community. The worldly *community* represented by Nicodemus must undergo a change of social location by openly acknowledging the messiahship of Jesus and in so doing will become part of the messianic community. They are called on to abandon the world and its continuing self-centeredness and to be integrated into the community of love.

Contemporary perspectives

New Gnosticism and Reincarnation

The conversation between Jesus and Nicodemus is one of the Johannine texts that have attracted great interest among the new religious movements. According to Steiner, the conversation reflects a deep secret regarding the development of humankind, and he would translate the words of Jesus in 3:5 thus: "Verily, verily, I say unto thee, except a man be born of water and air he cannot enter the Kingdom of Heaven."[15] The argument is that in New Testament times *pneuma* (Spirit) meant "air," and had "exactly that meaning."[16]

---

14. Rensberger, *Overcoming the World*, 148.
15. Steiner, *The Gospel of St. John*, 104.
16. Ibid., 103.

> If we wish to characterize the significance of this evolutionary process, we may say that formerly, when the human being was still living with the gods, his physical and ether bodies were fluidic and gaseous in form, and were only gradually, simultaneously with the solidification of the earth, condensed to their present material form. That is the descent, but just as he has made this descent, so will he also ascend again. After he has had the experiences that are to be in solid substance, he will again mount into those regions where his physical body will be fluidic and gaseous. He must bear within him the consciousness that if he wishes to unite himself again consciously with the gods, his true existence will be in those regions from which he has sprung. He has become condensed out of water and air and he will again become diffused into them. He can only spiritually anticipate this condition today by gaining within his inner nature a consciousness of the future state of his physical body. Only by becoming conscious of it today, however, will he gain the power to do so.[17]

In his commentary on John 3 Richard Damm considers various understandings of being born again "of water and the Spirit" in verse 5. One way is to see it as a reference to the Baptism of John or to Christian Baptism, another is to see it as a reference to a divine emanation or a creative energy—an idea which is found in Jewish mysticism.[18] Of special interest is Damm's *excursus* on translating *pneuma* as "air" rather than "spirit" (cf. 3:8). He argues that Nicodemus may have been talking about a birth from *earth* (birth in the bodily sense) and John the Baptist may have talked about birth from *water*. John 3:5 may then refer to a birth from *air*, and the Synoptic Gospels refer to a birth from *fire*. In this way we have to ascend through the four elements: earth (the solid element), water (the fluid element), air (the gaseous element), and the element of fire. In antiquity it is presupposed that humankind descends from the pure spiritual sphere to the earthly sphere: from ether (the lower over-sensual sphere) through fire (the higher material sphere), air, water to earth—and that we shall ascend again: from earth through water, air, and fire.

According to Damm these ideas should not be seen as an explanation, but rather as an expression of the many associations that the language of John 3 would evoke in the consciousness of his contemporary audience. "It is quite natural to think that the readers of the Gospel who were

17. Ibid.
18. Damm, *Johannesevangeliet*, 64.

Hellenists, would understand the words in verse 5 in the following way: In order to enter the Kingdom of God you need to ascend the same ladder that was used for descending."[19] Other aspects of John 3 might also be interpreted in gnostic manner, but Damm nevertheless argues that the author of John's Gospel does not subscribe to a radical dualism like gnostic dualism. However, in a later book on Christianity in an anthroposophical light, he seems to have changed his mind. At least he argues that the Gospel should be interpreted in a clear dualistic and gnostic manner. A similar position is taken in his book on Paul, which clearly reflects his approval of Steiner's understanding of Christianity.[20]

Reincarnation as a concept is a widespread religious phenomenon. In recent times some interpreters think that the idea of reincarnation is confirmed by John 3:1–21[21], but there is nothing in the text to support this interpretation. First, the Kingdom of God is not just a fulfillment of our religious quest. There is no straight line from the "inner" man—be it the soul or a personal core—to the Kingdom of God. The Greek original in verse 3 uses the word *anothen* which means both "again" and "from above." Humankind has to be born again and from above. Second, the context holds the key to the meaning, and this shows that Jesus was speaking of a rebirth in *this* life as a precondition for eternal life.[22] As argued previously, the main emphasis in John 3 is on the element of discontinuity. Rebirth means a radical transformation and is *not* something that can be attained through human effort.[23] It is offered in the giving of God's Son through the love of God and in the community of individuals who have believed in him.

---

19. Ibid., 66.*

20. See Damm, *Kristendommen i antroposofiens lys*; and Damm, *Paulus mellem øst og vest*. On the importance of the new initiation Steiner notes: "John still baptized by submersion with the result that the etheric body withdrew and man could see into the spiritual world. But if a man opens his soul to the Christ impulse, this impulse acts in such a way that the experiences of the astral body flow over into the etheric body and clairvoyance result.—There you have the explanation of the phrase, "to baptize with the spirit and with fire," and those are the facts concerning the difference between the John baptism and the Christ baptism" (Steiner, *The Gospel of John and Its Relation*, 130).

21. E.g., Kirkegaard, *Reinkarnation*, 55.

22. Albrecht, *Reincarnation*, 36.

23. Rebell, *Gemeinde als Gegenwelt*, 151.

The Man Born Blind

The issue of reincarnation has been discussed in relation not only to John 3 but also to the story in John 9 of the man born blind:

> As he walked along, he saw a man blind from birth. His disciples asked him: "Rabbi, who sinned: this man or his parents, that he was born blind?" Jesus answered: "Neither this man nor his parents sinned; he was born blind so that God's works might be revealed in him. (9:1–3)

The disciples' question assumes the link between sin and the punishment of blindness. Behind the possibility that the man has sinned there may lie a gnostic speculation in pre-existence or reincarnation from the beginning of our era. The other option is that the parents had sinned, and their son was being punished, according to Jewish thinking.[24] However, the story clearly shows that Jesus rejects both options. First he states that neither the man born blind nor his parents have sinned (v. 3), and then the man is healed (v. 6–7). If Jesus wanted to defend the teaching of reincarnation, this event would have been a fine opportunity to explain the doctrine. But he abstains from doing so; he refuses to talk about guilt and punishment in relation to the blindness. This is a position that is contrary to the doctrines of reincarnation and karma.[25] Instead Jesus sees it as a symptom of the condition of the whole of humanity that he has come to restore.[26] The crucial point is that God has revealed his true nature and love in Christ; he has entered a suffering world and has helped those who suffer.

---

24. Despite the Book of Job, the older theory of a direct causal relationship between sin and sickness was still alive in Jesus' time; cf. Brown, *The Gospel According to John*, 371.

25. Olofson, *Så I bliver som Gud*, 211.

26. Even some of the researchers who consider reincarnation to be very significant in John's Gospel concede that Jesus rejects it in this passage. On the other hand it is often said that the blind man episode in 9:2 shows the familiarity of the disciples with the idea of more successive courses of life stemming from the many ideas circulating in the Mediterranean world of the time (MacGregor, *Reincarnation as a Christian Hope*, 43). Hick is also open to the idea of reincarnation but is more cautious. Having discussed the problem he states: "I . . . conclude concerning the New Testament evidence (a) that it is possible, but not very probable, that there is a reference to the idea of reincarnation in John 9:2; and (b) that there is no reason at all to think that Jesus or any of the New Testament writers were sympathetic to the idea; on the contrary, if John 9:2 is a reference to reincarnation, the following verse is a repudiation of it." (Hick, *Death and Eternal Life*, 367–68; see also Nørgaard-Højen, "Kristendommens absoluthedskrav," 316–18).

This has consequences for how we perceive love today. Love is alert; it cannot be postponed to another time. If we see somebody drowning, we must try to rescue them. It is useless to say that there will be another chance in another life. If a society is marked by great injustice, for instance in relation to the caste system in India, there is no point in saying: These people suffer because of sins they have committed in a previous life; in addition, they have the chance of a better life in the next reincarnation. In contrast to this, a Christian understanding of love demands action *immediately*, one cannot postpone the good opportunities to a later occasion. Those who act in love are strongly aware that they have to work now, because "night is coming when no one can work" John 9:4.[27]

Love and compassion are two fundamental dimensions of Christian faith. Both play a role in Buddhism too, but with a different meaning. Pity should be felt for others who are suffering, mostly because they are unable to understand *why* they suffer, but also because they have not realized that their suffering can be overcome through the teaching and practice of Buddhism, which will liberate them from the recurrent, painful reincarnations. The Christian understanding of compassion is different. It means *to suffer with*,[28] to be present and responsible in situations where suffering takes place, an understanding clearly exemplified in the parable of the Good Samaritan (Luke 10:30–37). This is not to say that the idea of sacrifice is totally unknown in Buddhism—as can be seen in the tradition of the boddhisatvas: totally enlightened human beings who refrain from entering nirvana in order to save others in this world. See also the paragraph "The understanding of sacrifice in Buddhism and Christianity" in chapter 9 of this book.

Reincarnation and Resurrection

The doctrine of reincarnation differs not just from the Christian understanding of love and compassion, but also from other fundamental Christian values, including the concept of humankind, the belief in grace and forgiveness, and the *fact* of the resurrection. In this context I shall limit myself to the last issue.[29]

27. Martensen, *Kirke og reinkarnation*, 26.

28. For further reflections on the importance of love as compassion, see the chapter on "Spirituality as Sharing in God's Compassion" in my book, *Poverty and Mission*, 153–67.

29. On the other issue see also Albrecht, *Reincarnation*, esp. 106–19.

Rebirth

The teaching on the bodily resurrection of Christ is crucial in the New Testament. The Fourth Gospel is no exception, with John's story about the raising of Lazarus in chapter 11 having a paradigmatic role. When Martha says that she expects that Lazarus will rise again in the resurrection on the last day, Jesus replies: "I am the resurrection and life. Those who believe in me, even though they die, will live" (11:25). This is an affirmation of Jesus' own belief in the resurrection and it is intrinsically linked to that. And indeed, after his resurrection Jesus returns to the community that is gathered for worship. A major point in John 20:19–29 is that the crucified Jesus is identical with the Resurrected Lord. The death of Jesus was not just apparent or pretended—as is sometimes argued by the new religious movements and also by Islam (see chapter 14 of this book). Christianity emphasizes that Jesus really did die, and in the cruelest of ways. And it is the *crucified* Jesus who has arisen. The coherence and the *identity* of the crucified Jesus and the resurrected Christ are crucial.[30] Together they indicate that belief in the resurrection is not a denial of the reality of suffering but an overcoming of it.

Belief in the resurrection is thus an indispensable part of Christianity. The question today is: What are the consequences of this for the church's response to people influenced by Eastern religiosity and spirituality. They too are seekers and in some cases they are also members of Christian churches, even though they believe in reincarnation. The Danish document *Tro i tiden* has reported extensively on these people. Some think that reincarnation was originally part of Christianity, but when the biblical texts were canonized the church renounced this belief. Others hold that there need not be a conflict between reincarnation and resurrection. The Eastern circular thinking and the Western linear thinking may be united in Christ.[31]

By contrast, none of the Christian conversation partners in *Tro i lære* think that belief in karma and reincarnation can be combined with belief in Jesus Christ. Nevertheless, the issue has not been a hindrance for their

---

30. Arias argues that in John 20 we have the climax of the Johannine incarnational Christology, blending the divine and the human, the historical and the eternal. "The experience of the historical Jesus without the Resurrection was not enough—the crucifixion left the disciples behind locked doors. The experience of a divine presence, the eternal Christ, without the knowledge of the historical Jesus, would have left them with a philosophy or a mystical system of religion—lacking the concreteness of revelation through incarnation in human life and missing the contagious power of experienced good news" (Arias and Johnson, *The Great Commission*, 80).

31. *Tro i tiden*, 23–28.

conversation and contact with spiritual seekers who are inspired by Eastern thought. Instead they have tried to encounter people where they are and with the ideas they hold. And in this encounter they have pointed to another understanding of life marked by "concepts like sin, grace, and Our Lord."[32] It is important that we all listen to the concrete experiences of others. These experiences can be interpreted differently, and the theological reflections will be different because the superior frame of interpretation is different.

The Wind Blows Where It Chooses

This statement in John 3:8 is relevant for a modern understanding of mission as well as of dialogue. In the context of the Gospel there is an interesting similarity between what is said about the Word in the Prologue, and what is said about the Spirit in other Johannine passages.[33] The similarity is due to the fact, among others, that the Logos Christology of John is based on motifs from the Wisdom tradition, and the acts of Wisdom correspond to the Holy Spirit; cf. Prov 8. In John's understanding of the wind (or the spirit) the wind blows from Jesus, who is called the Logos, in the beginning with God and Himself God (1:1–2). It is life which breaks a path where it chooses.[34]

The link between the Prologue and John 3 is seen from the parallel between the motifs: children of God/"born of God" and rebirth. John 1:12–13 states: "But to all who received him, who believed in his name, he gave power to become children of God, who were born, not of blood or of the will of the flesh or of the will of man, but of God."[35] There is no direct mention of being born of God in John 3; instead the text speaks about being born again or from above, and this birth is due to the Spirit. It is self-evident that humankind cannot give birth to itself and therefore

---

32. *Tro i lære*, 26.

33. Thelle argues that the concept of the Spirit in John 3:8 should be linked with John's Logos Christology, Thelle, *Hvem kan standse vinden?*, 11.

34. Vogel, "Nicodemus," 80–81.

35. Dodd notes that the term "from above" in John 3 echoes the expression "born by God" in 1:13. There it was explained that to be a "child of God" is not a result of any process comparable with that of physical birth. It is by receiving the Logos that we gain the right to be God's child. "This effectively dissociates the idea of rebirth in the Johannine sense of the term, from all mythological notions of divine generation such as were current in wide circles of Hellenistic society" (Dodd, *The Interpretation of the Fourth Gospel*, 305).

cannot perform a rebirth. This is the result of a divine miracle and not an improvement of the inner nature of man; the Kingdom of God means a radical new creation—here and now.

The Johannine metaphor of birth is a continuation of creation, based on the model in Genesis where God blows his spirit into the earthly clay (Gen 2:7). At the new creation it is said: "What is born of the flesh is flesh, and what is born of the Spirit is spirit" (3:6). The resemblance to the original creation is also evident in 3:8: "The wind blows where it chooses, and you hear the sound of it, but you do not know where it comes from or where it goes. So it is with everyone who is born of the Spirit." Notto Thelle correctly indicates that this Spirit, the Spirit of Truth, at the same time is the wind of Logos that we cannot stop. We might try to divert it, or build walls of defense, but we will still hear the sound. In various ways we can try to drown it. But when our attempts stop, we sill hear the sounds of it. Who can stop this wind, this Spirit that gives life, blows into creation and gives life to our lives? We can drown the wind/the Spirit with out words, with our evasions and with the warnings of our friends, but when words and warnings have come to an end we still hear its sound. It gives life to words of the Bible that we previously did not understand. But there is even more than this: We are often afraid of the unknown—perhaps we are afraid of being introduced to faith because we are secularized, or we are afraid of loosing our faith. "Even when we know that it is the Spirit of Truth that blows into our lives, we resist. But ultimately we are well aware that no one can stop the wind . . . Should anxiety for the unknown be a hindrance to following its way? Who can stop the wind?"[36]

The metaphor in John 3:8 adds one thing more about the Holy Spirit, namely that it is hidden in itself, but is open in its *effects*. If we ask, in the analogy between wind and spirit: "Who is the Holy Spirit?" the answer is: "Look at Jesus Christ and how the Spirit works in him." Then: "Look at the church and how the Spirit operates in it." And finally: "Look at the world and see if you can recognize the Spirit operating in it." These three cannot be separated. The Spirit that works in Christ, must enlarge its work to the church, and the church does not exist for itself but for the sake of the world, the consummation of which has been prepared by the Spirit of the Creator from the beginning.[37] The new life "in the Spirit of Christ" cannot be seen immediately, but all those who are born of water and Spirit (John 3:5) can

---

36. Thelle, *Hvem kan standse vinden?*, 12.*
37. Martensen, *Dåb og Gudstro*, 169–70.

be recognized by their care for their brothers and sisters and by their faith, hope, and love—*the fruits* of the Spirit.[38] The sign of the presence of the Holy Spirit is the new life that is disclosed in love for the other brothers and sister. In 1 John 3:23–24 the characteristics of the Spirit are clearly lives marked by mutual love.[39]

What Jesus says to Nicodemus is in effect that life cannot be *reduced* to the life given by our parents. What is born of the Spirit is spirit. We are encouraged to see *with new eyes*. Our biological, social, and historical identities have not fallen away but they mean less than before. The name of the new community is sisterhood and brotherhood or just friendship.[40]

---

38. Aagaard, *Identifikation af kirken*, 251.

39. However, 1 John also reflects the difficulties of implementing such a life of mutual love. Two groups in the Johannine community seem to be at odds with each other, cf. Brown, *The Community of the Beloved Disciple*.

40. Aagaard, *Identifikation af kirken*, 257–58.

5

Water

Historical Perspectives

Water as a Universal Symbol

BRIEFLY AFTER THE CONVERSATION about rebirth in chapter 3 follows another conversation which also demonstrates how Jesus met with persons from other faith traditions. The first part of chapter 4 is about Jesus' encounter with the Samaritan woman (John 4:1–42). The specific character of this conversation is its focus on the "living water." Water is a fundamental and universal symbol, basic to survival and a requirement for all plant growth. Within human history and experience it conveys three dominant possibilities that affect our life:[1]

- as *life-giving* water for consumption, growth, preservation, nurture
- as *cleansing* water to purify our bodies, our communities, our food
- as *threatening* water in flood, storm, torrent, and through contamination

Water, then, can be both a blessing and a threat. The question is what kind of associations the image of water has for us. Do we consider it as a great blessing or a major threat? Both aspects are found in the Bible. In the first story of creation the symbol of water is ambiguous, with chaotic and desolate waters in the beginning (Gen 1:2). God's creative activity first

---

1. *Images of Life*, 26.

concentrates on ordering these waters to allow "space" for creations.[2] In the second story of creation (Gen 2) water is conceived of as a life-giving power. It is this positive conception of water that characterizes John 4. Here the "living water" refers both to water in a literal sense (spring water) and to water in a symbolic sense (Jesus or the Holy Spirit as living water). Let us first look at the dialogue form of the story and then at the use of the words "the living water" and the issue of the place for the true worship.

The Dialogue between Jesus and the Samaritan Woman

The dialogue between religions is often marked by enmity, hate, and rivalry. In some cases, the hate is so deep that it brings about a war of religion. In Jesus' time there was a great enmity between Jews and Samaritans—indeed the two had previously been to war with each other. However, the story in John 4 shows that a real dialogue can arise despite differences and contrasts. The encounter between Jesus and the woman has two dimensions, closely related and of equal importance: the social and the religious.

(a) As regards the *social dimension* the woman is an example of those who are rejected by this world. Seen from a traditional Jewish way of thinking, she has at least three factors working against her.[3] First, she is a *foreigner*, a Samaritan, and therefore in Jewish eyes ritually impure, for Samaritans mixed with the pagan population after the Babylonian captivity. Nor did they worship God in Jerusalem but at Garizim. She too is aware of the difference: "How is it that you, a Jew, ask a drink of me, a woman of Samaria?" (v.9). Second, she is a *fallen* woman. She was not just a "common stranger" like the Good Samaritan (Luke 10:30–37), she was also a sinner. In her own society she was expelled because of the way she had lived. Previously she had had five husbands, and the man with whom she now lived, was not even her husband (v. 18). Third, she is a *woman*, and therefore out of bounds in the public sphere. Jesus is therefore violating Jewish norms and conventions in speaking to her, and this explains his disciples' reaction in 4:27: "Just then his disciples came. They were astonished that he was speaking with a woman."

---

2. Ariarajah, "The Water of Life," 272; Ariarajah rightly notes that in many religious traditions water represents the "formless" and the "potential," signifying the primal substance from which all forms came into being and into which all would return. Water is the first and primary element; it is potential and germinal and hence the source of all creation (ibid., 271).

3. Russell, *Becoming Human*, 23–26.

It is noteworthy that Jesus talks to such a person about the great existential questions: the living water and the place for true worship. He demolishes all the barriers that had made the woman an outcast. He brings the message of love which cannot be hindered by human intervention. In the course of the conversation different things are revealed to her. She realizes who she is (cf. v. 29). She is given a new life, a radically new beginning. At the same time she realizes who Jesus is; she recognizes that he is Messiah (v.26). This is the only time in the Fourth Gospel that Jesus says about himself that he is Messiah, and this he says to a woman with an inadequate faith!

(b) Here we touch upon the second aspect of the story: the *spiritual dimension*. The dialogue between Jesus and the Samaritan woman has the character of faith meeting faith. It concentrates on two issues:

The *first* part deals with *the living water* (vv. 6–15). We are led from the daily problems with the supply of water and food to something deeper and more comprehensive, though this is not to say that the needs of everyday life are without importance. It begins with Jesus asking for water (v. 6), and it ends with the woman who says: "Sir, give me this water . . ." (v. 15).

It seems that the woman is not quite sure what she is asking for. Is it water in a literal sense, or in a figurative sense? Probably both aspects are included. Jesus is the living water, the water of life—in the same way as he is the bread of life (6:35). This means that he is the one who gives both things: water in the literal sense and water as an expression of the Spirit. He is both the creator of life and the renewer of life. The living water is the renewal which the gospel brings into daily life.

The *second* part of the dialogue deals with the question of *the place for true worship* (vv. 16–26). The woman asks whether it is on this mountain (Garizim) or in Jerusalem. Jesus answers that worship has nothing to do with geography. Worship is not bound to a particular place. This is in line with the statement of the Book of Revelation that there is no temple in the new Jerusalem (Rev 21:22). "God is spirit, and those who worship him must worship in spirit and truth" (John 4:24). The words "spirit and truth" are not to be understood as conceptions which can be acquired or owned once for all. Spirit and truth cannot be achieved through philosophical and religious speculations, as it is argued in some religions and philosophies.

The statement about worship in "spirit and truth" does not refer to the form of worship. Rather, it refers to a worship that has its origin in the encounter with God's revelation which in itself is the truth (cf. 14:6).

This means that the statement does not express a contrast between inner worship of a more private character and the worship of a congregation that assembles around words and sacraments. Worship is a praise of the Word that became flesh and lived among us.[4] The only way to know God is through his revelation, irrespective of who we are and irrespective of where we worship.

For the Samaritan woman the situation at the well becomes worship when Jesus reveals himself to her (v.26). In this way any daily situation can become worship, and any daily situation in a similar way can become a witness and mission. When the woman has heard the self-revelation of Jesus she leaves her jar at the well and runs to the town to tell people what has happened: "Come and see!" Through her witness other people go to the well, and many of them come to believe in Jesus (v. 39).

In summary, John 4 is a paradigm for mission.[5] Jesus' method is fundamentally dialogical, following the questions and issues raised by the Samaritan woman and pursuing his revelation purpose to the very end. The climax of the dialogue is Jesus' self-revelation in 4:26, but the core of the entire dialogue is the woman and her needs (vv. 10.13–14). Jesus uses the opportunity as a medium for revelation and proclamation, but for the woman it becomes a journey of self-discovery. The astonishing thing is that she immediately becomes a missionary. "Because of her sex, nationality and deplorable history (9.17–18.27), the woman represents the lowest grade of humanity to whom Jesus' mission of salvation could be directed. If such a woman, then, can be deemed worthy of Jesus self-revelation, then nobody can be excluded from his saving mission."[6]

Dialogue as a Self-Critical Learning Process

Like the other conversations in the Fourth Gospel Jesus' conversation with the Samaritan woman is relevant to the religious dialogue of today. The interaction of question and answer has a crucial function, though the outcome may be different. This is exemplified by a comparison between John 3 and 4.

Within the literary unit of John 2–4 the Samaritan woman is clearly contrasted with Nicodemus. Whereas he comes to Jesus at night and

---

4. Mogensen, *Således elskede Gud verden*, 82–83.
5. Nissen, *New Testament and Mission*, 89.
6. Okure, *The Johannine Approach to Mission*, 184.

disappears into the shadows, confused by Jesus' self-revelation, she encounters Jesus at high noon, accepts his self-revelation, and brings others to him by her testimony.[7] Apparently Nicodemus and Jesus do not "find" each other. We notice a tension between question and answer which has to do with the content of the discourse. Nicodemus cannot understand the distinction between physical and spiritual birth. The Kingdom of God is not a prolongation of our religious quest. By nature we are unable to enter it but have to be born anew and from above before entering. As mentioned in the chapter on "Rebirth" the destiny of Nicodemus is unclear. He slips out of the picture, though he later reappears twice (7:58; 19:38ff.); and there is a hint that he becomes a sympathizer or perhaps a "secret Christian." Perhaps he in the end understands what it is all about; yet the focus in John 3 is on the "confrontation." It seems that the encounter between the two persons is without success.

The development of the dialogue in John 4 is different. Here too a change is called for; and here again there is an encounter between two worlds. The story takes the form of a dialogue on daily issues between the two partners, but unlike the conversation in chapter 3 it leads to a new insight in the mind of the questioner. She recognizes who Jesus is (4:26). Thus, the communication of the gospel has the character not of confrontation but of a thorough-going change of heart.[8]

John 3 and 4 may serve as an offer of identification for readers. However, it is interesting to note that the character with whom we best identify in John 4 is a person who belongs to the fringes of society. It is the foreign, fallen woman who first "sees," and brings others to "see" him. In this context we should also notice the role of *misunderstanding* in the Johannine dialogues. Nicodemus and the Samaritan women both misunderstand Jesus. Understanding is also on occasion a problem for his own disciples (e.g., 11:11–15). The purpose of the Johannine dialogues is to lead the readers into a self-critical *learning process*. Contrary to what is often argued the interest of John is not the sharp contradiction between belief and disbelief, but rather the grey zone between them. He demonstrates how one gradually comes from blindness to sight, from ignorance to insight (cf. John 9).

---

7. Schneiders, *The Revelatory Text*, 187.
8. Rebell, *Gemeinde als Gegenwelt*, 177–210.

Part One: Images of a Greater Reality

CONTEMPORARY PERSPECTIVES

The Living Water—Indian Interpretations of John 4

As mentioned in the first part of this book the Fourth Gospel plays an important role in Indian theology. In relation to chapter 4 there are two quite different ways of treating the gospel: the mystical interpretation and the social interpretation.[9]

a. The mystical interpretation. One of the most interesting contributions within this category is Sister Vandana's book *Waters of Fire*. Based on a number of Johannine texts she attempts to show the kinship between this gospel and classic Hindu texts, and in doing so she emphasizes the importance of the symbol of water. This is illustrated by the titles of each chapter of her book:

1. Waters of Recognition—John 1:29–34
2. Water—God's Extravaganza—John 2:1–11
3. Waters of Rebirth—John 3:1–13
4. Jeevan-Dhara (Living Streams)—John 4:14
5. Healing Waters—John 5:1–15
6. Walking on the Waters—John 6:16–21
7. Water to Drink—John 7:37–39
8. The Guru's Pad-Puja—John 13:1–20
9. Waters of Salvation—John 19:31–37
10. Epilogue—Waters of Awakening—John 21:1–23.

Vandana's interpretation of John's Gospel stands in the mystical tradition, especially an ashramic spirituality. Although the aim of this spirituality is union with God, it will also, as a by-product, produce changes in society.[10]

9. Spindler, "Indian Studies," speaks of six main trends: "Some see the emphasis in a mystical union with God in a more or less cognitive process, some place the union with God in the sphere of love, others in the area of decision and commitment, some others again identify a strong eschatological and historical frame in John, others insist upon universal symbols in the Gospel of John, and others use the Gospel as a resource and direction for meditation in the technical sense" (ibid., 4).

10. The transformation of inner being will in turn lead to transformation of social structure, which according to Vandana is the "Asian, Marian, Gandhian way" to bring about justice in the world; cf. Kim, *Mission in the Spirit*, 95.

Water

The story of the Samaritan woman is central to the book, and its method and message may be summarized with reference to this story.[11]

John 4 is seen as a universal story about the fundamentals of life. Its setting is compared to a typical Indian village. "For a Jew to request water of a Samaritan was like a Brahmin asking for water of a Harijan (outcast) woman."[12] Vandana takes as her text, "The water that I shall give will turn into spring inside him, welling up to eternal life," (John 4:14; her translation), and ends with a Hindu-hymn, "Lord, give me the waters of life, the living waters, the waters of Ganges that flow from out your heart."[13] For Vandana, water in John is a symbol of the Holy Spirit, which she equates with the life-force of which the Ganges is a primary symbol. Jesus offers the woman himself, which is the Holy Spirit. The religion that he offers is essentially one of the "inside," of the interior.[14] It is a religion of the Spirit, the *atman* which comes from within, from the heart. The woman's deepest needs are satisfied by the water that pours from the heart of Christ.

According to Kirsteen Kim, Vandana's approach to John 4 is indicative of her approach to the Gospel as a whole, which is highly symbolic, less concerned with the root meanings of words than with their associations and their beauty. The emphasis on the mystical means that she downplays the element of human struggle in the story. "Jesus' weariness is not referred to and his thirst is spiritualized. Despite her professed sympathy for the feminist and *dalit* movements, Vandana ignores the reciprocal nature of the conversation between Jesus and the woman, making the role of the woman entirely passive, and what begins as an illustration of Jesus crossing caste boundaries comes close to an uncritical endorsement of brahminic spirituality as Vandana interprets Jesus in terms of *advaita*."[15]

Like the Indian Christian theologian Bishop Appasamy, Sister Vandana represents a mystical interpretation of the Fourth Gospel.[16] Many of her works are reflections on John in the light of the Upanishads or *vice*

---

11. Kim, *Mission in the Spirit*, 93–100.
12. Vandana, *Waters of Fire*, 45.
13. Ibid., 58.
14. Ibid., 51.
15. Kim, *Mission in the Spirit*, 99.
16. This is not to say that the concrete (material) aspect is totally neglected. See Vandana's interpretation of John 13 referred to in chapter 9 of this book. The same chapter contains a description of Appasamy's interpretation—cf. the paragraph: "Bhakti-devotion in Hinduism and the Johannine concept of love" below.

versa. The emphasis is on inculturation into the Hindu culture. The outcome is a specific focus on the mystical or spiritual aspect of the Gospel.

b. The social interpretation. This approach is taken by among others the catholic, D. S. Amalorpavadass. He has written a lengthy foreword to Vandana's book, and it is interesting to see his critical remarks: "While we commend the author's positive appreciation of religious traditions of India and her usage of Indian culture as a medium of communication, we feel that *one important dimension of Indian reality is absent* from the consideration and treatment of the author."[17] In relation to John's use of "living water" one should ask:[18]

- What is the symbolism of water or lack of it for the teeming millions of people in a situation of oppression, exploitation and injustice?
- What is the religious significance and challenge of the painful fact that millions of people in village and urban slums do not have clean drinking water even 34 years after independence?
- What is the connection between the holy streams of our land (Ganga, Jamuna etc.) *and* the lack of water to drink for people and animals, not to speak of the many harvests that fail?

Amalorpavadass adds that his critical suggestion does not take away his genuine appreciation for other merits of the book. But according to him there can be no truly indigenized theology which is not liberationist.[19] Other Indian theologians points in the same direction. According to Christopher Duraisingh the idea that the background of John is the Hellenization process of Christian faith, that it was written by a Greek to Greeks, and that it therefore finds an immediate meeting-point in the Indian mystical soul, is untenable. To interpret it in Hellenistic, pietistic, or merely spiritualistic terms is wrong. "Its message has the cutting edge relevant for those who

---

17. Amalorpavadass, "Foreword" (to *Waters of Fire*), xii; italics in the original.
18. Ibid., xiii.
19. For a similar point of view see Soares-Prabhu, "From Alienation to Inculturation." The author criticizes ashram spirituality from a liberationist point of view. He argues that *ashrams* are not a true inculturation because they disregard the economically oppressed and they merely dress up the gospel in indigenous clothes (cf. also Kim, *Mission in the Spirit*, 114).

struggle for reconstruction of a modern India."[20] The importance of the incarnation is emphasized.[21] In particular three aspects are underlined:

First, in John all traditional attributes of God are expressed not as adjectives but as adverbial modifiers of divine social relationship to all else, that is, divine attributes in John are divine modes of relation, love being the supreme mode. God is conceived of as a *societal relationship*.[22] Second, this authentic societal relation between Father and Son, Christ and his people, is described in terms of an *organic model* of the vine and the branches. Bishop Appasamy develops this image to point out how on the one hand it avoids any notion of mystical identity where individuation is totally lost, and on the other hand it negates notions of mere individualistic-subjective inwardness, for example that of Bultmannian existentialists (see also chapter 11 of this book). Third, the new commandment of love (John 13:34) is the *law* of this authentic sociality. Christ's selfless love with which he loved his own to the very end (John 13:1) is the *pattern* of such a social togetherness. The life, death, and resurrection of Christ as a single movement of this love can also be the movement of human sociality.

According to another Indian theologian, Samuel Rayan, the mysticism of John's Gospel is a historical mysticism. "The Fourth Gospel is mystical because it is alive with concern for the plight, the needs and the possibilities of the multitudes whom God loves."[23] The Samaritan woman in John 4 must be seen as one of the victims of Jewish discrimination: "Bringing them liberation from the oppression of contempt and marginalization and from the prisons of narrow religious traditions and from conceptions of God which are unworthy of him and of us was central to the ministry of Jesus."[24] In contrast, Vandana in her commentary on John, uses the same chapter in a way that appears to reinforce the status quo, arguing that the

---

20. Duraisingh, "The Gospel of John," 42.

21. Ibid., 44: "The Prologue, even though, it is Hellenistic in its categories, is in a sense anti-Hellenistic in its basic motif."

22. This focus on the triune God as societal relationship is a critical note to other Christian traditions, e.g., neo-orthodoxy or protestant pietism in India that tend to see God in "monarchical" categories (Duraisingh, "The Gospel of John," 50). A similar understanding of the Trinitarian loving fellowship is expressed by the Indian Orthodox theologian Mar Osthatios (*Sharing God and a Sharing World*) and by a number of Western theologians (e.g., Moltmann) and Latin American liberation theologians (e.g., Boff). See also Nissen, *Bibel og økumeni*, 187–88.

23. Rayan, "Jesus and the Poor," 213.

24. Ibid., 220.

Harijans' deepest needs are satisfied by the truth which flows from contemplative traditions, including brahminism.[25]

Sharing the Living Water

Vandana mentions other dimensions in the story in John 4. For instance, it is interesting to see how immediately the woman, having drunk of the "living water," herself becomes a believer—like the other woman Mary Magdalene who was the first believer in the Risen Lord; John 20:11–18.[26] The role of the Samaritan woman as missionary is hinted at in the end of the story. She enters the Samaritan city and tells about Christ and many of her townspeople believed in him because of her testimony (4:39–42), cf. the notice that the field *already* is ripe for harvest (4:35–36).

The new task of the Samaritan woman is interpreted by Vandana as "sharing waters": The living water becomes already now a "spring" in her, and the water begins to stream to other people. There is a reference to the Indian artist Jyoti Sahi who has painted the scene in John 4 (the only illustration in her book): the woman is seen—almost on her toes—being drawn up and into the Heart of Christ, from where she yearningly "draws" the living water, and simultaneously she herself becomes a living stream of that great gushing water. This corresponds to the saying of Jesus on the last day of the Booths, John 7:37: "Let anyone who is thirsty come to me, and let the one who believes in me drink. As the scripture has said, 'Out of the believer's heart shall flow rivers of living water.'"

Jyoti's own explanation of the painting is reproduced: "Water flows from what in Hindu terms might be called 'the cave' of Christ's heart. The woman at the well becomes part of that stream, in that she herself seems to impersonate the feminine force of nature which is here spoken of as having its true source in Christ. In Indian art the spirits of rivers and wells are often personified in the forms of woman (cf. Ganga-mata)."[27] In the painting, Christ is seen sitting in lotus posture above the well, meditating. The woman is reaching up toward his heart, her hands cupped to receive the living water that—channelled by Christ's hands—streams from it and

---

25. Cf. Kim *Mission in the Spirit*, 200. Kim finds that both Vandana's and Rayan's studies of John's Gospel are selective, Rayan favouring the act of Jesus that reveal a deeper meaning of the Spirit, and Vandana preferring to dwell on the symbolic meaning expressed in the discourses and its parallels with Hindu thought.

26. Vandana, *Waters of Fire*, 57.

27. Ibid.

simultaneously transforms her into a living stream of water. Christ sits between a papal tree and a neem tree which is sacred to both Buddhists and Hindus. There is a wind blowing and the whole painting is bathed in the fiery glow of the sun behind Christ's head.[28]

The statement "God is spirit, and those who worship him must worship in spirit and truth" is seen to be a critique of all cult. Vandana notes that many people who are "religious"—devout templegoers or churchgoers, offerers of *Puja* and *Yagna*—may not be truly "spiritual" at all. Contrariwise, as in the West and increasingly among the youth in some parts of India, there are among many post-Christians sincere "spiritual" people, seeking God and worshipping Him "in spirit and in truth"—people whom one may ignorantly condemn or pity as irreligious.[29]

It seems that this critique reflects a tendency to spiritualize the text in a way that is untenable. The point in John 4:24 is not a contrast between spirit and flesh or between the spiritual and the material. To say that "God is spirit" means to say that God acts in a way which breaks boundaries and renews. As mentioned previously worshipping in truth and spirit does not refer to the form of worship, but to its core root: it is a praise of the Word that became flesh and lived among us.

On the other hand Vandana is correct in regarding 4:24 as a critique of religion as an institution—whether it be church or temple. This criticism of cult is supported by John 2:18ff., a passage in which the old temple is replaced by a new temple that is Jesus himself.[30] Matthew Vellanickal, another Indian theologian, states that "every cult undertaken by man, which has its initiative in man, is inadequate, in whatever form or place it is celebrated. Adequate worship can only be given as a response to God's self-revelation in Jesus Christ. There can be no true relationship between man and God, unless it be grounded on and is in response to God's dealings with man."[31]

---

28. Cf. Kim, *Mission in the Spirit*, 98.

29. Vandana, *Waters of Fire*, 54.

30. In this context it is worth mentioning an interesting investigation by the biblical scholar Nereparampil, *Destroy this Temple*. Even though the author himself does not comment directly on the actual situation in India, the choice of title might not be a coincidence, cf. Spindler, "*Recent Indian Studies*," 36: "It is not impossible that this study may have a hidden relevance to the Indian context, where so much importance has been attached to the saying 'Not to Destroy But to Fulfil' (Mat. 5:17; quoted p. 43). The idea of the beginning of the new economy of salvation in the person of Jesus, who will be the new 'Temple' (91) for all Christians, may be applied in very controversial ways."

31. Vellanickal, "Drink from the Source," 317.

Part One: Images of a Greater Reality

Worshipping "in spirit and truth"—Material Reality and Johannine Mysticism

The German biblical scholar Gerd Theissen has suggested an understanding of John 4 that includes historical as well as actual perspectives. His entry point is the opposition between Jews and Samaritans. In the light of the hard reality of religious animosity the dialogue between Jesus and the woman at the well stands out as an example of how to worship in spirit and truth. In this interpretation the story reflects the unique Johannine mysticism in which water and food become images of a mystical experience that forms a contrast to hate and prejudges. Theissen argues that there are three ways of reading the story:[32]

The first has to do with *the level of relations*. The focus is on the relation between Jesus and the woman. Theissen wonders if the description of the mutual relations between the two persons bears traces of eroticism—as is the case with the Old Testament scenes at Jacob's well. However, Jesus' statements on her matrimonial conduct show that this is not the case. Furthermore, there is no hint at all that Jesus condemns her present way of relating to men. The main point of the story is that Jesus meets her as the Messiah who shows how God should be worshipped in spirit and truth. Such worship transcends the traditional division of gender roles and subverts the barriers of communication.

The second reading deals with *the material level*. It is imperative first to read the story concretely. Despite its sublime, mystical spirituality the Fourth Gospel often gives a surprising glimpse of this world with its hard realities. In fact, the story in John 4 reflects the most elementary questions, such as how we procure something to drink and to eat. The woman provides for the water, and the disciples have left Jesus in order to provide for some food. Jesus appears as a person who is in need of water and food, and others take care of bringing these things to him. These vital necessities are made accessible through the work of human beings: at noon—in the midst of the heat of the day—the woman goes to the well in order to draw water, and it is other people who sow and harvest in order to provide for the bread (cf. 4:36–38). It is in the context of this shortage of water and bread that religion for the first time comes to the fore.

All this seems to be quite natural, and yet, it is very important. It is precisely in this narrative we get an idea of the hard struggle in the distribution

---

32. Theissen, *Lichtspuren*, 152–56.

of basic goods and the scarcity of vital things. This story also suggests that religious traditions are often just accompanying music to give people a clear conscience in their fight for the distribution of the goods of life. Finally, the story also discloses the misunderstanding of the woman—as long as she only remains on the material level. When Jesus refers to "living water" he does not have the well in mind, and when he speaks of the water of life he does not think of Jacob. However, the misunderstanding of the woman is not just that of a "typical Johannine" character. This misunderstanding is seen several times in the history of Christianity and in the history of religion. Religion is misused to legitimize the combat about distribution of basic goods. Belief in Jesus should not be a meditative and mystical accompanying music to the struggle about distribution.

The third reading takes place on *the symbolic level*. In the Fourth Gospel events and words often have a symbolic meaning in addition to their literal meaning. In this story water becomes a symbol of the energy that gives eternal, true life (cf. 4:13–14). The term "living water" designates the power that gives life (e.g., the Spirit). Later on Jesus says (with reference to the Scripture) "Out of the believer's heart shall flow rivers of living water." These words are explained in the following way by John: "Now he said this about the Spirit, which the believers in him were to receive" (7:38–39). This confirms that in John 4 Jesus makes a promise of God's Spirit to the woman.

Based on this analysis of John 4 Theissen points to three distinctive marks in Johannine mysticism.[33] First, it is a mysticism of will, i.e., it is a conjunction of God's will with human will, cf. 4:34: "My food is to do the will of him who sent me and to complete his work." This mysticism is not an individualist but social in nature, its main focus being on Jesus' love. Union with God is experienced in loving action. The decisive aspect of this mysticism is expressed in 1 John 4:16: "God is love, and those who abide in love abide in God."

Second, John's mysticism ends the struggle for the distribution of the limited goods of life. This mysticism is related to the contrast between a literal and symbolic sense. Water and bread (in a literal sense) are limited goods; hence they must be distributed. If a person gets more, there is less to another person. But water and bread in a symbolic sense exist in unlimited quantity. God's Spirit, God's will and God's love are not diminished when we are given a share in the divine reality. Here there is no struggle over the distribution of vital goods. When we enter God's new reality, we enter a

---

33. Ibid., 156–58.

"space" that is beyond the struggle for distribution. This insight should have an effect on everyday life. Those who have discovered this will naturally share with others (cf. 1 John 3:17).

Third, John's mysticism serves to liberate people from dependence on religious traditions, in that it leads from an encounter with God mediated through the religious institutions to a more immediate encounter with God outside these institutions. Our worship of God "in spirit and truth" presupposes this inner liberty over against our traditions, because in our own lives we experience that which we have witnessed.

Theissen's study is interesting since it combines a historical and a topical reading of the gospel. He underlines that John's mysticism and his spirituality must be seen in close connection with material reality. This interpretation differs from that of Sister Vandana and resembles more that of Samuel Rayan who in a similar way insists on the connection between history and mysticism. The distinctiveness of Johannine mysticism will be further elucidated in Part Two (see the paragraph, "Love alone is absolute").

Confrontation and dialogue

Jesus' conversation with the Samaritan woman is often considered to be a kind of dialogue of religions. To illustrate this point it may be relevant to refer to Jean-Marc Chappuis (1982) who points to no less than ten layers of this story:[34]

1. *Perverted communication or poisoning.* The story begins with a note on Jesus leaving Jerusalem, when he learns that "the Pharisees had heard he was making and baptizing more disciples than John" (4:1–3). Public communication is often built on rumors and falsifications.

2. *Everyday communication or personal relations.* After the public aspect of communication comes a more personal aspect. Personal relations begin here on the level of everyday communication, that of commonplace utilitarian exchanges. Most often, personal relations remain on this level and everyday communications remain superficial. It sometimes happens, however, that relations become more intense, deeper, acquire more character, and then communication assumes the substantial character of interpersonal encounter, genuine meeting face to face. The most commonplace communication may expand to become suddenly substantial. That clearly is what happens in

---

34. Chappuis, "Jesus and the Samaritan Woman."

the meeting between Jesus and the Samaritan woman. She is attentive to this stranger, and this stranger (Jesus) shows empathy towards her.

3. *Impossible communication or the walls of separation.* Walls of separation do in fact exist between people, walls that make communication impossible: between men and woman, between generations and between nations. In this case the walls of separation are high and thick (ethical, cultural, religious, and the Samaritan knows it). "Give me a drink." "How is it that you, a Jew, ask a drink of me, a woman of Samaria?" The two speakers have a collective history behind them.

4. *Verbal communication or language and speech.* The verbal communication is important ("Give me . . ."), but so is also the non-verbal communication. Non-verbal communication always precedes and constantly accompanies verbal communication. "Give me a drink"—the language and accent probably gave her unmistakable clues. Even before that his clothes had no doubt marked him out. Yet, it is of equal importance to know who is speaking. To the woman's question if Jesus is "greater than our father Jacob . . . ," he answers unambiguously: Jacob our father and his well leave you thirsty, but "whoever drinks of the water that I shall give him will never thirst." The speaker and the change he produces are both in the foreground.

5. *Communication in dialogue or personal encounters with others.* Jesus does not seek to hold up a mirror, but rather an icon, to the woman he is talking to. His intention is not in fact therapeutic but soteriological. There are two characteristics of the authentic dialogue: (a) it is a confrontation; cf. the irony in the text; (b) it is a true dialogue that changes those who engage in it.

6. *Poetic communication or symbolic expression.* "Water" can become a symbolic expression of the Spirit (cf. 7:37–39).

7. *Existential communication or disclosure of man.* Some conversations do not really involve the speakers. When Jesus appears, the moment comes when existential communication is established. Jesus changes the subject and therefore the language. Enough talk of God. Let us now talk about you: "Go, call your husband, and come here." Revelation is for man the disclosure of his own life.[35] The existential communication is the opportunity offered man to pass from death to life.

35. Cf. Bultmann, *Das Evangelium des Johannes*, 138. Bultmann entitles this paragraph in his commentary "Die Offenbarung als Aufdeckung des menschlichen Seins." See also the paragraph at the end of this chapter, "Love discloses who we are as human beings" and the paragraph, "Seeking God—sought by God" in Part Two.

8. *Theological communication or the manifestation of God.* She asks about the place where such communication occurs: is it on Mount Garizim or in Jerusalem? In other words: Where does God communicate himself? On a mountain? In my conscience? Through the text or the sacred book? By the instrumentality of the infallible magisterium of a religious community? Jesus' answer is in total contradiction to the prevailing ideas of his age and also to those of the modern age on the matter. God does in fact communicate himself, but not at any of these places. The place of his communication is a person: "I am he, the one who is speaking to you" (4:26).

9. *Narrative communication or Christian witness.* The communication of the gospel can take the form of teaching, of preaching, of witnessing. In John 4 the content of communication consists in costly personal witness and its form is a challenging narrative. The Samaritan woman does not proclaim anything. She relates and questions. She does not teach but she tells her own story. The communication of the gospel is not in the first place a doctrine or a liturgy, but a history.

10. *Our daily bread and the fields white for harvest or the secret and horizons of communication.* Everything began at the side of the well with the misunderstanding about water. And everything finishes there with the misunderstanding about bread. "I have food to eat that you do not know about." (4:32). The disciples misunderstand the meaning, just as the Samaritan woman had done, by taking the symbol in its material sense. Then Jesus explains: "My food is to do the will of him who sent me and to complete his work." (4:34). Such is Jesus' secret food, his daily bread and ours. And that is the secret of communication. In a world of perverted communication, of the walls of separation which divide peoples, of superficiality of human relations, of ambiguity of language, the future of communication between human beings belongs to those who do the will of God.

The concrete realty of everyday life is the starting-point for the conversation between Jesus and the woman. The conversation might have remained at that. But it develops and becomes an authentic dialogue that is characterized by two traits.[36]

The first trait is *the confrontation*. Among some commentators there is a tendency to blur this aspect of the conversation. But in fact there is mockery and scorn between the two persons. Jesus says to the woman that she would ask him about water if she had known the gift of God; she

---

36. Chappuis, "Jesus and the Samaritan Woman," 19–20.

replicates that he has no bucket, and the well is deep. And later when she asks him whether he thinks himself greater than Jacob she is jeering and gibing at him.

Jesus for his part attacks her openly; on the respect due to Jacob, one of the patriarchs, which he declares out of date, on her marital status which he discloses, on salvation which "comes from the Jews." True dialogue is confrontation; here a radical one. And because it is confrontation, true dialogue produces *change;* that is its second trait. It changes those who engage in it. Genuine dialogue can lead neither to a facile consensus nor to one-way proclamation, nor to conciliary syncretism. True dialogue leads to the indeterminate. The partners change each other and only the end of their confrontation shows where their dialogue has led. The Samaritan woman has emerged from this dialogue changed.[37] Jesus, too, has changed. The disciples were surprised. They had left him tired, hungry, thirsty but they found him strengthened, his thirst was quenched and he was satisfied.

There is a tendency to contrast proclamation and dialogue. That is a superficial antithesis. This story shows that dialogue is an important aspect of the proclamation. The authentic Christian encounter with others must be personal and open in character.[38] The term "personal" is used to underline that Christians do not "have" the truth, because truth does not belong to the order of possession. Jesus never said "I have the truth." What he said is quite different: "I am the truth" (John 14:6). "Christ does not bring truths which one can acquire; he is the truth. He uncovers the human condition and reveals man to himself."[39]

Love Discloses Who We Are as Human Beings

Finally I want to highlight one important aspect of John 4. The story demonstrates how Jesus discloses not only himself but also the woman's true nature. This twofold dimension of revelation is a distinctive mark of John's Gospel.[40] Again and again we see how Jesus is *revealed* to a number of

---

37. In v. 15 the woman asks for water and at the end of the story (vv. 38–42) she has become one who believes in Jesus.

38. The WCC Uppsala Assembly rightly says: "A Christian dialogue with another implies neither a denial of the uniqueness of Christ, but rather that a genuinely Christian approach to others must be human, personal, relevant and humble . . . Each meets and challenges the other" (*The Uppsala Report*, 29).

39. Molla, quoted by Chappuis, "Jesus and the Samaritan Woman," 20.

40. See also the paragraph "Seeking God—sought by God" in chapter 16.

Part One: Images of a Greater Reality

people, beginning with a wedding (2:1–11), continuing with Nicodemus and the Samaritan woman, and ending with Mary Magdalene's "I have seen the Lord" after her experience in the garden. In a sermon on John 4 Johannes Møllehave underlines that in her conversation with Jesus the Samaritan woman suddenly realizes not only who she is but also that if she had not met Jesus, her life would have been lost.[41]

A crucial point in this story is that the truth about the woman was revealed, and such a revelation might be burdensome. To another woman who was in a similar situation Jesus said that her sins which were many have been forgiven since she had demonstrated a great amount of love (Luke 7:36–50, v. 47). Jesus did not say the same to the Samaritan woman. Perhaps she might not have loved that much. Nevertheless, the Samaritan woman discovered a new aspect of love. The divine love was revealed to her. In the same way, it was revealed to Simon Peter and he reacted by saying: "Go away from me, Lord, for I am a sinful man!" (Luke 5:8).

Both the sinful man in Luke 5 and the sinful woman in John 4 realize that when love comes to them, the true nature of their life is revealed. But what they meet is not the truth in the sense of an ice-cold truth. Even though Peter says, "Go away from me," love remains beside him—even when he renounces Jesus on a later occasion.

A crucial point in John 4 is that Jesus reveals to the woman at one and the same time who she herself is and who she has been. All the odds have been stacked against her. She is a woman, she is licentious, she is a foreigner from Samaria. Nevertheless when Jesus meets her, a new reality opens up to her. Love accepts her, not because she is naïve, but because that is love's nature.

It has been argued that Jesus' conversation with the woman from Samaria is a fine example of a proclamation that does not manipulate or moralize; rather, it is open-ended and close to the recipient. From Jesus' side the conversation takes the form almost of a retreat, and there is certainly no hint of spiritual imperialism in this story. "Jesus is just the person he is, and he is close to people. And then comes the moment when in her attempt to justify herself the woman stumbles over the truth about the emptiness of her life. At this precise moment she is open to the encounter with Christ: 'I am he, the one who is speaking to you' (John 4:26)."[42]

---

41. See Møllehave, *Den livsild som forbrænder*, 53–61.
42. Falk, *Kærlighedens pris*, 176.*

In the person of Jesus the woman meets a love that is boundary-breaking. This love is *infectious*. The woman is caught by what she meets. She becomes a witness to love and begins a mission among her own townspeople (John 4:38–42).

6

Bread

Historical Perspectives

Bread as a Universal Symbol

IN MOST CULTURES BREAD—LIKE water—is one of the basic elements on which life depends.[1] This is the reason why bread is a fundamental symbol in a great number of cultures, and many a custom is related to its production and consumption. It is often conceived of as a holy gift from God, to be handled with veneration and gratitude. As a symbol bread is closely related to other symbols like sowing and harvesting in a complex of symbols for growth and sustenance.[2]

The Gospel of John also employs bread and its symbols in images of sowing and harvesting (John 4:34–38), while we also find the grain of wheat expressing the transition from death to life (John 12:24). The image of Jesus as "the bread of life" in John 6 has a specific significance: "Bread is a biblical image which evokes responses in many cultures, but not all. Known as the 'staff of life' in some parts of the world, it is unknown elsewhere. Nevertheless, the need for nourishment, for food, is a universal human reality, and

---

1. In some cultures, that of Asia for example, rice has a corresponding role. Unlike rice, bread is not simply a product of nature. In the case of bread, the gifts of creation—grain, water and salt—have been combined with the human labour of the baker to produce this basic food; Link, "The Bread of Life," 249.

2. Mogensen, *Tro, håb og kærlighed*, 46–47.

the shortage of it which brings hunger and starvation to millions of people is an unfolding tragedy in today's world, as it was in ages past. Bread is of course one of the most familiar Christian symbols because of its use in the Eucharist."[3]

Leonardo Boff, a Latin American theologian, points out that the need for bread is an individual matter, but the satisfaction of that need is not an individual effort; it must be that of the community. Bread is *human* to the extent that it is shared and supports a bond of communion. When the bread that we eat is the result of exploitation, it is not a bread blessed by God. Unjust bread is not really our bread; it is stolen; it belongs to someone else. Only *our* bread is God's bread.[4]

The Feeding of the Five Thousand

One of the most important chapters in the Fourth Gospel is John 6, which in many ways is also typical for the theology of the Gospel. Helge Kjær Nielsen even calls it "the gospel within the gospel."[5] The chapter can be divided into four: Jesus' feeding the multitudes (vv.1–15), Jesus' walking on the water (vv.16–21); Jesus in dialogue with the people followed by a discourse on the bread of life (vv. 22–59); and Jesus in dialogue with his disciples (vv. 60–71). In what follows the focus is on the miracle of feeding and on the understanding of Jesus as the bread of life in 6:35. The first of these texts may be divided into five parts:

The introduction: Jesus and the multitudes (vv. 1–4)

The conversation between Jesus and Philip (vv. 5–7)

The prelude to the miracle: a little boy and the many people (vv. 8–10)

The miracle itself and its confirmation (vv. 11–13)

The closing: the effect of the miracle—an attempt to make Jesus king (vv.14–15).

In the midst of the account (v. 9) we have the reply that formulates the theme of the five loaves and the two fish which are not sufficient to feed the multitudes. The choice of words illustrates the problem: the contrast between the "little" boy and the "many" people. The event takes a turn in

---

3. *Images of Life*, 15.
4. Boff, *The Lord's Prayer*, 76–78.
5. Nielsen, *Johannesevangeliet*, 224.

Part One: Images of a Greater Reality

two directions.[6] The first turn is a miracle that changes *reality itself*. The few loaves nourish the many people. The second turn occurs in v. 14, where the multitudes come to a new insight; they interpret the sign, but misunderstand it. They have come to him because "they saw the signs that he was doing for the sick" (v. 2), and after being fed they also "saw the sign that he had done," (v. 14) but they interpret it wrongly—leaving Jesus to withdraw into loneliness. We are left with the realization that it is crucial to 'read' the significance of the bread.

The relation between account and discourse here throws light on how John understands the concept of "sign." In 6:26 he says to the crowd: "You are looking for me, not because you saw signs, but because you ate your fill of the loaves"; and in 6:30 they say to him: "What sign are you going to give us then, so that we may see it and believe you?" While the term "sign" is used negatively in the last passage, it has a positive connotation in the first. Hence, the crowd is mistaken in not perceiving the miracle as a sign, but only as a physical event. They see a sign without seeing *the* sign, i.e., the divine reality that comes to the fore in the acts of Jesus.

The disciples' reaction is marked by a certain division. The account itself only tells how the multitudes react. It is quite possible that the story of the walking on the water (6:16–20) serves to indicate how the disciples experience what has happened. They see how Jesus nourishes those who are hungry and how he defeats the forces of nature; they see his "glory" (cf. 2:11). However, other disciples react differently; for them Jesus' discourse is very hard to accept (6:60) and for this reason many of them leave him (6:66).

How to "read" the Meaning of Bread

In line with other Johannine miracles the multiplication is called a "sign" (6:14), a term that has often been misunderstood as signifying something else, usually something exclusively spiritual. If that were the case, Jesus as the bread of life (6:35) would aim at a spiritual and otherworldly reality in contrast with the concrete, material bread. However, it is a misunderstanding to contrast the spiritual dimension with the material dimension. First, it should be noticed that in several cases the miracles in John are more realistic than in the Synoptic Gospels. Second, the fundamental concepts of life, bread, and water are not just spiritual entities that make creation void; they

---

6. Bjerg, *Øjnenes faste*, 122.

are on the contrary about basic needs. Seen in relation to Jesus (e.g., 6:35) their intention is not to reduce creation. The Johannine Jesus is active not only in the new creation, but also in the old creation (cf. John 1:1; 5:17). In other words, all miracles must be understood in the light of the Prologue.[7]

A similar argument is proposed by Elsa Tamez.[8] When we reflect on the two accounts in John 6:1–15 and 6:22–59, we see that in both accounts two inseparable and essential elements are kept constantly together: bread and the word; the satisfaction of eating and the satisfaction of living life in all its fullness; matter and the spirit which inspires matter; bread and the blessing of the bread that will not perish. In other words, we are concerned with a human experience embracing both the immediate and the transcendent. Christian tradition has often separated this human experience and been content with the spiritual side: the word, the spirit, the blessing, while disregarding the material side: the bread. But the spirit without the flesh is useless—as of course is the flesh without the spirit. The multiplication of the loaves into bread for all signifies the abundance of life provided by Jesus, himself the bread of life.

Similarly, Svend Bjerg underlines that Jesus does not establish a contrast between bread as a material reality and bread as a spiritual sign. "He presupposes that there *is* eternity in the daily bread but he also tests our way of looking at things. He tests the ability of people to see a connection. The only person to pass the test is the one who can see the invisible *in* the visible, the eternity *in* the temporal. It is a specific ability to comprehend, the ability to see two realities at the same time."[9] "In the bread, daily life is linked to eternal life. Jesus maintains the interlinking of bread with the sign that it denotes. He does not invite us to localize the meaning of the bread in something that transcends this daily world, whether it be its internal or external space. It is *in* the daily bread that we find the heavenly bread. This life is eternal life."[10]

Unlike the Synoptic Gospels John concludes his account of the feeding by stating that Jesus refuses to be a king, i.e., a national king of bread. This is not in itself a critique of power as such but a warning against living by bread alone (cf. Matt 4:4). In other words, the Jews should not use the bread to establish an existence without God. In fact according to John 6

---

7. Nissen, "Kongemagt og discipelmenighed," 162.
8. Tamez, "The Bread of Life," 506.
9. Bjerg, *Øjnenes faste*, 124.*
10. Ibid., 24.*

Jesus is both the one who *gives* the daily bread (6:1–15) and the one who *is* the bread (6:35). Unlike John 18:28–19:16 the feeding of the multitudes does not point to Jesus as a king—the time for his glorification has not yet arrived.[11] For the use of the title of "king" in John 6:14 see also the chapter "Images of Christ" in Part Two.

"I am the bread of life"—the Human Quest and the Revelation of God

The significance of John 6:35 can hardly be overestimated. This passage is the first of the Johannine "I am" sayings in which the divine name is linked to such predicates as bread, truth, life, and way. The predicates are symbols of the human quest for God. The hungers and longings signify the long search for the face of God, a search depicted in Wisdom literature precisely in such forms. John intends with such declarations as "I am the bread of life" (6:35) and "I am the light of the world" (8:12) to present Jesus as God's manifest presence and the goal of the human search for God.[12]

We should note that the emphasis is on the positive search rather than the negative rejection. In this sense the "I am" sayings reflect the inclusivism and universality of the gospel. At the same time John insists that Jesus is fulfilling the human search in a surprising manner. This is especially evident in chapter 6. The crowd reacts to his miracles by saying: "Sir, give us this bread always." (6:34)—a reaction that is parallel to the woman's reply in John 4:15: "Sir, give me this water . . ." In both cases Jesus corrects the requests of the interlocutors, yet he also declares that although they do not realize it, he himself is the fulfillment of their search: "The food that you are looking for and which all people are looking for, and for which there are a great number of replacements—that is me. I am the bread of life."[13]

The Holism of the Fourth Gospel—the Theology of Life

In conclusion, it would be a misunderstanding to interpret John 6 as a denial of our material needs. According to such an understanding we have

---

11. Nissen, "Kongemagt og discipelmenighed," 163.

12. Cf. Brown, *The Gospel According to John*, 533–38. The predicative "I am" sayings are to be taken as recognition-formulas in Bultmann's famous classification: "What you understand by the bread of life and long for in it is fulfilled in me" (cf. *Das Evangelium des Johannes*, 168).

13. Davidsen, *Komponenter til kristendomsundervisningen*, 97.* See also the paragraph "The language of symbols and metaphors" in chapter 2 of the present study.

Bread

first the act (the miracle of feeding), the corporeal dimension which is of less importance, and then we have the words (the discourse about the life of bread), the spiritual dimension which is the most important. However, there is an indissoluble link between the material bread and the spiritual bread.[14] The statement in 6:35: "I am the bread of life" has a twofold meaning: Jesus is the one who nourishes man in a literal meaning; at the same time he is the one who provides the spiritual food. The Fourth Gospel presents a holistic theology by pointing to the intrinsic connection between creation and salvation. The Prologue in a similar way demonstrates this connection: "In it was life; and the life was the light of all people" (1:4).[15]

The gift of the Creator to his world is life (1:4), but this is also penetrated by the devil—he who is a "murderer from the beginning" (8:44). John gives a definition of the evil reign of the parasite which is very much to the point. Evil is a power that is unable to create; it can only destroy what God already has created. "The thief comes only to steal and kill and destroy" (10:10). By contrast, Jesus is depicted in the phrase: "I came that they may have life, and have it abundantly" (10:10). Salvation in Jesus Christ means to regain the life that we have been deprived of by the devil and sin. This new life is to be in an authentic communion with God, with our fellow human beings, and with the rest of God's creation.[16]

The Gospel of John is marked by an authentic holism that we may call the theology of life. It is about *life in its fullness*. In this theology there is no contrast between material life and spiritual life. The theology of life means a fight against death and a fight against the lie, the untruth, and all falseness. In this fight there is no grey zone between life and death, so neutrality is not an option— a continual decision *for* life has to be taken.

---

14. Cf. the following comment by Rene Padilla (on John 6): "[W]herever Christian compassion is present there is no room for the type of dichotomies which we oftentimes make between spiritual needs and material needs, between evangelization and service, between word and deed. People are hungry—Jesus feeds them" (Padilla, "Bible Studies," 326).

15. The first sentence of 1:4 is rendered differently in modern translations; according to some translations the best rendering is "in him was life" (so for instance NRSV).

16. Månsus, *Shalom jord*, 164–66.

Part One: Images of a Greater Reality

Contemporary Perspectives

The Bread of Life and the Spirit of Life—an Indian Reading of John 6

As mentioned previously the Gospel of John is interpreted by many Indians in a mystic or a spiritual way (see chapter 5 of this book). However, it has also been argued that some Indian scholars underline the *social* dimension of this Gospel. This is exemplified by Samuel Rayan who argues that the "mystic" reading of the Gospel needs to be supplemented with a "historical" reading—meaning not merely the reliability of details of places, times and events, but in a deeper sense what concerns the life of the people, what relates to the sorrows, hopes, struggles and movements of the often oppressed masses. Rayan suggests that the mysticism of the Fourth Gospel is historical mysticism, and that its contemplation fixes on the glory of God as revealed in Jesus' love and service of the people. "The Fourth Gospel is mystical because it is alive with concern for the plight, the needs and the possibilities of the multitudes whom God loves."[17]

Rayan draws attention to the poverty inherent in the introduction to the feeding of the five thousand—a great number of people are following Jesus because they have seen his signs and are hungry and tired (6:1–6). In Cana Jesus is witness to the embarrassment of a poor family who cannot afford enough wine for so festive an occasion as a wedding (2:1–11). And again, in the colonnades of the sheep-pool in Jerusalem "there lay a crowd of sick people, blind, lame and paralyzed (5:1–7)."[18] All these people are short of bread, of wine, of health, of help, of hope, and of dignity. As Rayan writes, "Bringing them liberation from the oppression of contempt and marginalization and from the prisons of narrow, religious traditions and from conceptions of God which are unworthy of him and of us was central to the ministry of Jesus."[19] "Within the Fourth Gospel, their faith stands in sharp contrast to the unbelief of the learned, the wealthy and the powerful in Jerusalem."[20]

---

17. Rayan, "Jesus and the poor," 213. Kim notes that Rayan attaches a great deal of significance to the signs in John's Gospel, which he sees as concrete, historical events that have a deep meaning. "The method of the Fourth Gospel is to posit a sign first which is 'flesh' and 'work', and then unlock its meaning and message through reflection and discourse" (Rayan, quoted in Kim, *Mission in the Spirit*, 145–46).

18. Rayan, "Jesus and the Poor," 215.

19. Ibid., 220.

20. Ibid. For a similar reading of the Gospel of John see Samuel, "The Kairos of the Galilaioi."

In the context of death and the threat to life Jesus stands as life and life-giver, as victor over death, as resurrection. Thus he appears throughout the Fourth Gospel, as bearer of abundant life to a ravaged flock (John 10), of sight to the blind and acceptance of the rejected (John 9), as giver of bread and new life to hungry crowds (John 6), as bringer of hope and wholeness to a cripple as good as dead (John 5), as provider of wine and joy in situations of want and diminishment (John 2).[21]

In Rayan's thought, not only breath but also bread is a symbol of the Holy Spirit. "Bread and breath" is a richly poetic way of combining the two natures of Christ, the secular and the sacred, the immanence and the transcendence of God. It is a way of bringing earth and heaven together. For Rayan, sharing bread, living for the other is the authentic sign of the Spirit's presence. The bread of life that is both Christ and the earth is broken and shared and this is inspired by the Spirit, the breath of God, who brings about movements for liberation.[22]

For the Life of the World

It is suggestive that the idea of Jesus as the bread of life seems to play a minor role in the religious dialogue and in the contemporary interest in spirituality. Perhaps the reason is that the new spiritual awakening is among other things a reaction to materialism and the consumer mentality. We must be wary not to end up in the opposite ditch so that the focus is merely on spiritual issues.

The last part of the discourse on Jesus as the giver of bread is just such a counterweight to a reading of John 6 that is too spiritual and too individualistic. The text has clear references to the Eucharist, particularly obvious in the last part of 6:51: "and the bread that I will give for the life of the world is my flesh." In this text the Eucharist is not an inner magic rite. On the contrary, it reaches out into the world, for Christ is proclaimed as the savior of the world. The broken bread is not only a confirmation of forgiveness for

---

21. Rayan, "Jesus and the Poor." The author notes that the Fourth Gospel shows this action already in the opening chapter by presenting Jesus as surrounded by laborers, those "whose work is hard and whose load is heavy" (Matt 11:28). Some of these disciples reappear in the closing chapter as fishermen who, after the agony and the ecstasy of the Paschal events, must go back to their boats and nets to earn their daily bread (21:1–3; 1:35–51). Jesus is with the poor in their quest (1:38) and their toil (21:3–5). The fish-haul in chapter 21 is a sign and promise of ultimate victory for the laborers despite the real or apparent fruitlessness of the toil (ibid., 217–18).

22. Cf. Kim, *Mission in the Spirit*, 192–93.

Part One: Images of a Greater Reality

the faithful; it is also a proclamation of God's love for the world. The bread of the Eucharist that is Christ himself is intended "for the life of the world."

The coherence between the faithful and the world is also emphasized by the churches in their common understanding of the Eucharist. In this context it should be noted that the World Council of Churches at its General Assembly in Canberra came to an agreement on the Eucharist as a source of inspiration for the life in the world:

> Eucharistic spirituality lived by a local Christian community is in itself the most valuable diaconal service that can be given and a missionary witness of immeasurable significance. No congregation lives for itself. As Jesus gave himself up for the life of the world, so the church is called to surrender power, resources and interests to God in serving society, world and creation. The prayers of the worshipping community join the voice of the voiceless. Both repentance and thanksgiving are expressed also on behalf of those who are absent. Bread and wine and water brought before God with thanksgiving represent all creation. The sharing of partaking of communion symbolizes justice and love. Our dependence on the fruits of the earth for our physical and spiritual life makes every Eucharistic celebration a call to preserve the integrity of creation. Through all this the Spirit keeps flowing, renewing the face of the earth.[23]

This understanding of the Eucharist reflects a holistic thinking that is also characteristic of John's understanding of Jesus as the "life of the world." There is an indissoluble link between the bread *for* life and the bread *of* life. Any attempt to separate the gift from the giver runs the risk of reducing Christianity to an ideology or a social program. That is the temptation which the multitudes present to Jesus.[24]

Daily bread and the Word of God

As with all texts we must ask who is the speaker, who are the intended recipients, and what is the context. For text and context interpret each other, as can be seen in the following examples.

The first is the beatitude in Luke 6:20: "Blessed are you who are poor, for yours is the kingdom of God." Here it is important to ask who is speaking to whom. Is a rich person speaking to a poor person? Is a well-educated

23. *Signs of the Spirit*, 118–19.
24. Padilla, "Bible Studies," 326–30.

person speaking to an illiterate? Is one who is satisfied speaking to one who is hungry? It is not wrong for a rich person to make this statement but he must apply it *to himself*, otherwise he loses all credibility. But if he does speak the words meaningfully to himself, they become an invitation to entrust all wealth to God and work for a just society.

The second example is from the account of Jesus' temptation in the desert. If a person says: "One does not live by bread alone but by every word that comes from the mouth of God" (Matt 4:4), we also have to ask: Who says these words to whom? If a rich person says the words to a poor person the message is no longer credible, as when the rich in the North tell the hungry in the South that all that matters is listening to the word of God.[25]

Jesus' words are not addressed to the hungry, nor are they the words of a satisfied person; they are spoken by a hungry person (Jesus), and they cannot be used to idealize poverty. The meaning is not that the word of God is more important than the bread. We are in need of both: the word of God and the bread of life. It is a widespread misunderstanding that the "word of God" in Matt 4:4 refers to the word of the Bible; this verse is *not about the word of the Bible but about the word of the Creator*. The word of the Creator is the word by means by which God creates and sustains the world. He is life and he gives himself as life. To live by bread alone means reserving it for ourselves and failing to share it with the others. In the fourth petition of the Lord's Prayer the material needs and spiritual needs are linked to each other, without the one taking precedence over the other. In the founding period of the church, daily bread was seen as a sign of the messianic meal, and conversely the messianic meal was a remembrance of the indispensability of daily bread.

Turning to John 6 we must therefore consider these three viewpoints:

a. Man cannot live without bread. This aspect is emphasized by *poor* Christians in the South. The liberation theologian Ernesto Cardenal notes that the five thousand see the miracle that love will effectuate in the world. He compares this with our present situation of food in abundance in some places and the lack of food in others. Any shortage is surely due to egotism, for if love prevailed there would be an abundance for all.[26]

25. Cf. the following remarks on Matt 4:4: "This text is often used in our churches, but in an ambiguous way. It is used to still the physical hunger of people who have nothing to eat: in doing this we are ignoring the word 'alone' in the text, yet it is of fundamental importance and without it the 'word which proceeds from the mouth of God' loses its meaning" (Tamez, "The Bread of Life," 507).

26. Cardenal, *Evangeliet fra Latinamerika*, 42.

b. Man dies by bread alone. For *rich* Christians the temptation is to read the feeding of the five thousand to install Jesus as king of bread and God as guarantor of health and happiness (6:14–15). René Padilla rightly notes that the wholeness that all people need "will not come through an ideology or program separated from Jesus Christ but through a Christ-centered mission in which the bread *of* life and the bread *for* life are offered side by side and the power of God is allowed to touch every aspect of human life."[27]

c. Man can only live by having a share in the bread of life. The meaning of life is hard to grasp for both the poor and the well-off. While the former are dying from lack of bread, the latter are dying from a surfeit of bread alone. We can only live truly if we receive the bread of life. This is reflected most clearly in the discourse of John 6, in particular in the reference to the Eucharist in 6:51. It is in the Eucharist that people are given a share in the life of Christ, and it is here that people are inspired to share their bread and their life with others.

---

27. Padilla, "Bible Studies," 330.

7

Light

Historical Perspectives

Light as a Universal Symbol

LIGHT IS ONE OF the most important key symbols in the world of religions. The interaction of light and darkness is fundamental to human existence. Day and night, brightness and shadow, establish the contours of the world we see with an evocative potency that has prompted people everywhere to ascribe religious significance to them. Light and darkness have been called archetypical symbols.[1] Because the symbolism of light is so much a part of human experience, it calls forth a host of varied and even contradictory associations on both the cognitive and affective levels. The symbolism of light is of great importance in the Old Testament tradition and in the Graeco-Roman world.

Images of light and darkness pervade the entire Gospel of John. The Prologue depicts God's Word as a source of life and as light shining in the darkness (1:5) The night conversation between Jesus and Nicodemus concludes with remarks about those who love darkness rather than light (3:19–21). The symbolism of light culminates with Jesus' proclamation in 8:12 that he is "the light of the world," exemplified literally by Jesus' enlightening

---

1. Koester, *Symbolism in the Fourth Gospel*, 123–24; Biehl, *Symbole geben zu lernen*, 63.

the eyes of a man born blind (9:4–7), while simultaneously intensifying the hostility toward him by many in Jerusalem. As their eyes narrow, the light disappears. In the story about Lazarus the public work of Jesus is seen as a period of daylight, but the night is coming closer (11:9–10). With a final appeal to believe in the light, Jesus leaves the public scene (12.35–36; 12:46), before he goes into the night of death (cf. 13:30).

Jesus as the Light of the World

In line with the other "I am" sayings the statement in John 8:12 consists of two parts: a word of revelation and a promise.

Word of revelation
self presentation ("I am")
metaphor/symbol with a definite article ("the light of the world")

Promise
invitation ("whoever follows me")
promise ("will never walk in darkness but have the light of life")

The historical background of the statement in John 8:12, is disputed. It is often suggested that these words should be interpreted in the light of some sort of Gnosticism, presupposing a physical dualism with a contrast between the superior, divine world and this material, evil world. Against this it could be argued that "the light of the world" terminologically and objectively is not gnostic, since Gnostics do not think that salvation has a universal scope. The point in Gnosticism is a metaphysical dualism: The aim is that "the messenger of the light" should lead the elected back to the upper world of light, but not be a light for the lower world and dark world.[2]

While the gnostic interpretation must be rejected, the "dualism of decision" characteristic of the Qumran community might be applicable. Yet, here too there are significant differences. For this community the struggle between light and darkness will be settled at the end of time, since it is apocalyptic in character; whereas the Fourth Gospel underlines how the struggle is taking place here and now in the encounter with Jesus.[3] In addition, the concept of a universal salvation is absent in the Dead Sea Scrolls.

---

2. Biehl, *Symbole geben zu lernen*, 65.
3. Værge, *Johannesevangeliet*, 110.

This is in contrast to Second Isaiah, according to whom the servant of the Lord is called "the light to the nations," e.g., 49:6: "I will give you as a light to the nations that my salvation may reach to the end of the earth" (cf. 42:6, 51:4). In Judaism the term "the light of the world" is often used with reference to the law, the temple, and Jerusalem, but also with reference to persons, in particular Adam, and finally also with reference to God himself. Characteristic of the Fourth Gospel is that "images with strong roots in Judaism are expanded and universalized enabling them to evoke a broad range of associations. Manna becomes bread for the world, and the light in the temple becomes the light of the world."[4]

The symbolism of light is connected to other symbols, in particular that of *life*, as we can already see in the Prologue. As the Word stems from God, is active in creating life, and has now appeared in the world, so Jesus is the only one who is entitled to call himself "the light of the world"—and he has that light within himself. The images of the water of life, the bread of life, and the light of life articulate our search for our origin, for paradise, but this is now realized in the person of Jesus. The Gospel simultaneously insists on the *universal* scope of salvation and its *exclusive* bond to Christ.

Following the Light of the World—on Christology and Discipleship

Among the various symbols used in the first century light seems to be the one with the most pronounced ethical connotations. In Jewish sources it is related to divine wisdom and the Law, and in Graeco-Roman texts it is linked to philosophy and virtue. Enlightenment signifies that one's understanding and way of life are shaped by the light of wisdom through the study of the Mosaic Law or a training in philosophy. By presenting Jesus as the light of the world, the Gospel identifies him as the true source of wisdom and moral transformation.[5]

In the Fourth Gospel, the symbol of light is also connected to "the way": "Whoever follows me will never walk in darkness but will have the light of life" (8:12). Jesus' statement about light begins at the level of Christology but moves on to discipleship. Previous passages similarly reflect this close link. For instance, the conclusion to Jesus' conversation with Nicodemus insists that the true character of our deeds will be disclosed by our

---

4. Koester, *Symbolism in the Fourth Gospel*, 234.
5. Ibid., 234–44.

response to Jesus: "those who do what is true come to the light, so that it may be clearly seen that their deeds have been done in God" (3:21).

The combination of Christology and discipleship is expanded in the story of the man born blind in John 9. On the surface it is a simple story of a miraculous healing of a blind person. But the physical healing of his sight is interpreted by John as the outer sign of the inner enlightenment that people experience when they meet Jesus, the light of the world; cf. 12:46: "I have come as light into the world, so that everyone who believes in me should not remain in the darkness."

The man born blind gradually acquires a greater understanding of Jesus' identity. From the first simple affirmation that he has been healed by "the man called Jesus" (9:11), he comes to the acknowledgment that Jesus is "a prophet" (9:17); then to the vigorously defended assertions that his mighty works show him to be "from God" (9:31–34), and last of all, in response to Jesus' own self-revelation, to an adoring faith in the "Son of Man" (9:35). The self-disclosure of Jesus (v. 37: "you have seen him, and the one speaking with you is he") recalls the revelation made to the Samaritan woman at the well of Sychar (4:26). Conversely the Pharisees are gradually becoming more self-blinded.[6]

Contemporary Perspectives

In the second part of this chapter we shall see some examples of the great significance of the symbolism of light in the world of religions and in mysticism. The first two examples are about the encounter of Christianity with the great religions; then follow some examples of the role of the light in new religious movements, Christian mysticism and spirituality. The frequent references to "light" in the new spirituality and mysticism are often linked to a gnostic understanding, so we shall also reflect on the relationship of John's Gospel to Gnosticism.

---

6. Soares-Prabhu, "The Man Born Blind," 72–73. In the story of the man born blind we are led from questions about the identity of the healed man through questions about his healing to questions about the identity of Jesus.

Jesus as the Enlightener and the Enlightened One

The first example concerns the use of images of Christ in a contemporary Asian context.[7] In Part Two of this book I discuss what kind of criteria can be established for the use of new images of Christ. An important point is that such images have to be recognizable in the cultural context in which they are used, as well as being in accordance with the basic aspects of the biblical representations of Christ. Some of today's images certainly have a solid basis in the biblical tradition, while others seem to miss it. Under the former we can cite the image of Jesus as the Enlightener of the world; under the latter we hear how some Christians in Asia refer to Jesus as the "Enlightened One" (or *"the Buddha"*).

The Asian theologian Peter C. Phan asks if Jesus ever had a profound experience comparable to that of Siddhartha Gautama, as a result of which he gained new insight into reality. In other words, is there any meaning in understanding Jesus as the Enlightened One (*the Buddha*)? Phan's purpose is not to compare Gautama's experience under the Bodhi tree with a possible, similar event in the life of Jesus. Instead of focusing on such an *inter*-religious dialogue between Christianity and Buddhism on enlightenment, he pursues an *intra*-religious study of the Christian basis and justification for calling Jesus the "Enlightened One."

Phan's thesis is that it is meaningful to understand Jesus both as the Enlightener and as the Enlightened One. Light is a crucial theme in the Bible. In John's Gospel it is closely related to other themes. Light, truth and life are synonymous ways of describing the one and the same reality that is Jesus, cf. 14:6. Because Jesus is the way, the enlightenment he brings is never a mere dispelling of intellectual error or ignorance but always includes a total transformation and liberation of the person from oppression, sin, and death. But can Jesus also be understood as the Enlightened One? Phan argues that throughout his public ministry Jesus seems to have changed

---

7. Cf. Phan, *Being Religious Interreligiously*. His entry to this issue is the Special Assembly of the Synod of Bishops of Asia (1998) convoked by Pope John Paul II. This synod suggested a number of images of Christ relevant for Asian Christians. Among these images several have a distinctly biblical flavor, e.g., "the Compassionate Friend of the Poor," "the Good Samaritan," "the Good Shepherd." Others are more generic, albeit solidly based on the Bible, such as "the Teacher of Wisdom," "the Healer," and "the Liberator." The remaining two, namely "the Spiritual Guide" and "the Enlightened One," may appear rather alien to Western Christians, but to Asian ears they sound quite familiar, especially if they are translated into their equivalents, the former as "the Guru" and the latter as "the Buddha" (ibid., 128).

his mind about his mission as a result of his encounters with others. So, for instance at the wedding at Cana, Jesus changes the timing of his mission by anticipating his "hour" in response to his mother's entreaty (John 2:1–11). There is very likely a gradual enlightenment, a growing self-awareness, in Jesus' consciousness as to the shape of his vocation and destiny.

According to Phan, Jesus is the enlightener of the world precisely *because* and *to the extent that* he himself is enlightened. To be sure, he is the light, but to use the language of the Nicene-Constantinopolitan creed, he is not simply the light but "light from light." It is only because he originates as light from the Light that he can enlighten and reveal the Light perfectly, and in this way liberate humans from darkness. Perhaps no Gospel has spoken more extensively about the derived character of Jesus' light than the Fourth Gospel. Jesus states again and again that whatever he is and receives comes from his Father: "Very truly, I tell you, the Son can do nothing on his own, but only what he sees the Father doing; for whatever the Father does, the Son does likewise" (5:19; cf. 5:30). Even more explicitly Jesus affirms that his teaching is received: "My teaching is not mine but his who sent me" (7:16). And: "I do nothing on my own but I speak these things as the Father instructed me" (8:28).[8]

It is no accident that in the great Johannine themes of Word, Wisdom, Light, Life, Truth, Way, and Son come together as different ways of describing Jesus as the Enlightener of the world. Later christological doctrine would elaborate in ontological terms the relationship between the "Father" and the "Son" and affirm the divinity of Jesus by saying that he is "one in substance with the Father." But because Jesus' divinity is a "derived" divinity, a gift eternally poured out in love on him by his Father, so that he is "true God from true God," it is equally important to remember that before the Son can enlighten the world, he is himself enlightened by his Father. Phan therefore concludes that the Enlightener is himself the Enlightened—and vice versa.[9]

In assessing Phan's study we must ask if it represents a syncretism or a (necessary) contextualization. This question is not easy to answer. Previously we have referred to another Asian theologian, Kosuke Koyama, who argues that Jesus as the Enlightened One need not reflect a syncretistic approach.[10] The crucial issue is whether this title can be combined with Jesus

---

8. Ibid., 136.
9. Ibid.
10. See the paragraph "Syncretism and accommodation" in chapter 3 of this book.

as the Light; moreover, Jesus' unique position must not be abandoned. Here it is important to note that Phan maintains both aspects: Jesus is seen both as the Light and as the Enlightened One. The twofold nature of Jesus' divinity and humanity is preserved. See also the chapter "Images of Christ" in Part Two.

Light as Symbol of God's Hidden Presence—a Possibility for Dialogue

The metaphor of light points to an important theological insight: It is beyond our capacity to comprehend God in the same way as we may comprehend the created world. Light cannot usually be seen directly, but is nevertheless the precondition for our ability to see other things. In the same manner, it is not possible for us to see God's actions in the world as we can see man's. This basic insight regarding the difference between God's activity as creator and human activity is common to the three Abrahamic traditions: Judaism, Christianity and Islam. Perhaps Psalm 36:9 is the best metaphorical expression of this insight: "For with you is the fountain of life; in your light we see light." In all three religions light is seen as symbol of the hidden presence of God.[11]

In the Jewish tradition light is not only conceived as the beginning of creation (Gen 1:3), but it is a symbol of divine presence and salvation as well. Light is used in Jewish worship—first in the temple and later in the synagogues—as a metaphor for God's glory but also as a symbol of God' s presence in God's absence.

In the Christian tradition Jesus' statement in John 8:12 is central. Also important are the words of the Nicene Creed: "God from God, Light from Light." Christians took over many Jewish traditions, but gave them a new interpretation, including the use of oil lamps and candles in the liturgy. The reference to Christ gave these ceremonies new meaning. Of particular interest is the understanding of light in Christian spirituality. The awareness that God as Light is not visible to human eyes leads to such paradoxical phrases as "dark light" in mystical writings from Pseudo-Dionysius to John of the Cross.

In the Muslim tradition the so-called "light verse" in the Qur'an attracts our attention:

> God is the Light of the heavens and earth. His Light is like this: there is a niche, and in it a lamp, the lamp inside the glass, a

---

11. Valkenberg, *Sharing Lights*, 212–13.

glass like a glittering star, fuelled from a blessed olive tree from neither east nor west, whose oil almost gives light even when no fire touches it—light upon light—God guides whoever He will to his Light. God draws such comparisons for people; God has full knowledge of everything—shining out in houses of worship (Sura 24:35).[12]

This famous verse has been interpreted by many Muslim theologians, for instance al-Ghazali (1058–1111), whose major contribution to Islamic thought is his effort to reconcile theology with philosophy, Islamic orthodoxy with Sufism, and tradition with reason.[13]

In his book *Sharing Light: On the Way to God* Pim Valkenberg demonstrates a number of parallels between the Christian theologian Thomas Aquinas and the Muslim theologian and mystic al-Ghazali. Three insights are drawn from the teaching of Aquinas: the doctrine of God's hiddenness or incomprehensibility, the play of analogy in speech about the divine, and the consequent need for many names of God.[14] Al-Ghazali follows Aquinas in speaking of God's incomprehensibility. With respect to the use of the word "light" he remarks—in a treatise on above verse—that God alone is the real, true Light, and that all other uses of the word are metaphorical (p. 236).[15] Like Aquinas, al-Ghazali is preoccupied with the idea of God's hidden presence, but there are nevertheless certain differences between the two which have to do with the fact that al-Ghazali is a very practically oriented theologian. "The connections between the mystical level, the theoretical level, and the practical level are very strong in al-Ghazali, which makes him a guide for interreligious dialogue not only at the level of the theological experts but at the levels of religious experience and ritual lifestyles as well."[16]

The idea of God as light offers a possibility for a dialogue between Christianity and other religions. So, for instance, the Danish book *Samtalen er nødvendig* (Conversation is Essential) analyzes the conception of

---

12. *The Qur'an*, trans. Haleem, 223. Cf. Valkenberg, *Sharing Lights*, 213.

13. Moucarry, *Faith to Faith*, 301.

14. Valkenberg, *Sharing Lights*, 214.

15. Ward's study *Concepts of God* deals with both al-Ghazali and Thomas Aquinas. The chapter entitled "Al-Ghazzali and the God of Unveiled Light" has several interesting passages, for instance: "The idea of the essential hiddenness of God is part of Islam. God shows us only what is required for us to live well. We have the Book of God, but not the Being of God, within our grasp" (ibid., 126).

16. Valkenberg, *Sharing Lights*, 252.

God in Christianity and Islam. In Christianity the emphasis is on the Trinity. A paragraph on the Trinitarian God is introduced as follows:

> The center of the Christian faith is the comprehension of God's love in Jesus Christ, his act in the creation, the reconciliation and the consummation of the world. We find this testified in a great variety of expressions in the Bible that speaks of the pluriform acts of the one God. When approaching the divine reality, trying to perceive it and giving expression to it in a correct manner, we obviously have to think in more than one dimension. The phrase "God is light" (1 John 1:5) reflects the creative power of God. In a similar way this idea is conveyed in other religions, for example Islam (Sura 24:35). "God is spirit" (John 4:24) is another phrase that connects the biblical experience with other religions. "God is love" is a phrase that in the Christian confession is bound to Jesus Christ in a particular way. It can be experienced personally in the creation and in the world, yet it is a specific Christian statement.[17]

Similarities and differences in the concept of God in the two religions will be taken up again in the paragraph "The image of God in Islam and Christianity" in chapter 9 of this book.

In the Service of the Light

The symbolism of light is important in many of the new religious movements and new spirituality, and in particular in the network of theosophy. In a recent study Rene Dybdal Pedersen has demonstrated that most of the theosophical groups in Denmark practice different kinds of service that may be called "Sun meditation by full moon," "light service" etc. Even though these are formed according to the specific characteristics of each group, they have many things in common, such as sitting in light rooms in a circle around a table with composite candles, a glass of water or a bunch of flowers, and "spiritual" music playing. For an hour or so participants seek to channel the energies from superior spiritual planets in order to improve the living conditions of the earth.[18]

This particular form of light service characterizes the *Golden Circle*, founded by Asger Lorentsen.[19] The Golden Circle sees itself as one of the

---

17. *Samtalen er nødvendig*, 42.*
18. Pedersen, *I lysets tjeneste*, 45.
19. The Golden Circle is a modern spiritual group with its main focus in Denmark. It has activities in Scandinavia and stimulates a retreat in Crete. In a wider sense, the

forerunners of the New World Impulse, which is perceived as new revelations intended to give the spiritual basis for the New World Religions as well as for the enlightened civilization of the 3rd millennium. Included in these revelations are new divine outpourings from the center of the Cosmic Logos, from the heart of the Sun, from Shamballa, where the Will of God is known, and from the close cooperation between the Lord Buddha and the Lord Maitreya, the Christ. Asger Lorentsen emphasizes the development and improvement of the Earth that have been stimulated in particular by virtue of the Christ Impulse that was instituted with Christ's manifestation on Planet Earth about 2000 years ago. This impulse seeks to raise human civilization to a new level of understanding and insight into the form and purpose of the universe and to spread an ethic marked by humanism, care, and human-kindness.

According to its website the *Golden Circle* movement has three aims.[20] The first is to educate spiritually oriented people in modern theosophy, in world service, and in spiritual transformation stimulated by God. The second is to focalize various downpourings from the Kingdom of God, the Buddhic plane, into humanity, so that emanations from cosmic, solar, and planetary sources may eventually transform the veils of our collective human consciousness and stimulate new life within the hearts of humanity. And the third aim is to share the outpourings of the Christ in the awakening of the heart of humanity and thus partake in the healing and initiation of humanity.

The theosophy of Lorentzen and the Shan-movement are a challenge to Christians.[21] According to these theosophical groups the redemptive work of Christ is the transformative energy emanating from the Solar Logos; but it is not an active saving act from outside fallen humanity. It is rather a release of what is hidden in man, since he is essentially a minor aspect of the divine. The Christ is an archetype of the human soul. This is

---

Golden Circle is a network of spiritually oriented people throughout the world responding positively to the heart vibration of the New Word Impulse which emanates from the Heart of the Sun (information from Den Gyldne Cirkel, http://www.dengyldnecirkel.dk/en/purpose).

20. Cf. http://www.dengyldnecirkel.dk/en/purpose.

21. The Shan-movement or Shan The Rising Light was founded by Jeanne Morashti (also known as Ananda Tara Shan). For many years there was a close cooperation between her and Lorentsen, but it was ended when Lorentzen considered Morashti to have too strong a position as the connecting link between humanity and the divine origin; cf. Pedersen, *I lysets tjeneste*, 50.

a consequence of an impersonal understanding of the divine. The ultimate source of life is not conceived by the Theosophists in personal terms. By contrast—as will be demonstrated in the next paragraph—the Christian experience is that of a personal encounter with God, a communicating with him and a resting with him in adoration.[22]

In the Master's Light

Even though it is not stated explicitly, such neo-spiritual ideas are inspired by a gnostic understanding of the Fourth Gospel. Many other new religious movements are similarly influenced by gnostic thinking, e.g., the Martinus Institute of Spiritual Science, a New Age organization founded in the 1930s. *In the Master's Light* (IML) is a movement founded by the theologian and pastor Ole Skjerbæk Madsen. This movement is obviously inspired by Christian thought and has been successful in using a terminology and forms of praxis that are recognizable among people involved in new esoteric circles and New Age. For instance, Jesus is usually called "the Master" and in some cases also "the Light," while the Holy Spirit is merely referred to as "the Spirit."[23]

Yet, at crucial points the IML disassociates itself from what is considered to be significant in esoteric teaching, not least the principle of emanation. Humankind is not understood as being part of the divine. Skjerbæk Madsen thinks that the major reason that people love themselves is their experience of being identical with the divine, which in turn makes them turn their back on God and life with him. Skjerbæk Madsen works with a personal concept of God,[24] and recognizes only one master, namely Jesus. A third issue relates to reincarnation. It is argued that every creature is unique and has just this life on earth. Death is followed by the resurrection to eternal life in God's kingdom—on a new earth.[25]

---

22. Madsen, "Theology in Dialogue," 261–62.

23. Pedersen, *I lysets tjeneste*, 105.

24. See also the paragraph "From the impersonal to the personal image of God" in chapter 3 of this book.

25. Despite this criticism of reincarnation, Skjerbæk Madsen does not refuse completely the idea that man can experience or remember what has happened in a former life. However, in these cases the decisive thing is not one's own former (life) history, but the events of others that are anchored in the collective un-consciousness (Pedersen, *I lysets tjeneste*, 106).

Part One: Images of a Greater Reality

Skjerbæk Madsen argues that to be a disciple of Jesus is to acknowledge him as Master, and to follow the Master is to become like the Master. Furthermore, he considers this concept to be very important in the dialogue with those elements in the spiritual environment that follow or are inspired by gurus or by living or ascended masters, and the uniqueness of Jesus Christ as the Master and world teacher has been highlighted in comparison with the idea of the world teacher or world teachers appearing in the different dispensations of human history. "It is not because of his realized humanity as a master that Jesus is considered the world teacher; rather, he is the world teacher in a unique sense because I AM through God's eternal Logos teaches us in the Master."[26]

Light in Christian Mysticism and Spirituality

The classic forms of Christian mysticism and spirituality also employ light as a symbol, there being an obvious coherence between the Jesus prayer and the mysticism of light. The background for this mysticism can be found in the Bible, in particular the Johannine writings.[27] John is regarded by Orthodox Christianity as the first of the so-called "theologians." Thus, 1 John 1:5 gives the following definition of God: "God is light, and in him there is no darkness at all." This is often combined with the words of creation in Genesis 1:3: "Let there be light." In John's Prologue this eternal and creative light is identified with the Word becoming flesh.

Light is an important part of all spiritual guidance; the inner way of this guidance is described by Ove Wikström, who in accordance with the mystical tradition reckons with seven stages. In his book *Det blændende mørke* (*The Dazzling Darkness*) he outlines these stages as: 1) the want—God is perceived; 2) the foretaste—God is living; 3) the reckoning—God is demanding; 4) the grace—God is offering; 5) the night—God is hiding; 6) the light—God is dazzling, 7) the journey—God is accompanying.[28]

The description of the sixth stage underlines the ineffability of God; God is described as a fascinating and an eternal mystery. "Therefore one cannot say that much about this light which is rather un-light, or about

---

26. Madsen, "Theology in Dialogue," 278.
27. Lönnebo, *Religionens fem språk*, 143.
28. This is a refinement of Origen. Origen originated the notion of *three stages* of the mystical journey: purgation, illumination and union with God (Thompson, *Christian Spirituality*, 23).

Light

the fire which is dazzling. They defy all human attempts to define them."[29] In the dazzling darkness we may find the immanent light, and the most important thing is no longer the church or the congregation but the creation, the world, society and other human beings. The so-called profane is becoming part of the holy. When light is shed, a change comes about, a "rebirth" or a birth from above. We see all things in God and we see God in all things. We are granted an *openness* so that we see the eternal presence in all things, in all people and in all that we do. God is not more present in peculiar psychic experiences than in everyday life. The light makes us see the world both as truth and as sacrament. We regain the feeling that each part of divine creation is something specific and "peculiar"—and a sign pointing to the Creator. Every aspect of creation regains the intensity in its existence and at the same time becomes transparent, like a window that reflects the divine reality. The creation becomes a theophany.[30]

This understanding of spirituality and spiritual guidance maintains that creation is good in itself. In other forms of Christian spirituality the stance to the creation is more ambiguous. This is to a certain extent characteristic of Lene Højholt who apparently uses a language which seems to be dualistic or even gnostic[31] Yet, in her comment on John 8:12 she notes that the disciples now are enriched by a new insight into Jesus' nature. "They realize that his union with the light in the world brings him in relation to the creative power itself, and in this way he also stand in relation both to the creation of the world when God's light for the first time penetrated the darkness, and to all of God's creation since then, and to all what occurs just now."[32]

Today's spirituality often has an individualistic purpose; it serves the unfolding of the self. By contrast, Christian spirituality is marked by a holistic approach to reality, characterized by two things: The life of the Spirit is

---

29. Wikström, *Det blændende mørke*, 170.*

30. Ibid., 170–72.

31. Højholt, *Vejen*; see the quotation from her book (ibid., 21) given in paragraph "The way of faith—the meditative reading of the Fourth Gospel" in chapter 10 of this book. The reason might be that the author has her focus on the "I in the world," this being the center in human beings that is turned away from the divine source of light. "This 'I' will always be opposed to the spiritual life, because it is directed merely towards its own existence, while the spirit means self-surrender. 'The I in the world' wants to create its own life and control it. Its intention is to unfold itself in the physical and material part of reality where it will dominate and control" (ibid., 26*).

32. Ibid., 108.*

everyday life and the life of the Spirit is bound in mutuality to "the other."[33] Hence, authentic Christian spirituality reflects a critique of dualism and Gnosticism and differs from "spiritualization," which may be defined as a refusal of life as created life.

A Dualistic Language—not a Dualistic Understanding of Reality

We shall briefly return here to the question of how the Gospel of John relates to Gnosticism.[34] It is clear that John uses dualistic language on many occasions, most obviously in pairing opposite symbols such as light/darkness (1:5; cf. 8:12), from above/from below (8:23), spirit/flesh (3:6), life/death (3:36), truth/falsehood (lie) (8:44f.), heaven/earth (3:31), God/Satan (13:27). This is often interpreted as an absolute dualism between two worlds: on the one side we have the true, spiritual world of the light, on the other side we have the bodily and material world. However, what is evil is not the world in itself, the natural life, or the body. John's use of the term *kosmos* is not consistent. It often has a negative meaning—but not always. In a number of passages this term is employed in a neutral or even positive sense when applied to the creation itself—the physical reality of this world (cf. 17:24; 16:21). The world is the object of God's love (3:16). It is the realm in which the light enlightens persons (1:9).[35]

The reason for John's use of a dualistic language is both theological and sociological.[36] The Johannine dualism is a result of theological minds coming to grips with a social as well as a religious crisis. The church with which he was affiliated seems to have undergone social dislocation; that is, these Christians had been expelled from their original home in the synagogue alongside their Jewish colleagues (cf. 9:22; 12:42; 16:2). This uprooting experience must have resulted in a kind of social trauma. One result of the subsequent social reorientation was that a dualistic view of the world developed. The split between "us" and "them" was natural. Along with it came a tendency for them to think of themselves as born from above, as the truth, as the light in a dark world etc. Conversely, they thought of others who opposed them and their religious faith as born from below, as the

---

33. Aagaard, *Ånd har krop*, 133. 150.
34. See also the paragraph "As Gnostics to the Gnostics," in Part Two, chapter 12.
35. Kysar, *John the Maverick Gospel*, 50.
36. Nissen, "Rebirth and Community," 129.

world, as darkness, as "Jews." Dualistic thought satisfied both a theological necessity and a sociological one.[37]

To conclude, then, Jesus' statement in John 8:12 should not be understood as an example of physical dualism—as some would argue (e.g., Steiner). The Johannine dualism is not a physical or cosmological dualism but rather a "dualism of decision." Instead of understanding themselves as creatures human beings are putting themselves in the position of the Creator. In John 8:44–45 we see the contrast between truth and falsehood. These words should not be interpreted in a gnostic way about a physical or natural origin in the Devil or the realm of the darkness, but rather as a two opposing ways of perceiving oneself and existence.

---

37. Kysar, *John the Maverick Gospel*, 63. The Johannine dualism between spirit and flesh, the world above and the world below, is not a dualism between interior and exterior, personal and social. The realm of the spirit includes both interior and exterior, and so does the realm of the flesh. "It is not that the world above is that of the individual and God, while the world below is that of society that is 'from above,' namely the community of the Johannine Christians" (Rensberger, *Overcoming the World*, 137).

8

Truth

Historical Perspectives

Truth is not a metaphor but rather a concept. However, it is connected to various metaphors and plays a significant role in the dialogue between Christianity and other religions. The word is rarely used in the Synoptic Gospels, but is frequently employed in the Fourth Gospel. In the following we shall analyze the most important passages on the concept of truth.

Truth as a Person

The concept of "truth" is used for the first time in the Prologue: "The Law indeed was given through Moses; grace and truth came through Jesus Christ" (1:17). The wording is interesting, since two founders of religion, Moses and Jesus, are mentioned in two parallel sentences. Yet, the two figures are not quite parallel. The wording implies that grace and truth are more important than law. A more fundamental difference is that the law *was given* by Moses while grace and the truth *came* through Jesus. He himself is the truth.

Other Johannine passages similarly insist that truth has a personal character. The most famous example is John 14:6, which will be analyzed in more detail in chapter 10. This passage indicates that truth does not refer to a doctrine but to a person: "I *am* the truth." The corollary of this statement is a profound transformation of the ordinary meaning of truth. For most of us, statements are true or false; people may or may not *have* truth; but how can they *be* truth, even *the* truth? When Jesus says, "I am the truth," he indicates that in Him the true, the genuine, the ultimate reality is present, in other words, that God is present, unveiled, undistorted, in his infinite depth, in his unapproachable mystery. Jesus is not the truth because his teachings are true; but his teachings are true because they express the truth which he himself is.[1]

The challenge is how to get to this truth. The answer of the Fourth Gospel is obvious: By doing it. This is not to say that we must merely accept, obey, and thereby fulfill the commandments. *Doing* the truth means living out of the reality which is his who is the truth, thereby making his being the being of ourselves. Such a personal understanding counteracts an objectification of the truth. First and foremost, truth is not something to be formulated, but something to be done, and when it is done, it shows itself authentically and with authority.[2]

In John's Gospel Christ is not seen as a teacher of truth among, or even above, other teachers of truth. This would *separate* the truth from him; the message of the Prologue is different: grace and truth "came" through Christ (1:17). Doing the truth, being of the truth, the truth has come, I am the truth—all these combinations indicate that truth in Christianity is something which *happens*, something which is bound to a specific place, to a special time, to a special personality. Truth is life, personal life, revelation and decision. Truth is a stream of life, centered in Christ and actualized in all who are connected with him.[3]

The Truth Will Set You Free

The significance of truth in the Fourth Gospel is underlined by the argument between Jesus and "the Jews who had believed him" initially (John 8:31–37). The text has a concentric structure:

---

1. Tillich, *The New Being*, Religion-Online, http://www.religion-online.org/showbook.asp?title=375. Danish translation: Tillich, *En ny skabelse*, 64–65.

2. Nørgaard-Højen, "Kristendommens absoluthedskrav," 234.

3. Tillich, *The Shaking of the Foundations*, Religion-Online, www.religion-online.org/showbook.asp?title=378. Danish translation: Tillich, *Grundvoldene vakler*, 111–12.

Part One: Images of a Greater Reality

> v. 31: If you continue in my word . . .
> > v. 32: the truth will make you free
> > > v. 34: Everyone who commits sin is a slave to sin
> > v. 36: the Son makes you free
> > v. 37: . . . because there is no place in you for my word.

This passage places an equation sign between Jesus and the truth. There is an obvious parallel between v. 32 (the truth will set you free) and v. 36 (the Son sets your free). The concepts of truth and freedom are combined. The Greek word for truth (*alētheia*) means to make manifest the hidden, to unveil, to disclose. Truth liberates from the tie to falsehood by unveiling it, by demonstrating what it really is. The truth about the lie and the falsehood is that one imagines one can live on one's own and without God. Falsehood leads to captivity, described as a captivity to sin (v. 34).

John 8 sees liberation as a totality. It encompasses the *entire* human being and *all* that is human. Jesus' care is not limited to those with mental inhibitions or guilt complexes.[4] When Jesus says: "So, if the Son makes you free, you will be free indeed" (v. 36), it is an either-or issue: *total freedom or no freedom at all*. To be without Jesus is to *lose* the truth and the freedom, and thereby be bound to death, guilt, and a meaningless life.[5]

According to this passage the Jews remain in captivity. They do not understand what Jesus means and they claim that they are Abraham's descendants who have never been slaves to anyone (v. 33). In other words, they point to *their* traditions. Since they have Abraham as their father, they have the whole truth and they need not worry further on the issue. Jesus' answer makes it plain that freedom has nothing to do with a transmission of privileges and rights from one generation to another. To be slave to sin means to be captive to selfishness and lovelessness. In one of his sermons Tillich puts it thus: "The truth that liberates is the power of love, for God is love. The father of the lie binds us to himself by binding us to ourselves. Love liberates from the father of the lie because it liberates us from our false self to our true self—to that self which is grounded in true reality." Consequently, Tillich calls us to distrust every claim for truth where we do not see truth united with love. We are of the truth and the truth has taken

---

4. See also John 7:23: "[B]ecause I healed a man's *whole* body on the Sabbath?" Brown translates the verse as follows: "because I cured the *whole* man on a Sabbath?" (Brown, *The Gospel According to John*, 310).

5. Nilsson, *At giva de förtryckta frihet*, 34–45.

hold of us only when love has taken hold and begun to make us free from ourselves.[6]

John 8:31–37 is undeniably about a truth that liberates people, but often we react like the Jews in the text. We protest emphatically and point to *our* tradition, which goes back to the church fathers, or the popes, or the reformers. In this way we transfer the words of the Jews into our own context, claiming that we do not need anyone to set us free.

The Praxis of Life versus the Praxis of Death

On several occasions John indicates how truth and love liberate the individual. A single example will suffice here: the woman caught in adultery in John 8:1–11. Its origin is debatable. Some scholars even think that it originally belonged to one of the Synoptic gospels, but that is of no importance in our context.

The narrative is about the love that sets free. When confronted with the Mosaic Law stipulating stoning to death as punishment, Jesus *says* nothing but bends down and writes with his finger on the ground. As the scribes and Pharisees persist, he straightens up and says: "Let anyone among you who is without sin be the first to throw a stone at her" (v. 7). When Jesus reminds them of their own guilt, the men suddenly become part of the problem. Yet Jesus is also reminding them of God's mercy, which is the foundation of his teaching. Left alone with the woman Jesus makes it clear that he is not indifferent to what she has done. But crucially he calls her to a new life. What has occurred should not be overlooked or even forgotten. The woman was lost, but now she is saved—not to continue her past life, but to enter into a new life.

This story illustrates the main point in John 8: the contrast between life and death, between truth and falsehood.[7] Basically all the dualisms in this chapter refer back to a single, fundamental dualism, namely that of life and death. The opening narrative (vv. 1–11) shows that the problem is not a philosophical but a *practical* problem—a question of how to live concretely. The context is specifically Jewish; what is at stake is how to interpret the Law. According to the juridical and ideological interpretation of the Pharisees and Scribes the woman deserves the death penalty. Jesus takes

---

6. The quotation is taken from the very end of the sermon; cf. also the Danish translation: Tillich, *En ny skabelse*, 68.

7. For a more detailed analysis see the article by Critical Theology Group, "Truth Will Set You Free—Bible Study of John 8."

Part One: Images of a Greater Reality

the opposite approach. He seeks to break their authority as interpreters of the law, and to set the woman free. He can do so only by setting the *praxis of life*, the original meaning of the law, against their *praxis of death*.

This assertion may be supported by comparing John 8:1–11 with in John 8:31–37. An important aspect of vv. 31–37 is that even though the Jews can refer to their descent from Abraham (i.e., being part of the elect people), this is no guarantee of their freedom. Freedom must be judged on one basis only, which is the question of whether it implies life or death. In vv.1–11 the praxis of the Pharisees and the scribes would have led to death.[8]

One cannot be a descendant of Abraham without doing his works, and it is precisely on this point that the Jews fail, cf. 8:39: "If you were Abraham's children, you would be doing what Abraham did." The works of Abraham should have led to life, but his descendants were unsuccessful. They tried to stone the woman caught in adultery, and at the end of chapter 8 they tried to stone Jesus (8:59).[9] His adversaries lived, as it were, by the logic of death. Truth is where the praxis of *life* takes place; John maintains that the praxis of life is to live in community with Jesus. To abide in the words of Jesus (cf. 8:31) is to do them and to do them is to promote life.

The Truth of Power or the Power of Truth

One of the most profound reflections on the concept of truth in John's Gospel is the dialogue between Jesus and Pilate in 18:28—19:16. John's aim is to point to Jesus Christ as the truth; the primary intent of the account is the question of salvation. But, as demonstrated by Miroslav Volf, this soteriological perspective on truth also has an important social and political dimension.[10]

At the beginning of the dialogue Jesus is asked if he is the King of the Jews (18:33). John reports the following exchange of words (18:36–38):

> Jesus answered: "My kingdom is not from this world. If my kingdom were from this world, my followers would be fighting to keep me from being handed over to the Jews. But as it is, my kingdom is not from here." Pilate asked him: "So you are a king?" Jesus answered: "You say that I am a king. For this I was born, and for this I

---

8. Critical Theology Group, "Truth Will Set you Free," 46–47.

9. Ibid., 48: "The opponents stay in their logic, ending up with the attempt to stone him, that is the same praxis as they wanted to use against the woman (vv. 1–11)."

10. Volf, *Exclusion and Embrace*, 264–73.

came into the world, to testify to the truth. Everyone who belongs to the truth listens to my voice." Pilate asked him: "What is truth?"

During his trial Jesus is caught in the field of social forces with religious, ethnic, and political aspects. All are interested in maintaining their position of power. The main actors are the Jewish leaders and Pilate. As is made clear in John 11:45–54, the chief priests and the Pharisees are afraid of Jesus' popularity: They argue that if he continues his ministry, "everyone will believe in him, and the Romans will come and destroy both our holy place and our nation" (11:48). In order to prevent this they are planning his death. They couch their desire for power in a concern for the well-being of the people (v.50), but the rhetoric of benevolence cannot conceal their real motives. As Caiaphas says, "It is better for you to have one man die for the people than to have the whole nation destroyed" (v. 50).

Trials usually seek to find the truth. But in the case of Jesus neither the accusers nor Pilate are interested in the truth. Jesus is already judged guilty: "If this man were not a criminal, we would not have handed him over to you" (18:30), say the accusers, and although Pilate asks for the truth (18:38), he seems uninterested in the answer. At least he leaves the scene of dialogue with the accused and returns to the place outside the headquarters where the play of clashing forces determines the outcome.

There are other forces at work than "truth," namely the maintenance of power. For both the Jewish accusers and the Roman judge, the truth is irrelevant because it contradicts their wish to maintain power. The only power they will recognize is the *"truth of power."* It is the accused (Jesus) who raises the question of truth by subtly reminding the judge of his highest obligation—to find the truth. And significantly Jesus, the innocent and powerless victim, remains alone in his interest in truth—as judge of the judge.

In John's account we sense a counter-trial taking place in which judgment will be passed on *Pilate*. Whereas he argues for the truth of his power, Jesus argues for the *"power of truth."* When Pilate asks Jesus if he is the King of the Jews, Jesus does not deny the title of "king," but he changes its content: His kingship is not "from this world" (18:36). The point is not that this kingship is a purely spiritual matter, without connection to the created world. In fact, Jesus "came into the world" (18:37) and the disciples are living "in the world" (17:11)—that is, they are part of the play of social forces.

Nevertheless, the kingship of Jesus is different from all other kingships. It does not rest on the use of force.[11]

Jesus' instrument of power is the "witness," one who does not strive to bring anything but the truth. Indeed Jesus has already called himself a witness: "My teaching is not mine but his who sent me" (7:16). So, to be a witness means to strive to do the self-effacing work of telling the truth. If we insert something of our own, there is the risk that we begin to manipulate others instead of witnessing to the truth.

Jesus says to Pilate: "Everyone who belongs to the truth listens to my voice" (18:37).[12] This statement does not mean that the witness is addressed to a few or that access to the truth is limited to the elect. On the contrary, during the interrogation before the high priest Jesus speaks distinctly: "I have spoken openly to the world; I have always taught in synagogues and in the temple, where all the Jews come together. I have said nothing in secret" (18:20). The truth to which he has come to witness is not restricted to his own community; his truth-claims are universally accessible.

In conclusion, there are two assertions in the Johannine concept of truth: That we can know the truth and that the truth sets us free. Both of these challenge our modern and post-modern consciousness. Or as Volf has put it: "What audacity to insist that one knows *the* truth! What naiveté (or is it malice?) to maintain that *the* truth will make people free! No, *the* truth does not liberate, our postmodern sensibilities tell us; it enslaves. The one big Truth is but the one big Lie made to pass as truth in order to garb the evil holders of the oppressive Power with the vestments of the holy guardians of liberating Truth. To make people free we must disperse the one big Truth into many little truths."[13]

Truth and Non-Violence

Modern society is marked by conflict over truth-claims. What are the implications of the encounter between Jesus, Caiaphas, and Pilate in this context? According to Miroslav Volf two issues must be considered.[14]

First, we should notice that *the truth matters more than my own self*. Jesus was crucified as witness to the truth. Though he was threatened by

---

11. Ibid., 267; see also Nissen, "Kongemagt og discipelmenighed."
12. Literally the Greek text says: "being of the truth."
13. Volf, *Exclusion and Embrace*, 271.
14. Ibid., 271–73.

the power of Caiaphas and Pilate, "this marginal Jew" refused to place his own self above the truth—and he became the Messiah of the world. Why this self-denying refusal in the face of powers that threatened to crush both him and his project? Because when we place ourselves above the truth the consequences will easily be violence. If truth is reduced to our individual or communal interests, violence will reign and this will be most harmful for the weak among us.

But what about those who in the name of truth oppress the weak? The question brings us to the second implication of the encounter between Jesus, Caiaphas, and Pilate. *The self of the other matters more than my truth.* "Though I must be ready to deny myself for the sake of *the* truth, I may not sacrifice the other at the altar of *my* truth. Jesus, who claimed to be the Truth, refused to use violence to 'persuade' others who did not recognize his truth. The kingdom of truth he came to proclaim was the kingdom of freedom and therefore cannot rest on pillars of violence."[15] Commitment to non-violence has to accompany commitment to truth; otherwise commitment to truth will generate violence. Thus, what we can learn from the encounter between Jesus, Caiaphas and Pilate is that authentic freedom is the fruit of the twofold commitment—the commitment to truth and the commitment to non-violence.

This understanding is affirmed by John in 18:36. The statement of Jesus, "My kingdom is not of this world," has often been taken to mean that his kingdom is only spiritual in nature. This is a misunderstanding, as can be seen from the succeeding lines: "If my kingdom were from this world, my followers would be fighting to keep me from being handed over to the Jews . . ." Jesus means that his kingdom is not a part of this violent and selfish world. John 18:36 is not a refusal of Jesus' kingdom as such, but a refusal of the idea that his power is based on the use of violence.[16] Jesus is regarded as the king who came to witness to the truth (18:37).

---

15. Ibid., 272.

16. Cf. Nissen, "Kongemagt og discipelmenighed," 152–53. Jesus' kingship will inevitably come into conflict with the kingships of this world, but precisely because it is "not of this world" the conflict is not carried out on the world's terms. Jesus' followers do not fight and his enthronement is on the cross. John 18:36 means that the values of the Kingdom are different from and opposed to the values of this world; cf. Nissen, "Community and ethics," 208.

Part One: Images of a Greater Reality

The Spirit of Truth that Liberates

Another important aspect of John's concept of truth links it to the Holy Spirit. Several passages in the Fourth Gospel refer to the Holy Spirit, most clearly in the Farewell Discourses (John 13–17). Here we have five statements about the Holy Spirit (14:16–17; 14:26; 15:26–27; 16:7–11; 16:12–15). In what follows I shall comment on the last two passages.[17]

John 16:7–11 is about the relation between the Holy Spirit and the world. In v. 8 Jesus says: "And when he comes, he will prove the world wrong about sin and righteousness and judgment." In this passage the Spirit is conceived of as a person engaged in a lifelong fight against evil and the power of the sin, i.e., all forms of alienation in the world, be they spiritual, physical, moral, or social. The decisive struggle has already been won, as "the ruler of this world has been condemned" (v. 11). By virtue of his death Jesus has liberated humankind from any form of alienation and sin. But after his death the struggle against sin continues by means of the Holy Spirit, *the liberating Spirit*, who is sent into the world. The Spirit should not be conceived of as a comfort for the already comfortable or as belonging primarily to the religious experience of grace and forgiveness. It seems an indispensable function of the Spirit to make our witness for Christ and the kingdom of justice and peace on earth bold enough to confront and rattle the powers that be.[18]

Life in the Spirit is not lived in the comfort zone, it is a constant struggle against those powers that enslave human beings. It is life that looks forward to the resurrection after Good Friday. A new humanity is born, but only after a long and painful process. John's metaphor is apt: When a woman is in labor, she has pain, because her hour has come, but when her child is born, she no longer remembers the anguish because of the joy of having brought a human being into the world (John 16:21).

In proving the world wrong about sin, righteousness, and judgment, the Spirit initiates the world's transformation, though this will not come about without conflict: Even though or exactly because the fruits of the Holy Spirit are love, joy and peace, there will be resistance from those forces of the world that provoke enmity, quarrel and envy. As Hans Martensen puts it, "The liberation is on its way, but the closer it comes, the more forceful will be the oppression and the more maliciously will the power-holder,

---

17. Nissen, "Helligånden sprænger grænser og sætter skel," 28–29.
18. Stendahl, *Energy of Life*, 32.

the ruler of this world, fight to maintain power, even though it is doomed beforehand. The Spirit touches our life so that evil comes to the surface like boil that grows and bursts."[19]

The spiritual movement by means of which the Spirit proves the world wrong about sin, righteousness and judgment has been interpreted as a "stream against the stream" in the midst of this perishable world. It is the beginning of the new reality of the Holy Spirit: Sin is recognized and forgiven, the power of evil is broken, and justice is becoming a reality.[20]

This reference to the negative, disclosing function of the Spirit is followed by a statement about its positive function in 16:12–13: "I still have many things to say to you, but you cannot bear them now. When the Spirit of truth comes, he will guide you into all the truth . . ." There are three points to be made here.[21] First, what can be granted to and grasped by this group of first-century Jews is limited to the time, place, and circumstances of their lives. It is true knowledge of the only true God and in that sense it is the full revelation of God (17:3.6). But it is not yet the fullness of all that is to be manifested. Second, it will be the work of the Holy Spirit to lead this little community, limited as it now is within the narrow confines of a single time, place, and culture, into "the truth as a whole" and especially into an understanding of "the things that are to come"—the world history that is still to be enacted. Third, this does not mean the community will be led beyond or away from Jesus. Jesus is the Word made flesh, the Word by which all that is came to be, and is sustained in being. Consequently all the gifts which the Father has lavished on humankind belong in fact to Jesus, and it will be the work of the Spirit to restore them to their true owner.

In short, the Paraclete will receive everything that is to be said from Jesus but it will be contemporized in each period and each place. In this the Spirit will not only pass on what was received from Jesus but will also ensure the element of the contemporary and original, to face new situations meaningfully.

The function of the Holy Spirit, then, is to lead the community into *all* the truth. There is the prospect here of coming into a new understanding beyond what the group has already reached. A similar dynamic understanding of the Spirit is reflected in John 3:8: The promise in John 16:13 is a remarkable one. We are plainly told that there is more to be learned than

---

19. Martensen, *Dåb og Gudstro*, 220.*
20. Martensen, *Dåb og Gudstro*, 202–3.
21. Newbigin, *The Open Secret*, 202; Nissen, *New Testament and Mission*, 92–93.

can be found in the recorded teachings of Jesus to his disciples during the years of his ministry (cf. 14:12). We might tend to think of the Bible as a book containing timeless truths. This, however, is not how John sees the work of the Spirit. Revelation is not the communication of a body of timeless truths which we only have to receive in order to know the whole mind of God. It is rather the disclosure of the direction in which God is leading the world. The stuff of the Bible is promise and fulfillment. It is the story of a journey, of a pilgrimage, of a movement, of a mission that is not yet finished. The Spirit plays a significant role on this journey. The Spirit is not only the witness who points men towards the coming kingdom, but also the one who leads the church through all its encounters with new experiences, new cultures, new languages and new forms of thought.[22]

As has been underlined several times the term truth has a christological content in the Fourth Gospel (cf. 14:6). Hence, the meaning of 16:13 might be that in the future there will be new revelations but not new truths. The new revelations will be a disclosure of *new aspects* of the fundamental truth that is a more profound acknowledgment of the full reality of Christ. The Holy Spirit makes Christ more present, more comprehensible, more transforming. In its Spirit-prompted mission to the world, the church discovers the true meaning of the Word made flesh.[23]

Truth as Knowledge and Practice

Although "truth" is clearly a key term in the Fourth Gospel, it is disputed whether John's use of the term must be seen primarily in the light of the Greek or the Hebrew understanding of the concept.[24] The Greek *alētheia* has the basic meaning of non-concealment; it describes what is unveiled. Thus, truth is a state of affairs insofar as it is seen or expressed. And for the Greek, truth and reality are closely related. In the Hebrew Old Testament *emet* is related to the root *'mn* "to be firm, solid," and thus *emet* is the essential solidity of a thing, or that which makes it trustworthy and reliable. A man's life is "true" if he is faithful to God's ways. Thus there is a moral element in the Hebrew concept of truth. Truth as knowledge and truth as practice both play a crucial role in the religious dialogue. For John knowledge and practice are probably not alternatives. Yet, there are several factors

---

22. Newbigin, *The Good Shepherd*, 123–24.
23. Senior and Stuhlmueller, *The Biblical Foundations for Mission*, 288.
24. For more details, see Brown, *The Gospel According to John*, 499f.

which point in the direction of a Johannine usage that is primarily rooted in the Old Testament and Jewish thinking.[25] In particular three aspects may be mentioned.

First, *the truth is connected to God's revelation in Christ*. Truth is not an idea but a person. Jesus is the way, the truth, and the life (14:6). The truth sets us free (8:32), meaning the Son sets us free (8:36). Everyone who belongs to the truth listens to the voice of Jesus (18:37). While the law "was given through Moses," "grace and truth came through Jesus Christ" (1:17), that, is in his person.

Second, *the truth is a form of life*. Truth is something which one has to "do" (3:21, cf. 1 John 1:6). To do the truth means to live out of the reality that is revealed in Christ. The truth is intrinsically combined with love. Truth and love are not two separated aspects of life—e.g., life as an affect and truth as a theoretical recognition of a matter of fact. On the contrary, truth and love throw light on each other and reflect the same divine reality.

Third, there is *a special relation between Spirit and truth*. God is to be worshipped "in spirit and truth" (4:23–24). The meaning of this passage is not that worship of God is limited to a spiritual issue; rather it is a praise of God's truth that has become flesh in Jesus as a human being (1:14). The Spirit is called "the Spirit of truth" (14:17; 15:26: 16:13; cf. 1 John 5:6). This Spirit will guide the disciples "into all the truth" (16:13). As mentioned above, the meaning is not that new revelations will supplement the one offered in Jesus Christ. Rather, the Spirit in a new situation points to new aspects of the same fundamental revelation of Christ.

The significance of the concept of truth for the religious dialogue will be analyzed in Part Two. At this moment it suffices to mention two present examples of the understanding of John 16. The first illustrates a disagreement among Christian theologians as to where to put the emphasis in the dialogue. The other example deals with a disagreement among Christians and Muslims.

---

25. In the theology of liberation the main emphasis is on truth as practice. Gutiérrez underlines that Christian life is to follow Christ: "The proper doing of theology (the method, the way) has its place within this movement (itself a way) toward the Father. Jesus calls himself the truth, but he also describes himself as the way, and the life (see John 14:6). His actions and words, his practice, show us the course to follow. The Lord proclaims a truth that must be put into practice" (*The Truth Shall Make You Free*, 97).

Part One: Images of a Greater Reality

Contemporary perspectives

Inner-Christian Dialogue on the Understanding of the Holy Spirit

The missiologist Kirsteen Kim points to the importance of John 16:13 for Stanley J. Samartha, an Indian theologian who represents a very open attitude to other religions. His theological basis for dialogue is pneumatological, that is, based on the Holy Spirit. Especially three issues should be noticed: (1) the incarnation as God's dialogue with humanity; (2) the open nature of the new community in Christ; and (3) the Holy Spirit leading into all truth as described in John 16:13. In Samartha's view, the Holy Spirit not only makes it necessary for us to enter into dialogue, but also to continue in it without fear, but with full expectation and openness.[26]

The precise meaning of John 16:13 was a bone of contention between Samartha and the English theologian Lesslie Newbigin who had a background in India (as bishop) and later played a significant role in the World Council of Churches. Samartha has described Newbigin's theology of the Holy Spirit as a "pneumatological Christology," while his own theology is characterized as "Christological pneumatology." The difference is revealed in their interpretation of John 16:13. The breadth of the one word "truth" is crucial to Samartha. He argues from the Greek that "truth" includes the truth of other religions, whereas Newbigin argues the opposite because the whole thrust of John's Gospel is that "the Holy Spirit does not lead to past, or beyond, or away from Jesus."[27]

Samartha's understanding of the dialogue may be called theocentric pluralism. He defends his approach by arguing that if Peter confessed Jesus as Messiah (using Hebrew thought) and the author of the Fourth Gospel spoke of the Logos (using Greek thought) "why should not an Indian Christian theologian accept one of the most hallowed notions in Indian heritage, namely that of the *Brahman* as the Ultimate Mystery?"[28] The disagreement between Samartha and Newbigin exemplifies how prominent mission theologians have different views on the encounter between people from different faith traditions. While Newbigin emphasizes the Christology (a Christocentric theology of religion), the focus of Samartha is on the

---

26. Samartha, *Courage for Dialogue*; Kim, *Mission in the Spirit*, 31.
27. Newbigin, *The Light Has Come*, 216–17; cf. Kim, *Mission in the Spirit*, 32.
28. Kim, *Mission in the Spirit*, 53; the quotation is from a letter that she has received from Samartha.

understanding of the Holy Spirit (a pneuma-centric theology of religion).[29] The difference has relevance for the understanding of God's revelation among Non-Christians—an issue that will be discussed in Part Two.

Christians and Muslims in Dialogue on the Understanding of Revelation

Christianity and Islam have different ways of understanding revelation. According to Islam it is definitive: Muhammad is considered to be the "seal of the prophets." When revelation strikes the earth, it is fixed, unmovable.[30] Christianity also regards revelation as a final event, but at the same time it is open-ended. It is noteworthy that the revelation is identified as a concrete, living person, and not as a dead scripture: "One may speak of Christianity as a continued revelation in the sense that the community is confessing Christ as a living and resurrected Lord who is present in the Word and in the sacraments. This means that man encounters the final revelation in a new way."[31]

The different understandings of the revelation in the two religions may be illustrated by the ways in which they interpret the Farewell Discourses, in particular Jesus' sayings about the coming of the Paraclete (John 14:16–17; 14:26; 15:26; 16:7; 16:12–13). According to Muslim tradition these sayings should be interpreted as a prophecy regarding the coming of Muhammad, cf. Sura 61:6: "And (remember) when 'Iesa (Jesus), son of Maryam (Mary), said: 'O Children of Israel! I am the Messenger of Allah unto you confirming the Taurat [(Torah) which came] before me, and giving glad tidings of a Messenger to come after me, whose name shall be Ahmed.'"[32]

Today some Muslims claim that Muhammad is the "Paraclete" whose coming was foretold by Jesus. Maurice Bucaille takes this view, his main argument being that the two Greek verbs "to hear" and "to speak" define

---

29. According to Samartha the understanding of John 16:13 is related to the struggle between the Holy Spirit and the spirits of this world, between truth and distortions of the truth. This struggle is going on *within* every religious community in history. Samartha reminds us that Christians should avoid the temptation to transform it into a struggle *between* Christianity and other religions in the world. To discern the movement of the Spirit not only in the church but also in the communities of people outside the visible boundaries of the church is perhaps the most challenging demand of our time (Samartha, "The Holy Spirit and People of Other Faiths," 261).

30. Arendt, *Gud er stor!*, 46.

31. Ibid., 54.*

32. Here quoted from: www.dar-us-salam.com/TheNobleQuran/. Brackets original.

concrete actions which can be applied only to a being with hearing and speech organs. He says that it is impossible to apply them to the Holy Spirit. Bucaille therefore suggests that "the presence of the term 'Holy Spirit' in today's text could easily have come from a later addition made quite deliberately. It may have been intended to change the original meaning which predicted the advent of a prophet subsequent to Jesus and was therefore in contradiction with the teachings of the Christian churches at the time of their formation; these teachings maintained that Jesus was the last of the prophets."[33]

According to Chawkat Moucarry, the problem with these suggestions is that there is no textual evidence to support them. None of the manuscripts we have today contains such variant readings. Moreover, Jesus identifies the "Paraclete" as "the Spirit of the truth" (John 14:17; 15:25; 16:13). Bucaille's difficulties could easily have been removed if attention had been paid to the fact that Jesus told his disciples that he was speaking figuratively (John 16:25). "There is no need to take his words literally by saying that the Holy Spirit is unable to hear or speak as a human being does. For, after all, is it not God who communicates his word through his Spirit?"[34]

Reading the Holy Scriptures of Other Faiths

The Swedish theologian Jan Hennigsson relates a conversation with a Muslim who with great energy underlined that the Johannine texts about the Paraclete should be seen as references to Muhammad. This approach to the Bible gave him a new insight and to begin with he was pleased that the Muslim apparently took the Gospel seriously. But later on he became irritated by what the Muslim had done with "my" text. The Muslim had completely misunderstood its content. A person who was not familiar with the Christian faith and the Christian interpretation of the Scripture should not confiscate "our" holy texts so that they became a kind of pre-stage to the Qur'an. At the same time he realized that the Jews might often have nurtured the same feelings towards Christians when we read the Law and the Prophets from "our" perspective, and when we call their holy scriptures for the *Old* Testament.[35]

---

33. Maurice Bucaille, *The Bible, the Qur'an and the Science*, 105–6, quoted in Moucarry, *Faith to Faith*, 246–47.

34. Moucarry, *Faith to Faith*, 247.

35. Henningsson, *Tro möter tro*, 30–31.

We are gradually realizing that the relation of the faithful to their holy scriptures is full of tension and that we must take heed of emotional attachments such as pride, envy, humbleness, and the desire to share with others. The dialogue raises useful questions about the "privilege of interpretation" and about how we read one another's scriptures. How should we react if, say the Jews, who are mentioned in both the New Testament and the Qur'an, do not recognize themselves in the descriptions given in these texts? What should we say if they in fact reject the assertions of the text and have good arguments as to why it is erroneous? Perhaps we might discover that given in its historical setting the text might have only limited validity. For instance, what is said about "the Jews" in the Gospel of John might not apply to all Jews, but to a group of Jews, e.g., the Pharisees. In a similar way, what the Qur'an says about the Christians applies to the isolated Arab church in Najran at the time of Muhammad and need not be representative of the Christian church all over the world at all times.

When we read a text which is considered to be holy we do not engage with it in the first place with our reason. Rather, we read it with our conscious and unconscious associations.[36] It is a peculiar dimension of a holy text that it grows together with us and opens up new viewpoints as our experience of life is enhanced. We are engaging with the word of God in a way that is quite different from other texts. It seems to be unthinkable that a committed Christian should ever read the Bible with the distance characteristic of literary criticism. This would be the equivalent of trying to be a psychiatrist in relation to a beloved relative.

---

36. Ibid., 26–27.

9

Love

HISTORICAL PERSPECTIVES

LOVE IS A CONCEPT rather than a metaphor—in the same way as truth. And yet, in several cases love is represented in metaphorical form, e.g., the parable of the Good Shepherd and the metaphor of the grain of wheat. Love is also described in an act that has a metaphorical meaning: the washing of the disciples' feet. And love plays a significant role in moral exhortations. One of these exhortations is related to the speech of the vine and the branches; cf. the following chapter 11 of this book.

Love as Self-Giving and Sacrifice

Love is a fundamental concept in Johannine theology. The concepts of God and of Christ are both marked by love and thus love has both a theocentric and a christocentric dimension. God is love (cf. 1 John 4:8.16), that is, God acts in love, which is his nature, his essence. At the same time love has a christocentric motivation, in the form of a radical self-giving (cf. John 3:16).

John's portrait of Christ is decisively formed by the concept of self-giving love, as evidenced by Jesus' words:[1] "I am the good shepherd; the good shepherd lays down his life for the sheep" (10:11). "No one has greater love than this, to lay down one's life for one's friends" (15:13). "For their

---

1. Nissen, "Community and ethics," 200–201.

sakes I sanctify myself" (17:19) that is: I give myself for them; I sacrifice myself for them. Finally we should note the saying of Jesus in 12:25: "Those who love their life lose it, and those who hate their life in this world will keep it for eternal life."

Central to the concept is the Greek word, *agapē*, also used in 1 John 4:8 in the phrase "God is love." Jesus reveals God's essence as a love that is devoted to others and which reaches its supreme expression in his self-giving sacrifice. It is in the passion that we see most clearly who God is. The divine power in the Fourth Gospel is not primarily manifested by miracles, although the Gospel reports some of them. The death of Jesus is not accompanied by signs like earthquakes or a story about the dead coming out of their tombs or revelations of angels etc., as is the case with Matthew's Gospel (e.g., Matt 27:53ff.). In John's Gospel the death of Jesus is simply an act of love that reveals the nature of God.[2]

The Fourth Gospel characterizes this death as a "glorification," the term "glory" being used in biblical writings as a technical term for God's essence. John regards the divine glory in the first place as God's love. In 1:14 we therefore have a formulation full of paradoxes, for the verse is about the earthly Jesus but says: "We have seen his glory, the glory as of a father's only son, full of grace and truth." In this earthly Jesus there are no remarkable exterior signs of the divine. And this is precisely the point. As the most supreme form of an act of love his death has to be a voluntary self-giving and it has to be a self-giving for others. Jesus did not surrender himself to death, but to the One who is the source of all life.[3]

Jesus as the Good Shepherd

Two texts in particular testify to Jesus' self-giving and sacrifice. These texts are the parable of the Good Shepherd and the account of the washing of the disciples' feet.

The parable of the Good Shepherd in John 10:1–18 consists of four different parts.[4] The first (vv. 1–6) makes it clear how to approach the sheep.

---

2. Jervell, *Større kærlighed har ingen*, 45.

3. Ibid., 45–46.

4. Værge, *Johannesevangeliet*, 128–31. According to Brown (*The Gospel According to John*, 301–400), the passage of John 10:1–18 consists of the following parts: vv. 1–5: the parable (s), v. 6: the reaction, vv. 7–10: explanation of the gate, vv. 11–18: explanation of the shepherd.

Thieves are strangers who cause the sheep to flee, whereas they will follow the real shepherd when he calls them by their name.

In the second part (vv.7–10) Jesus identifies himself with the words: "I am the gate for the sheep," a metaphor that is paralleled in the use of "the way" in John 14:6 and one which again underlines his unique claim. While the thief comes only to steal and destroy, Jesus comes in order that the sheep may have life and have it abundantly (v. 10).

The third part, vv.11–13, is the climax of the parable. "I am the good shepherd. The good shepherd lays down his life for the sheep." Here the naturalistic image of the shepherd is transcended. The "natural" shepherd may endanger himself for the sake of the sheep, but he would hardly lay down his life for them.[5] "However, since this is precisely what Jesus did, he is a qualitatively different type of shepherd—the *good* shepherd."[6]

The last part, vv. 14–18, contains another "I am" saying, but other aspects are added to the image. First, there is a reference to the relation between Father and Son (v. 15), and second, Jesus speaks of "other sheep that do not belong to this fold" (v.16). This is another way of proclaiming that Jesus is the savior of the world (cf. 4:42). Finally, it is underlined that Jesus lays down his life as an act of his own accord (i.e., voluntarily), vv. 17–18. It is the unity with the Father that gives Jesus the power to lay down his life and to take it up again.

John 10:18 is a cue to understanding the way in which John describes the account of Jesus' suffering.[7] Jesus is seen as king, with a kingly power as the background for his self-giving and sacrifice. He lays down his life as king and sheep. Unlike the thieves and the bandits he does not steal and kill the sheep, or flee from them; instead he acts in love. In the Fourth Gospel the power of the king is understood in the light of the concept of the shepherd who lays down his life for his sheep. Jesus is the true king who sacrifices himself.

Koester rightly observes that the imagery of John 10 is accessible enough to engage a spectrum of readers from different backgrounds, both Jewish and non-Jewish, yet it is transformed to convey a distinctly christological message. "When Jesus identified himself as the good shepherd, he

---

5. Cf. Nielsen, "John's Understanding of the Death of Jesus," 244–45: "That the shepherd can be called the good shepherd is primarily because his loving care for his disciples stretches so far as to laying down his life for them. He confronts the powers of evil and secures their lives. Again the crucial significance of Jesus' death is underlined."

6. Værge, *Johannesevangeliet*, 130.*

7. Nissen, "Kongemagt og discipelmenighed," 155.

appropriated these familiar associations but redefined them in terms of his crucifixion insisting that *the* good shepherd is one who lays down his life for the sheep."[8] [9]

The Washing of the Disciples' Feet

The character of love is specified in the Fourth Gospel not by an extended body of teaching, as in Matthew's Sermon on the Mount, but by a single enacted parable: Jesus' washing of the disciples' feet. A number of circumstances suggest that the account is of central importance to John, due to its position at the head of the second main section of the Gospel and the detailed introduction with which the story is introduced.

The episode has two dimensions. The first part of the story (vv. 4–11) reveals that the crucifixion was Jesus' consummate act of complete self-giving love. In the washing of his disciples' feet, as in his death, he gives himself completely.[10] The second part of the passage (vv. 12–17) elaborates the significance of the act as an example for the disciples to follow (13:15). John 13 describes the mastership of Jesus not as a hierarchical position, but rather as a counter-power from below. This is reflected in his action: Then Jesus "got up from the table, took off his outer robe and tied a towel around himself" (v.4). There is a reversal of expectations in the story, just as the reversal in the parable of the Good Samaritan. The disciples are really shocked. By acting like a slave their master is turning the world upside down.[11]

In the following verse we hear how Jesus pours water into a basin and begins to wash the disciples' feet (v. 5). In antiquity foot-washing expresses hospitality and love, and is a clear indication of the relations of power. When it comes to the service at the table (diaconia) the inferior person expresses their subordinate position.[12] The one at the bottom of the pyramid washes the feet and is servant at the table. Women, slaves, and children are inferior to the master of the house and they constantly have to confirm their position through actions like foot-washing and diaconal service. As Koester

---

8. Koester, *Symbolism in the Fourth Gospel*, 236.

9. Cf. Nielsen, "John's Understanding of the Death of Jesus," 240.

10. Jesus' remark to Peter in 13:8 indicates that his self-giving love will bring his followers into an abiding relationship with him; cf. Koester, *Symbolism in the Fourth Gospel*, 116.

11. Nissen, "Bible and ethics," 88–89.

12. Washing other people's feet was widely understood to be a task for slaves.

has put it, "Although people occasionally performed this task voluntarily as a gesture of devotion for someone of similar or higher social status, no one would expect a person in authority to do this for those beneath him. When Jesus, the Teacher, stooped to bathe the feet of his disciples, he acted contrary to social conventions."[13]

Peter is not prepared to receive such slave-like service from Jesus (v. 6); he regards Jesus simply as a master who exercises his power at the top of the hierarchy. He fails to understand that this reversal of hierarchy takes place in order for him to share in the glory of God (vv. 8–10). The last part of the account (vv. 12–17) points to the ethical impact of Jesus' action. "So if I, your Lord and Teacher, have washed your feet, you also ought to wash one another's feet. For I have set you an example, that you also should do, as I have done to you" (vv. 14–15). In this text we meet the same two elements as in Mark 10:42–45. The relation between Jesus' service and the disciples' service is seen both as motivation and as comparison.[14] Jesus' unique action is an anticipation and a presage of his own imminent death, while simultaneously being a prototype for the disciples, just as his laying down of his life for his followers (15:13) serves as an act of love and servanthood. John sees Jesus' death as an act of self-sacrificial love that establishes the cruciform life as the norm of discipleship. Those within the community may be called upon literally to lay down their lives for one another.[15]

The Love Commandment

The crucial significance of love in the Fourth Gospel is based on Jesus being the image of God, God's self-portrait, the face of God's love. The manifestation of divine love is self-giving. This fundamental character of Jesus must also be the mark of his disciples. "Love—even God's love, even *agapē*—seeks a response, an answering love. It seeks mutual love, and where it finds it, the heavenly realm is entered."[16] The commandment is found in two passages in the Farewell Discourses.

---

13. Koester, *Symbolism in the Fourth Gospel*, 244.

14. This twofold character is also underlined by Nielsen (*Johannesevangeliet*, 240–42) and by Koester. The foot-washing and the new commandment are structurally identical. "Both anticipate the love Jesus shows for his disciples through his death on their behalf and make it an example of the love his disciples should show to one another" (Koester (*Symbolism in the Fourth Gospel*, 244).

15. Nissen, "Community and Ethics," 202.

16. Verhey, *The Great Reversal*, 144.

The first passage is John 13:34–35: "I give you a new commandment, that you love one another. Just as I have loved you, you also should love one another. By this everyone will know that you are my disciples, if you have love for one another." The focus on mutual love does not mean that the world disappears from the picture. Love is seen as the badge of discipleship: "By this *everyone* will know . . ." If the followers of Christ reproduce in their mutual love the same love which the Father showed in sending his Son (3:16) and which the Son showed in laying down his life (10:18; 15:13), this will be the most powerful of testimonies to the world. John's community is a community of love. In and through their love for each other the disciples are called to give public witness to the life-giving power of God's love revealed in Jesus. By this *praxis of agapē* all people will know that they are Jesus' disciples.[17]

The second passage is John 15:12–13. Here, the commandment is followed by the famous words that there is no greater love than to lay down one's life for one's friends (15:13). Jesus continues by saying that the disciples are no longer his servants but his friends, and he adds: "I have called you friends, because I have made known to you everything that I have heard from my Father" (15:14–15).[18]

The new life that is love is exclusively bound to the person of Jesus. It cannot be acquired automatically, but is dependent on continuous fellowship with Jesus, and therefore is given again and again to human beings. This is affirmed by the way in which the image of the vine and the branches is related to the commandment to love. The eternal life, the unbroken community with the Father, is not to be found in a mystic, inner experience but in sober, concrete action in the community of love.[19] Most significantly, the existence of this community of love is in itself a testimony of God's own nature. Love (*agapē*) is nothing but a revelation of who God is. That is why we only have one commandment, the commandment to love.[20]

---

17. Schüssler-Fiorenza, *In Memory of Her*, 323; Nissen, "The Distinctive Character," 143. See also Arias, *The Great Commission*, 93: "The life of love in the community of disciples becomes the trademark and the credential of the missionary community."

18. For further reflections on this saying, see chapter 15 in this study.

19. Cf. Hays, *The Moral Vision*, 145: "Love within the community is not merely a matter of warm feelings; rather it is a matter of action."

20. Jervell, *Større kærlighed har ingen*, 37–38.

Part One: Images of a Greater Reality

Contemporary perspectives

What are the implications in a contemporary context of John's insistence on the importance of love? This question is discussed internally among Christians and also in the relation between Christians and people of other faiths. In what follows, the first paragraph is about a discrepancy among Christians, while the succeeding paragraphs deal with the Johannine understanding of love in relation to other religions.

"For God so loved the world..."—on Salvation and Judgment

Christians disagree on how to understand the relationship between salvation and judgment in the proclamation of the gospel. Some continue to hold that we depart this life to partake either in eternal life or in eternal perdition. Others argue that there can be no condemnation from God. Can he not open all doors? Is heaven a limited franchise? Will he not pardon all in the last resort? The difference between the two viewpoints is a disagreement regarding the concept of the "apocatastasis," that is, the restoration of all things to their original condition. There is no unambiguous answer to these questions, but there is a significance in distinguishing between the small hope and the great hope.

The *small* hope is the hope that the church has usually proclaimed: that all the faithful will be saved while all the unfaithful and the ungodly will be lost—in other words a *limited* salvation. By contrast, the *great* hope rests on the belief that the gospel is trustworthy: when we say that God is almighty in love, that really *is* his nature, so that ultimately *all* people are included in this love. Advocates of the great hope therefore ask: How can perfect love encompass a God who punishes disobedience eternally?

We must ask how the Fourth Gospel should be interpreted in relation to these questions.[21] Its essence is the proclamation in John 3:16 that God's love for the world is so strong that he sent his own son to save it. The determinant here is salvation and judgment, not salvation and perdition. The proclamation of God's salvation is foundational; the judgment consists in man's refusal to receive that salvation. Perdition is never a theme in Jesus' proclamation or in the proclamation about Jesus. The idea that God loves you, and *if* you believe, you will be saved is the erroneous gospel of retribu-

---

21. In what follows I am indebted to Kaj Mogensen who has given a thorough discussion of these issues. He has recently published a major book on Salvation and Perdition; see Mogensen, *Frelse og Fortabelse*, esp. 240–67 (on the Gospel of John).

tion. A God who says: "I love you, but if you do not love me, I will destroy you" is a God created by the fallen man in his own image. It is absolutely essential in Christian mission and dialogue to maintain that God's love is perfect, boundless, endless, and unreserved. God does not cease to love because *we* fail. God continues to love, until his love has transformed us into what we should be.[22]

People must not be frightened into the Kingdom of God; they are *invited*. There is still a need for conversion, and indeed those who do not believe "are condemned already" (3:18). However, conversion should be regarded as a consequence of the proclamation not of judgment but of salvation. The First Letter of John says: "Love has been perfected among us in this: that we may have boldness on the day of judgment, because as he is, so are we in this world. There is no fear in love, but perfect love casts out fear; for fear has to do with punishment, and whoever fears has not reached perfection in love. We love because he first loved us" (4:17–19). Although these words were originally written in the context of an internal Christian conflict, they are also a pointer to what is the basic motivation in Christian mission. It is never fear, but is always love. In communicating the Christian gospel it is not possible to separate the form from the content. A proclamation of God's love is inconsistent with aggressive forms of mission and the use of power; see also chapter 8 of this book. Another issue is how the Christian understanding of love affects its relation to other religious traditions, specifically Islam, Hinduism, and Buddhism.

The Image of God in Islam and Christianity

Although God's love is known in Islam, the concept has another position than in Christianity. Islamic theology distinguishes ninety-nine names for God, but the supreme name, which represents God himself, remains unknown. Among God's most beautiful names, the "Ever-Merciful"and the "Most Merciful," stand out. According to Chawkat Moucarry, the Christian gospel is not just about God's mercy; it is about God's love, and divine love is far more embracing than divine mercy: "A merciful person is not necessarily loving, whereas a loving person is always merciful. Without love, the

---

22. Cf. 1 John 3:2 "What we will be has not yet been revealed. What we do know is this: when he is revealed, we will be like him."

Part One: Images of a Greater Reality

mercy of God would not only serve to reveal more clearly his majesty as Creator and judge."[23]

In many passages the Qur'an speaks of God's love for his people (Sura 3:31; 5:54). But it is a love conditional on their obedience. Thus God loves those who fear him (Sura 3:76; 9.4), trust in him (Sura 3: 159), are steadfast (Sura 3:146) and equitable (Sura 5:42), and fight for his cause (Sura 61:4). But God does not love the unbelievers (Sura 3:32), the evildoers (Sura 3.57), the proud (Sura 16:23), or the prodigal (Sura 7:31). Above all, God loves those who love him and follow the prophet (Sura 3:31–32). "In the context of the Qur'an, God's love means that he is pleased with the obedient servants rather than knowing them in a personal and loving relationship."[24]

In Christianity on the other hand God is conceived as the unconditionally loving Father, his fatherhood being fundamental to his nature in the same way as his love. The greatest revelation of God in the Bible is that he is the eternal Father, which in a sense is his supreme name. "See what love the Father has given us that we should be called children of God; and that is what we are" (1 John 3:1). This way of thinking is foreign to Islam. In their perspective it is demeaning for God to be considered a father.[25] For God is transcendent, radically other than and totally separate from, his creation.

Most Muslims believe that there is no way in which we can experience God or meet him, (the exception being the Islamic mysticism, Sufism). But we can be obedient to his law. Like Muslims, Christians know the concept of the hidden God.[26] The Gospel of John can even say that "no one has ever seen God," but immediately after this statement, this restriction is invalidated by the coming of Jesus. "If you know me, you will know my Father also. From now on you do know him and have seen him" (14:7). The Christian understanding of Jesus influences the image of God. Unlike Islam, Christianity does not see a degradation of God in the idea of his humiliation.[27]

The difference between the two religions is also noticeable in their understanding of the christological title "the Servant of the Lord." For

---

23. Moucarry, *Faith to Faith*, 89.

24. Ibid., 90.

25. Ibid., 91.

26. Cf. the paragraph, "The Light as symbol for God's hidden presence," in chapter 7 of this book.

27. Arendt, *Er det den samme Gud?*, 76.

Muslims this title is a confirmation of the humanity of Jesus because they think that Jesus submitted himself to God like other human beings, whereas Christians understand the title as a pointer to the greatness of Jesus: he made himself a servant, even though he was the Lord; cf. John 13:1–7; Phil 2:6–11.[28]

Bhakti-Devotion in Hinduism and the Johannine Concept of Love

There are many forms of Hinduism, and the *bhakti*-spirituality is of particular interest in our context, since there seem to be a number of parallels with John's concept of love. This was already underlined by the Indian theologian A. J. Appasamy in his book *Christianity as Bhakti Marga: A Study of the Johannine Doctrine of Love* from 1926.

The Bhakti type of religious thought in India is chosen for the purpose of showing the intimate relation between the inner spirit of Christianity and the inner spirit of India's religious thought in three areas: (1) The type of religious experience expressed in Bhakti writings—with its longing for union with God and its enjoyment of such union—is of all the types of religious experience in India probably the nearest in affinity to real Christian experience. (2) The metaphysical background behind Bhakti experience is also closest to the metaphysical background of Christianity. Both agree in maintaining the separateness of the divine and human personalities, however much they may be eager for union. (3) The immense following which Bhakti has in India.[29]

The word "Bhakti" has often been translated into English as "faith," but for many this implies an intellectual assent to certain facts, and such an understanding does not do justice to the word's rich and complex meaning. The heart of Bhakti is strong love, through which the devotee can attain God. "Those who worship me with Bhakti are in me and I also in them" (*Gita* 9:29). In the *Gita*, Bhakti is constantly associated with action and knowledge and these three are spoken of as paths leading to God, though the first path (i.e., love) is of prime importance.[30]

There are many points of resemblances between the idea of love in John's Gospel and Bhakti mysticism. Nevertheless, the use of the Gospel in an Indian context will have a corrective function, or as Appasamy puts it:

---

28. Larsen, *Jesus i Koranen*, 23.
29. Appasamy, *Christianity as Bhakti Marga*, 21–22.
30. Ibid., 24.

"The study of St. John's Gospel will, therefore, be of peculiar helpfulness to thinking people in India."[31] Three points are mentioned:

First, Indian mysticism tends to live in eternity, conscious of its vastness alone and neglecting or even despising time. The Fourth Gospel, however, shows how in *accepting the historical Christ* we may live in eternity. In it history and metaphysics are woven together. In other words, the historical dimension and the incarnation are maintained.[32] Secondly, the danger of mysticism is the identification of the human soul with the divine. By contrast, John maintains the *difference between God and man*. John "seems to be quite aware of the possibility of man being metaphysically one with God but emphatically maintains the difference between God and man even in the deepest moments of religious experience."[33] Thirdly, in mysticism all over the world there is a constant tendency to ignore the laws of morality. "On this too, St. John has much that is of value to teach India. Wholly obedient to God as he is, he realizes that he has constantly to be on his guard against wrong doing."[34] In other words, John maintains that *ethics is an essential part of mysticism*.

There is a similarity between the Fourth Gospel and Bhakti on the idea that the initiative in human religious experiences is taken by God. The conviction that it is God who first calls us and implants in us deep and strong longings for himself is often found in the Johannine writings. We did not love him first but he loved us first. Hindu Bhaktas also have strong convictions on this point, but occasionally there are lines that seem to imply that man and not God begins the process.[35] This determination to be devoted or opposed to God arises, according to Hindu Bhaktas, from a man's previous karma. It is his karma which enables him either to have or not to have Bhakti. "In thus speaking of karma as the factor which conditions God's grace, Hindu Bhaktas withdraw from man his immediate responsibility."[36]

---

31. Ibid., 16.

32. Or as Appasamy puts it: "On the one hand, St. John is aware of the importance of history as he reckons with a person who has appeared in time. On the other, he fully realizes the significance of metaphysics, being aware of the eternal issues in time" (ibid., 15).

33. Ibid., 16.

34. Ibid.

35. Ibid., 50–51.

36. Ibid., 55. There are also many points of similarity between the Gospel of John and Bhakti as to the understanding of the relation between love and knowledge. "John and the Hindu Bhaktas are at one in their conviction that love is the supreme revealer. Men want to know God and in their anxiety try different methods. But all these are of no avail.

Love

The Understanding of Sacrifice in Buddhism and Christianity

In one of his books on the relation between Buddhism and Christianity, Notto Thelle underlines the fact that many Japanese are attracted by Jesus' teaching, whereas they are critical of the Christian church. He considers it a paradox that many friends of Jesus prefer not to associate with the Christian church. At best they see a pale shadow of what they read in the gospels. At worst they regard the church to be treasonable to Jesus.[37]

What Buddhists see in the gospels is above all the love sacrifice. While many Christians tend to summarize the essence of the gospel in the well-known, but often well-worn, words "God is love," Thelle has often heard non-Christians refer to Jesus' words about self-giving love: "Very truly, I tell you, unless a grain of wheat falls into the earth and dies, it remains just a single grain; but if it dies, it bears much fruit. Those who love their life lose it, and those who hate their life in this world will keep it for eternal life" (John 12:24–25). The strong appeal of these words may relate to the possibility that behind the façade of the competitive society we may find dreams and longings towards love and sacrifice.

For the idea of sacrifice is not unknown in Buddhism. The highest ideal of eastern Buddhism is not the ascetic who reaches his goal and enjoys the harmony beyond the constant transmigration of souls; it is the bodhisattva, who is willing to postpone nirvana in order to return to this world and save others. Some Buddhists therefore regard the life of Jesus as a realization of the Buddhist idea that authentic life arises when the "I" dies. This seems to be in line with the famous hymns to the Philippians (Phil 2:6–11). They argue that God's innermost essence is realized in Christ "emptying himself."[38]

The relation between love and knowledge plays a crucial role in the encounter between Christianity and Buddhism. The Sri Lankan theologian Aloysius Pieris points to similarities as well as dissimilarities in how the two religions understand their mutual relationship. He mentions two positions: on the one side "the 'Agapeic Gnōsis' of Christians" and on the other side "The 'Gnostic Agapē' of Buddhists." In Buddhism *knowledge* is of fundamental significance. "Though it is true that selfless, self-immolating

---

God, however, in the fulness of His love unveils Himself before His loving children and reveals to them the wonder and the depth of his personality" (ibid., 218).

37. Thelle, *Hvem kan standse vinden?*, 78.

38. Ibid., 86.

love may make one a bodhisattva (a candidate to Buddhahood), the fact remains that it is gnosis that finally makes him a Buddha."[39] By contrast, the fundamental thing in Christianity is *love*. "More specifically, *loving one's neighbor is the Christian way of knowing God*. In other words, love is Christian gnosis, because one who does not love one's fellows does not know God (1 John 4:7f.)."[40] It is characteristic not only of John but also of Paul that "the Sinai covenant of justice has received its final fulfillment in Jesus in whom mutual love among humans is the (path to) true gnosis or the knowledge of God through the Son in the Spirit."[41]

The Washing of Feet in an Indian Context

The insistence on Jesus' self-giving and sacrifice is a challenge in an age of individualism. It is also a challenge to those forms of spirituality that concentrate on self-salvation.

Jesus' washing of the disciples' feet is perhaps the best example of the Johannine concept of love colliding with Gnosticism's denigration of the body.[42] In the Indian context Sister Vandana calls the act "The Guru's *Pad-puja*."[43] The background for this designation is that in some Hindu ashrams every Thursday (called *guruvar*, day of the guru) there is a ceremony of *Guru-pad-puja* in which the disciples wash the feet of the guru, anoint them, and offer flowers and gifts at his feet. If the guru has already "left his body"—that is, has passed out of this world—the disciples perform the ceremony at his *paduka*: two feet or sandals made in stone or metal which symbolize the presence of the guru. Vandana compares this ceremony with a similar rite observed in her own Christian ashram on Thursdays. Here the rite is performed in memory of Christ's *pad-puja*, but the participants wash each other's feet, for "Jesus the Satguru instead of having his feet washed, as would be expected, himself washed the feet of the disciples and told them

---

39. Pieris, *Love Meets Wisdom*, 118.

40. Ibid., 114; italics in the original.

41. Ibid.

42. Davidsen rightly notes that from a comparative point of view in the history of religions there is a strong contrast between the gnostic idea of the degradation of the Savior—which is seen as negative—and the service of love which is the point of the foot-washing (Davidsen, *Komponenter til kristendomsundervisningen*, 122).

43. Vandana, *Waters of Fire*, 99–115.

to do as He had done—a symbolic gesture showing their willingness to serve and love, which means their willingness to die."[44]

This is an interesting attempt at inculturation, since the foot-washing in John 13 was in origin a critique of Jewish traditions in the first century, when disciples washed the feet of the rabbis. Jesus demonstrates a reversal of roles, which is a central motif in Christianity, and even more obvious in Luke's version of the Last Supper: "The kings of the Gentiles lord it over them; and those in authority over them are called benefactors. But not so with you; rather the greatest among you must become like the youngest, and the leader like one who serves. For who is greater; the one who is at the table or the one who serves? Is it not the one at the table? But I am among you as one who serves" (Luke 22:25–27; cf. also Mark 10:42–45).

---

44. Ibid., 99.

10

Way

Historical Perspectives

The Way as Universal Symbol

THE IDEA OR IMAGE of "the way" is important in every culture and religion. As to the cultural meaning it is useful to compare the two symbols "house" and "way." While the "house" as the centric space has a mid-point, the "way" points to "ex-centric space" drawing people towards something beyond in a world where people are never the same as before.[1]

The image serves two important functions.[2] First, *finding (or losing) the way*: In high mountains, in the desert, on the high seas, finding the way is a matter of survival—of life or death. But in a large city, surrounded by crowds of people, one can suddenly be overwhelmed by the feeling of having *lost* the way. Second, *opening (or blocking) the way*: The opening of new ways (waterways, highways, trade routes) has always brought with it a sense of expansiveness, of freedom. The open way is a symbol of a new opportunity. On the other hand, ways may be blocked, literally or figuratively.

Present experiences with ways are ambiguous.[3] On the one hand we have negative experiences among millions of people who are "in transit" because they are fleeing from war, terror, and persecution. On the other

---

1. Biehl, *Symbole geben zu lernen*, 98.
2. *Images of Life*, 6.
3. Biehl, *Symbole geben zu lernen*, 99–100.

hand we have positive experiences of the hiker or the wanderer, for whom the journey itself is a form of life. It is important to note the difference between way and path. The path follows the landscape and is not an artificial product. Hence, a path is not suited for marching. Path-travelers must accommodate their steps to the circumstances, the journey being more important than the goal.

The "way" is not only a significant image in the different cultures; it is also a key symbol in the world of religions,[4] as we shall see later in this chapter. To begin with we shall take a look at its role in Christianity, especially the Fourth Gospel.[5] Jesus' saying: "I am the way, and the truth, and the life" (14:6) is of special interest. This verse has often been seen as an argument in favor of the exclusivity of Christianity, an understanding that seems to be supported by the following words: "No one comes to the Father except through me. If you know me, you will know my Father also. From now on, you do know him and have seen him" (14:6–7). However, this is a simplification. The statement in John 14:6 reflects a continuity with other religions traditions as well as a certain discontinuity.[6] As we shall see, the text is about the exclusivity of Christ—which need not be the same as the exclusivity of Christianity.

John 14:6 is part of a greater unit (14:1–11) which has three themes: (a) departure and dwelling places, (b) the way, (c) Jesus and the Father.[7] Each of these themes will be considered in the following paragraphs.

---

4. See also the paragraph "The language of symbols and metaphors" in chapter 2 of this book.

5. Kaj Mogensen has demonstrated that the "way" is both a symbol of phenomenon and a symbol of situation. A *symbol of phenomenon* can be related both to nature (e.g., water) and the human world; the bread and the way are examples of the last category. A *symbol of situation* is found especially in narratives. Important symbols of situation are the "journey" and the "wandering." The journey can occur on the horizontal level (the journey to and from our home) as well as on the vertical level (the journey from earth to heaven and vice versa, the journey from time to eternity). The Fourth Gospel is an example of how the journey on the vertical level is crossed by a journey on the horizontal level, especially in connection with the Jewish feasts (Mogensen, "Symboler og symboldidaktik," 243–44).

6. Nissen, *New Testament and Mission*, 92.

7. Gjesing, "Tekstvejledning."

Part One: Images of a Greater Reality

The Father's House and Its Many Dwelling-Places

Chapter 14 is introduced by Jesus' appeal to his disciples not to be troubled. He continues: "Believe in God, believe also in me. In my Father's house there are many dwelling places. If it were not so, would I have told you that I go to prepare a place for you? And if I go and prepare a place for you, I will come again and will take you to myself, so that where I am, there you may be also" (14:1b-4). These verses are a continuation of the theme from the preceding chapter. Peter asks, "Lord, where are you going?" and Jesus replies, "Where I am going, you cannot follow me now, but you will follow afterwards" (13:36), a statement that Peter is unable to understand.

Most scholars agree that John's eschatology may be described as "present eschatology"; cf. John 3:18; 5:24-25.[8] Eternity is now! Only a few passages hint at the traditional understanding of eternal life as something that is to come ("futuristic eschatology"). John 14:1-4 is usually considered to be one of these in its affirmation that the disciples will one day be able to follow, for he has shown "the way" to what must be assumed to be heaven.

However, there are other ways of interpreting the text.[9] If it is seen as part of the Farewell Discourses as a whole and in relation to the passion narrative it is not unambiguous that the main emphasis is on Jesus going to heaven. The way from earth to heaven would then have its focus on being where Jesus now is (v. 3b) and therefore on taking up one's own cross. This understanding would be in line with the tradition in Mark 10:35-45 where the sons of Zebedee request honorary places in heaven but are corrected by Jesus who asks them if they can drink his cup. An additional argument is that the 'way' in verse 6 seems to have a twofold meaning. Jesus is both the guide who *is showing* the way and he himself *is* the way.

The language used in 14:2 is hardly accidental. "House" is a rendering of the Greek word *oikia* (rather than *oikos*, building) and it can mean "household" or "family." The "many dwelling places" is a rendering of the Greek words *monai pollai* which corresponds to the common Johannine verb *menein* ("abide"), cf. 6:56; 15:4-10 and also 14:23: "Those who love

---

8. Cf. The story of the resurrection of Lazarus in John 11. To Martha's statement that she knows that her brother will rise again at the resurrection on the last day, comes Jesus' answer: "I am the resurrection and the life. Those who believe in me, even though they die, will live, and everyone who lives and believes in me will never die." The point of the chapter is that a faith relation with Christ is itself a "resurrection" (cf. Kysar, *John the Maverick Gospel*, 88).

9. Gjesing, "Tekstvejledning."

me, will keep my word, and my Father will love them, and we will come to them and make our home with them."[10] The passage is known as the Johannine "Pentecostal text."

The temporary (eschatological) and the spacious understanding are not mutually exclusive alternatives but a coherent combination. The metaphorical language of "many dwelling places" points to the universal and spacious character of the salvation. John 14:1–4 is not just about the future; it is also about the present time. Again and again the Fourth Gospel proclaims that the eternal life has moved into the present time by virtue of Jesus' life and death. Or as Johannes Værge has put it: "The same may be said about the dwelling-places in the Father's house. In our faith they are *here and now* as a space where we can feel at home, where we can live and where we can breathe—in midst of this world, so that this world will not press the life and our free breath out of us."[11] The house of many dwelling-places cannot be localized in a concrete earthly building, but is to be found where there is worship in spirit and truth (4:23). It is the space of life that constitutes the fellowship of the believers.[12]

Means and Ends—the Twofold Meaning of Jesus as the Way

As we have seen, the image of "the way" is central to the Gospel of John. Those who follow Jesus are promised that they will never walk in darkness but will have the light of life (8:12). They might be uncertain and say like Thomas, "Lord, we do not know where you are going. How can we know the way?" (14:5). To this Jesus answers, "I am the way, and the truth, and the life. No one comes to the Father except through me" (14:6). There is no distinction here between means and end.[13] The opening of the way and the coming of Jesus Christ are one and the same.[14] But how then can anyone be "the way," even in a metaphorical sense. There is obviously a shift intended

10. Brown translates "our dwelling place" instead of "our home" (*The Gospel According to John*, 638).

11. Værge, *Johannesevangeliet*, 165.*

12. The authorized Danish translation is: "I min fars hus er der mange boliger" (English: "In my Father's house there are many dwelling-places"). An alternative translation says: "I min fars hus er der rum for alle" ("In my Father's house there is room for everyone"). Cf. also Brown, *The Gospel According to John*, 625: "The 'many' simply means that there is room enough for all."

13. This twofold aspect of Jesus as the way has its counterpart in the two dimensions: Jesus as the enlightener and Jesus as the light (cf. chapter 7 of this book).

14. Wieser, "The Way of Life," 225.

in the use of the image in 14:6, for the same shift is involved in the rest of the verse: "I am the truth and the life." Here, too, there is a departure from the common usage of terms. Normally we would expect someone to *speak* the truth and to *offer* life. This threefold alteration of the usage of terms produces an extreme concentration of meaning on the person of Jesus. He becomes the locus of the final purpose of the human enterprise, of human history, and the world.[15]

Thus, Jesus is not only the one who *shows* the way as guide, he *is* the way. This is not to say that the aspect of guiding is absent from Johannine imagery. We have already seen that Jesus' way has the character of a *via dolorosa*. Most importantly in this context is the definition of the way as Jesus himself. The way, in the sense of the life, death, and resurrection of Jesus, has been accomplished once and for all. When Jesus *is* the way, the way has been laid and traveled, and he is at the goal where the disciples will be together with him.

Jesus and the Father

In the last part of the text Jesus says to Thomas: "If you know me, you will know my Father also. From now on you do know him and have seen him" (14:7). The statement evokes a reaction from Philip: "Lord, show us the father, and we will be satisfied" (14:8). Here we come to the last major theme of the text, namely the relation between Jesus and the Father.

According to Old Testament and Jewish thinking no one has ever seen God—indeed no one can bear to see God and live. In this perspective, Jesus' answer to Philip is revolutionary: "Have I been with you all this time, Philip, and you still do not know me? Whoever has seen me has seen the Father. How can you say: 'Show us the Father'?" (14.9). In John's context there is a reference to the important theme of the Prologue: No one has ever seen God, but God, the only Son who is close to the Father's heart has made him known (1:18).

The answer to Philip is unambiguous. He asks to see the Father, but during his time together with Jesus, he has already seen his face! Those

---

15. Ibid., 224–25. Wieser continues: "One might ask whether the image of the way is really able to carry the meaning with which it is invested here, or whether it does not actually break down under the weight of the meaning placed on it. Or could such breakdown actually be intended by the evangelist in order to make the reader realize that something unique, something totally out of the ordinary has happened with the coming of Jesus?" (ibid., 225).

who have seen the Son have seen the Father. This is a fundamental claim of the Fourth Gospel. Lars Ole Gjesing comments that God on this earth is seen face to face, and the death penalty over the one who sees is not only suspended; it is replaced by its opposite. From now on all promises are related to this vision—in particular the promise never to see death. But at the same time the vision has lost its character of refusing admittance. It has to be *said* to Philip that it is God he has seen.[16]

Contemporary Perspectives

The Way of the Religions and the Way of Christ

The dialogue between Jesus and Philip is of great interest when we consider our present religious dialogue. It is surprising to hear a disciple of Jesus say, "Lord, show us the Father, and we will be satisfied." It would have been easier to understand these words if they were uttered by one of today's religious seekers. Nowadays we meet many people who are searching for the ultimate truth about life, a divine principle, a power behind the universe (see also chapter 3 of this book). Often they do not know what to do with Jesus. They may say: "Why is this Jesus the only way to the true God? You Christians say that he is the way, but it seems to us that he is standing in our way. Show us the Father, and we will be satisfied." This is how Philip has been thinking, but according to John it is an inadequate approach. Jesus emphasizes that there is no admittance *at all* to the Father without the Son; there is no chance for recognition of God and no fellowship with God except that which the Son gives. Jesus' statement in 14:9 is an accurate counterpart to that of 1.18.

It is interesting to note that in 14:6 John applies a terminology that is known throughout the world of religions. Similarly, the multiplicity of religious ways and paths was an issue in the New Testament period. For instance, among Jews it was customary to speak of the "way." In Jewish tradition we meet the term the "Way of the Torah," and the Qumran community designated itself as the Way. A third example is "the way" of John the Baptist.[17]

16. Gjesing, "Tekstvejledning," 372.

17. Cf. Brown who suggests that "John 14:6 reflects the whole chain of usage of the imagery of 'the way,' originating in the OT, modified by sectarian Jewish thought, illustrated at Qumran, and finally adopted by the Christian community as self designation" (Brown, *The Gospel According to John*, 629).

Part One: Images of a Greater Reality

Today we have a similar variety of "ways," the various religions being attempts to find direction. Religions are not in the first place institutionalized systems, but ways.[18] The first Christians are called those who belong to "the Way" (Acts 9.2). The first Sura of the Qur'an is characterized as "the way" (or straight path). In particular, in the Eastern tradition there are many references to religion as a way.[19] One of the most widespread terms for religion is Tao, which means the Way, the law of the universe, the innermost meaning of life. Buddhism may be characterized as the teaching of Buddha; yet it is as important to see it as the way of Buddha, its Eightfold Path.[20] And in Hindu tradition there are three ways to salvation.[21]

The subject of "the way" is a good starting-point for the Christian dialogue with people from other faith traditions.[22] When the first Christians used this terminology they acknowledged that such longings and aspirations reflected the universal condition of humankind, created in and through the eternal Word of God. Here is the element of continuity. But equally the Christian community believed then, as it must still do, that the Way of God has been most clearly discerned in the way that Jesus followed—the way of rejection and suffering, of abandonment and death. This way of Jesus is clearly discontinuous with all other religious ways that give false expectations and—in the last resort—are based on the self-sufficiency of man.[23] Jesus' way is different; it is the way of love, cf. also 1 Cor 12:31—13:13.

Even though there are similarities between the use of "the way" in Christianity and in other religions, there are also important differences. Notto Thelle draws our attention to the fact that Buddha pointed out the

---

18. Camps, *Partners in Dialogue*, 84.

19. For a more detailed analysis, see Amaladoss, *The Asian Jesus*, 64–69.

20. Thelle, *Hvem kan standse vinden?*, 28.

21. The three *margas* (i.e. ways or paths) are: *Jnana marga*, the path of knowledge; *karma marga*, the path or discipline of good works; and *bhakti marga*, the path of devotion (Cracknell, *Towards a New Relationship*, 81). Amaladoss, *The Asian Jesus*, 67, speaks of four ways to be released from futility, unreality, and the endless cycles of *karma* and rebirth. The fourth way is *yoga*, which is a psycho-physical discipline that leads to concentration.

22. Cracknell, *Towards a New Relationship*, 78–85.

23. One may add that this criticism of the self-sufficiency of man corresponds to the arguments of Mahayana Buddhism against the earlier Hinayana Buddhism. Mahayana Buddhism sees itself as the way for *all* people, and in its theology and in its religious history there are many examples of this criticism of self-sufficiency and justification by works.

way and he himself walked the way, but he never spoke of himself as The Way and The Life as Christ did. While Jesus said: Whoever has seen me has seen the Father, Buddha said: Whoever sees dharma (the doctrine) sees me; and whoever sees me, sees dharma. "Buddha becomes one who proclaims (preacher), an ideal and a model, but he is no savior. He discovered the way and pointed to it, but man must himself strive for it and walk the way."[24] This is not to say that the statement in John 14:6 necessarily reflects the exclusivity of Christianity, only the exclusivity of Christ. The decisive point is not Christianity or the church as systems and practices of faith, but instead the *person* of Jesus Christ.

"I am the way"—in an Esoteric Reading

An esoteric Bible reading is common in occult circles. Here it is presupposed that the Bible has two levels of meaning. The first is the immediate understanding of the *written* text, e.g., John 14:6, according to which Jesus Christ is the way, the truth, and the life. The occults consider such an understanding to be correct, but this reflects only a lower level of consciousness. It is argued that the words also have a deeper, spiritual meaning which can be comprehended only by the enlightened person. According to this esoteric reading of John 14:6 it is the "I"—the enlightened person—who is the way, the truth, and the life. Thus, the verse refers not only to Jesus, but to the inner, divine spark or "I" of all human beings. This is in line with Rudolf Steiner's understanding of the "I am" sayings (see chapter 3 of this book). It is natural that such an esoteric knowledge and understanding is only accessible to those who are on a higher level of consciousness than is the case with "normal" Christians.

The presupposition for this esoteric reading is a distinction made in new religious movements between "Jesus" and "Christ."[25] It is argued that "Jesus" was an advanced historical person within the limits of time, whereas "Christ" denotes a *state of consciousness*, the oneness with the eternal divine principal. This divine principle is to be experienced within the soul of any human who prepares for it. Jesus realized the "Christ within" as did Buddha, as indeed do all the great saints of religions. We may call this inner enlightenment "Christhood" or "Buddhahood," and according to this understanding, the word "Christ" as a designation for "Jesus" does not mean a

---

24. Thelle, *Buddhismen*, 21.*
25. Romarheim, *The Aquarian Christ*, 20–21.

person, but an "embodied idea." Every good individual, therefore, may find Christ in his inner being whether they be Jew, Hindu, or Christian.

Occult writers also stress Jesus' *prototypic significance*. His "Christ experience"—through baptism, death, and resurrection—was not primarily something which happened in history. Its greatest significance was that of *initiation*. In fact, this higher Self is identical with the all-pervading divine Christ Self of Jesus.[26]

"The people of the way"

The twofold character of John 14:6—Jesus as pointing to the way and himself being the way—corresponds to the manner in which the metaphors of "way" and "journey" are used in other biblical texts. These metaphors are already important in the Old Testament. Some scholars would even label the Israelite religion a "religion of the way" and the God of the Israelites a "God of the way," based on God's words to Abraham in Gen 12:1–3 and the Exodus traditions. In Psalms "the way" is used frequently, especially in the so-called psalms of Wisdom that deal with the life of the individual. In Judaism at the time of Jesus the theme of the way is prominent, not least in the idea of the two ways: to life and to death (cf. also Matt 7:13–14).

"Way" and "journey" are also important categories in the gospels and the epistles of the New Testament. For instance, Mark's Gospel can be seen under the perspective of "the Kingdom and the way."[27] In the central section of 8:22—10:52 Mark has linked his teaching on discipleship to three predictions by Jesus of his own suffering, death, and resurrection.[28] To be a disciple is to be on the way; it is to be in a process of learning; it is to follow the crucified Lord.

We should note that the biblical metaphor of the way refers both to the way itself and to being *on* the way. Christians are "a people of the way," a wayfaring people. The Synoptic Gospels have similar direct or indirect references to the theme of the way. Luke has shaped the tradition most clearly so as to elevate the itinerant aspect of Jesus' ministry into a major

---

26. Ibid., 22.
27. Nissen, *New Testament and Mission*, 41–44.
28. Three situations are described and each of these has three components: (a) a passion prediction (8:31; 9:31; 10:33–34); (b) an account of misguided behaviour on the part of one or more of the disciples (8:32–33; 9:31–34; 10:35–41); (c) Jesus' corrective teaching on the true discipleship (8:34—9:1; 9:35–50; 10:42–44); cf. Nissen, *New Testament and Mission*, 42.

theological theme. Acts depicts the believers as those "who belonged to the Way" (9:2). Finally, the way and the journey are two of the most frequent ethical concepts in Paul's letters. The life of the believers is considered to be a walking of this way (Rom 6:5). Moreover, Paul describes his teaching of the first congregations as "ways in Christ" (1 Cor 4:17), and in 1 Cor 12:31 love is called "a still more excellent way."

This understanding of 'way' and 'journey' gives the Christian faith a specific dynamic. The gospels make it clear that Jesus did not stay in any one place—cf. the question in John 1:38. This is also confirmed by the well-known words from Matt 8.20: "The Son of Man has nowhere to lay his head." Jesus is rightly called the Way in John's Gospel, but the problem with these words is that Christians often consider them to be absolute. "We have made Christ into the Way in the sense that there is no way to go."[29] We think that we have already attained the goal, that we possess the entire truth by means of which we can instruct others (see also the paragraph "The truth and the way" in chapter 15 of this book). This misunderstanding arises because we forget that Jesus called people to be his *followers*. When he spoke of the cross, he did not invite people to rest at the foot of the cross but to take the cross upon themselves and to *follow* him. "The Way of Christ is a way one walks—not a place to 'stay.'"[30] To be in mission is to be on the way towards a goal that is unknown. But God is accompanying us on that journey (Matt 28: 20).

It would be useful to make a distinction between "the way" and "the ways." On the one hand we may say that Christ is *the way* in mission. On the other hand there are several different *ways* in mission, because the gospel is proclaimed and communicated into our everyday lives. Pentecost means that the gospel becomes rooted in different local cultures in a process of "inculturation." And yet, Christians can never feel fully at home *in* it, for they are always "on their way" as pilgrims; they will always have a goal that transcends the boundaries of the given culture in their journey towards the Kingdom of God. The church is a people on its way; it is not a people that settle. "We have become settlers but it should not be so. We behave like the Israelites with the property we receive when we settle . . . we cling fast to it and it is almost impossible for us to leave the place. We forget the original purpose of the journey and are satisfied with a peaceful spot near the road."[31]

29. Thelle, *Hvem kan standse vinden?*, 29.*
30. Ibid., 28.*
31. Lundegaard, "At være menighed i håbets lys," 7–8.*

Part One: Images of a Greater Reality

The Way of Faith—the Meditative Reading of John's Gospel

For centuries the Fourth Gospel has regularly been interpreted in a spiritual or mystic way. A modern example is Lene Højholt's book: *Vejen. Meditativ fordybelse i Johannesevangeliet* ("The Way: A Meditative Immersion in the Gospel of John"), which she calls "a symbolic reading of the Gospel with special focus on the faith of the disciples, starting with their being called by Jesus, until they are sent into the world after his resurrection in order to continue his work."[32] Her purpose is not to present a classic academic or a theological hermeneutical reading of the Gospel; rather she wants to describe it as a mystic text which gives readers new spiritual possibilities and dimensions.[33]

Højholt regards the Gospel as bearing its own authority and its own inner universe. She has tried to penetrate this universe and to understand it on its own premises in order "to let the Gospel speak on its own without pressing foreign structures and definitions into it." Nevertheless, she adds: ". . . in order to facilitate the reading with a few compasses and classifications I have set the Gospel's structure and way of faith in relation to the four classic phases of mysticism as a description of the mystic way."[34]

These four phases are used as headings for the major sections of her book. After a brief description of "Man in the world" comes the first phase: "*Turning away from the world—vocation*" which is a commentary on John 1:35–51. The second phase is about John 2–9 with the heading: "*Purification—the way from 'the I in the world' to 'the psychically conscious I.*'" The third phase is called "*Illumination—'the psychical I' is opened, the image of God is awakened, and the new man is initiated*"; this is a commentary on John 10–13. The fourth phase deals with John 14–17 and is called "*Union—'The spiritual I' meets the Father.*" In the last part of her book Højholt comments on the Gospel's presentation of Jesus' suffering and resurrection and she also writes at length on the Prologue. She closes with a summary of the book in a chapter entitled "the Way of the Fourth Gospel."

Like any other interpreter Højholt approaches the biblical text with certain preconditions and a specific point of view, in her case the mystical tradition. The Gospel's structure and way of faith are described in the light of its four phases, a process which to some extent belies her intention to

32. Højholt, *Vejen*, 11.*
33. Ibid., 17–18.
34. Ibid., 19.*

let the Gospel speak for itself.³⁵ Højholt and other representatives of the Christian mystic tradition will probably reject the charge that the focus is hereby moved from away Jesus, and to be sure her commentary on many passages upholds his unique position. For instance, Jesus' words in John 1:51 mean that he is opening the spiritual way that the disciples have to follow by his help. At the same time Jesus tells them who he is. He is the ladder between earth and heaven, between the earthly and the spiritual, between man and God. He will guide them on the way, and simultaneously he himself is the way.³⁶ On the other hand Højholt seems to use concepts from the new spirituality in her interpretation of the Jesus figure. With reference to the "I am" sayings it is said that Jesus' divine nature is expressed in an "I" (a center of consciousness) that makes it possible for him to recognize and be in union with God. This superior center of consciousness is significant for her description of John's understanding of the human mind:

> The beam of light from God which is the essence of every human being contains or is an "I" of consciousness. The intensity of the light in this "I" decreases the farther away man is from God and the more mists that separate him from God. By contrast, the phases that man has to go through on his way back to God are characterized by greater and greater light of the "I" and the accompanying consciousness of God and of the person himself. The "I" is always present and is always the same, but the intensity of the light in it differs. Consequently I have chosen to give the phases or levels on the way of the faith designations that all contain the word "I." In so doing I wish to underline the basic connections between the levels—that they are all radiations of the same "I"—but with different degrees of consciousness or contact with the source of light.³⁷

In this quotation we see a usage of gnostic and mystical concepts to understand both God and humankind, cf. the metaphor of emanation and radiation from the light and "the consciousness" as the essence of the human being. Despite this affinity between Højholt's and gnostic terminology there is an important difference between her Christian spirituality and the

---

35. None of us read the texts in a completely neutral, objective way; any reading of the Bible will start with certain specific questions. We cannot jump to some privileged place of neutrality or complete objectivity; it is from within our "life-worlds" that we engage in the reading task (cf. the paragraph, "Mutual critical correlation" in chapter 1).
36. Højholt, *Vejen*, 110.
37. Ibid., 21.*

spirituality that is characteristic of the new religiosity. The document *Tro i tiden* refers to a conversation partner, an informant who as a young person had an experience that directed his spiritual search. In a kind of ecstasy he saw himself present at the Lord's Supper as depicted in Leonardo da Vinci's painting of the scene. All the disciples were present and Jesus distributed the bread and the chalice. Suddenly he looks directly at A (the informant) and says: "A, I did not say 'I am the way, and the truth, and the life'. I said: 'The 'I' is the way, the truth, and the life.'"[38]

In her commentary on John 14:6 Højholt underlines that Jesus has given the disciples a Way, he has led them on this Way, and He himself indeed is this Way. Jesus and his disciples form a unity. The Way is also "the truth" since Jesus is the truth. The Way and the Truth are essential to the nature of Jesus and cannot be separated from him. Jesus as the Way is the Truth about human life; this Way has Truth as its content, for it is only those who dare the truth about themselves who are able to walk on that way.[39]

On the Move towards a Greater Reality

"The way" is an important issue in relation not only to Christian mysticism but also to the idea of *pilgrimage*, which is becoming a common aspect of Christian spirituality; at the same time it has deep roots in history. The pilgrimage is the classic form of journey in the world of religions. There are many reports in the history of the church of holy persons on migration, people who become role-models through their outward and inward journeys. This journey can have three components: a *contemplative* (or introspective) journey, a journey *in time* in order to become synchronic with the faith stories, and a journey *in the footsteps* of holy men and holy women.[40]

Today's growing interest in the theology of pilgrimage has several causes, including the link between post modernity and new spirituality. The post-modern society is the post-traditional society (A. Giddens). In traditional society the framework for the individual was given by means of tradition, family, and locality. Identity was given more or less beforehand. In late modernity the bond to family, locality, and tradition has been loosened, so that is now up to the individual to develop their own identity,

---

38. *Tro i tiden*, 9.*
39. Højholt, *Vejen*, 185.
40. Wikström, *Det blændende mørke*, 115–16.

which then becomes the "project of the individual. However, identity is not something that the person develops once and for all and then takes a rest; it becomes a narrative project, a history of life that is constructed and reconstructed again and again."[41]

Post-modern society is characterized not only by individualism but also by a nomadic mobility. We are on the move all the time—in our daily life, in our existence, in our search. Our goal is not to find a place where we can become firmly rooted, nor is our identity bound to the destination of our journey. Life takes place on the way; the meaning of life is to be on the move.[42] A significant task of the church is to accompany nomads on their journey, though not by subjecting itself to a similar mobility and changeability. In a time of restlessness there is a need for places of rest, and the church can stand out here in two ways. First, it may be a place for silence, a place for reflection and an alternative way of relating to the phenomenon of time. Second, it may be a solid basis in life. Nomads are in need of oases. On their journey nomads have to rest at a spot with water and greenery. The oasis is the place for re-creation offering spiritual, and in some cases physical, food to the hungry and thirsty. In the years to come the church must include both dimensions: the way and the place, both the nomads and the oasis.[43]

It is important to find the balance between journey and place. The tendency in post-modern society is towards a distinct individualism that strives for life authenticity and realization of the true self. The goal is no longer to have contact with God outside the self, but to have contact with the inner source of the self. This helps to explain why people are turning away from institutional religion to different forms of spirituality and therapies which help them to realize their selves.[44]

A Christian theology of pilgrimage cannot be content with this. The church as an oasis is a reminder of the existence of something higher than the individual. The aim is not just that we as human beings realize ourselves through our own decisions; there is a greater reality outside ourselves. This perspective is underlined in a booklet by the Swedish archbishop Karl Gustav Hammar with reflections on Dag Hammarskjöld's *Vägmärken* published after his death in 1961. The first English translation was accessible in 1964

---

41. Mogensen, *Kristendom*, 33.*
42. Bollmann, *Kirke til tiden*, 158.
43. Ibid., 162.
44. Mogensen, *Kristendom*, 34.

Part One: Images of a Greater Reality

under the title *Markings*, but later editions have employed the rarer English word *Waymarks*,[45] The book is now recognized as a modern spiritual classic. It is an attempt by a professional man of action to unite in one life the *via activa* and the *via contemplativa*.[46] It reflects the author's effort to live his creed, his belief that all men are equally the children of God and that faith and love require of him a life of selfless service. In this book Hammarskjöld describes seven markings, and in his words of meditation he frequently points to that which is "greater."

Karl Gustav Hammar's book is entitled *Vägen valde dig* ("The Way has chosen you") which is a quotation from Hammarskjöld: "It is not we who seek the Way, but the Way that seeks us."[47] Although not stated directly Hammar's title refers to Hammarskjöld's Christian heritage, and perhaps even alludes to John 14:6 and 15:16: "You did not choose me but I chose you." Hence, it is worth considering whether the spirituality of Hammarskjöld is influenced by a Johannine spirituality.

The Way, the Place, and the Person—the Theology of Pilgrimage in the Gospel of John

The relation between way, place, and person in the Fourth Gospel is of interest for the understanding of a modern theology of pilgrimage. In the past the concept of pilgrimage was related to the conviction that the way brings you to a particular sacred place. On the surface it seems that this idea also played a significant role in the Gospel of John because on several occasions Jesus travels to the Jewish itinerant festivals. In practice, however, John relativizes the idea of the sacred place, replacing it with the holiness

---

45. Cf. Erling, *Waymarks*, viii: "While 'waymark' is not a common English word, it is to be found in unabridged dictionaries and it does significantly appear in Jeremiah 31:21 in both the King James and Revised Standard versions of the Bible. The 1917 translation of the Swedish Bible has also *vägmärken* in this verse. An additional reason for literal translation at this point is that it introduces 'way' into the title. Hammarskjöld has much more to say about 'the way' than about the marks or markings he makes along that way."

46. In his foreword to Hammarskjöld, *Markings*, from 1964, the English poet W. H. Auden quotes Hammarskjöld as stating: "In our age, the road to holiness necessarily passes through the world of action" (ibid., 23).

47. The full quotation is: "It is not we who seek the Way, but the Way which seeks us. That is why you are faithful to it, even while you stand waiting, so long as you are prepared, and act the moment you are confronted by its demands." Cf. Excerpts from *Markings* (Good Reads, Dag Hammarskjöld > Quotes, www.goodreads.com/author/quotes/946904 .Dag_Hammarskjold).

of Jesus' person. This is seen especially in the significance invested by the Jewish people in the Jerusalem temple and the festival pilgrimages that had the temple as their goal. Indeed, the Gospel reports no fewer than four journeys by Jesus to Jerusalem. The first (2:13–21) is for "the Passover of the Jews" (2:13). In the following verses John tells about the cleansing of the temple (2:13–22). Jesus' action temporarily brings to a halt the whole purpose of other people's pilgrimage, as the sacrificial animals are dispersed at Jesus' command: "Take these things out of here! Stop making my Father's house a marketplace!" (2:16). When he adds "Destroy this temple, and in three days I will raise it up" (2:19), he is of course referring to himself. God's presence, previously focused in the Jerusalem temple, is now to be found in the crucified and risen body of Christ.[48]

Also Jesus' last journey to Jerusalem is to celebrate the Passover festival, but this journey is towards his own death. According to John the death of Jesus does not mean the abandonment of God's presence. The glory of the divine presence is no longer to be found in the temple but in Jesus. This glory, which is to be seen in the Word that became flesh and "tabernacled among us" (1:14), and which was manifested throughout his ministry, has its own climactic hour when he is crucified. This brings about a radical redefinition of all human notions of glory.

The idea of pilgrimage in John's gospel is probably most clearly expressed in the conversation between Jesus and the Samaritan woman in John 4:21–24.[49] After Jesus' remark to the woman: "You worship what you do not know; we worship what we know," one would expect him to say: "Yes, you need to make your pilgrimage to Jerusalem to worship." Instead, the statement is prefaced and followed by two very surprising assertions that announce an eschatological change that affects both the previously erroneous Samaritan view and the previously correct Jewish view. First is the prediction: "the hour is coming when you will worship the Father neither on this mountain nor in Jerusalem" (4.21) and then comes the announcement of its present realization: "The hour is coming and is now here, when true worshipers will worship the Father in spirit and truth" (4:23). It is in and through Jesus that God is now revealing Godself and seeking worshipers.

To conclude, the divine presence must be localized in the person of Jesus. If God has an "address" on earth, it is no longer in Jerusalem but in the incarnated Word. Worship now is not so much in a place as to a person.

48. Lincoln, "Pilgrimage and the New Testament," 38.
49. Ibid., 39.

Part One: Images of a Greater Reality

The aim of pilgrimage and worship in the temple has been transformed by Christology. Jesus is the true place for worship. Since Jesus does not dwell in a particular place, the implication is that John's theology of pilgrimage has a dynamic of its own—cf. the previous quotation from Thelle: "The Way of Christ is a way one walks—not a place to 'stay.'"

11

Tree

Historical Perspectives

The Tree as Universal Symbol

"I am the true vine" is the last of the famous "I am" sayings. The statement introduces Jesus' speech about the vine and its branches in John 15. It resembles the other sayings in that it connects Jesus with a fundamental symbol. In all cultures the tree is depicted as a universal symbol of growth, life-energy, and renewal. In addition, the tree symbolizes development and cohesion in the history of the family and the people, cf. the image of the genealogical tree. The most important symbolic use of the tree is the tree of life, whose roots penetrate deep into the underworld and whose branches stretch up towards heaven. The holy tree of life is located in the axis of the Cosmos, being the center of the universe from which all life and energy arise. Cosmos is a huge, ancient tree that bears the earth in its crown, such as the huge ash Yggdrasil in Nordic mythology.[1]

At the beginning and end of the Bible we meet the symbolic tree; in Eden in Gen 2 and in the vision of the future tree of life in Rev 22:1–5. According to the creation story the tree of life and the tree of wisdom are two different trees. In Revelation the symbolism of water *and* the tree are united, with the tree bearing "twelve kinds of fruit, producing its fruit each

---

1. Mogensen, *Tro, håb og kærlighed*, 207.

month and the leaves of the tree are for the healing of the nations" (v. 2). This tree grows on both sides of the river, symbolizing eternal life as the restoration and eternal existence of all things.[2]

The True Tree of the Vine

The discourse in John 15 is based on the idea of Christ as the tree of life. The close relationship between Christ as the giver of life and those who belong to him is compared with a vine and its branches. The choice of words in v. 1—"the *true* vine"—hints at a polemic against the Mandean-gnostic religiosity in which the vine is seen as the tree of life.[3] Human souls are compared to branches that grow on the tree of life. However, the most important background for understanding the metaphor in John 15 is the Old Testament and its frequently used metaphor of Israel as a vineyard and God as its owner, cf. Isaiah 5.

In the Fourth Gospel this Old Testament use of the metaphor has been transformed. A people (Israel) has been replaced by a person (Jesus). "In the past Israel was God's vineyard in the world, but the grapes were poor. Now the true vine is planted in the world to produce the fruits of love (vv. 9–17) in spite of the world's hatred (vv. 18–25), in order that it can be a witness to the world" (vv. 26–27)."[4]

In the overall structure of the Gospel there seems to be a connection between the image of the vine in chapter 15 and the miracle of the vine in chapter 2:1–11. Furthermore, in both accounts we have allusions to the vine of the Eucharist. This is probably also hinted at in the words of Jesus in 15:4: "Abide in me as I abide in you."

This last statement is probably one reason why the discourse in John 15 has often been interpreted in a mystic or even gnostic direction. In his comment on the passage, the Danish theologian Richard Damm notes that a disciple cannot live spiritually unless he is *in Christ*. Then he continues: "In a similar way we may say: When a branch is a part of the tree, it has an intimate relation to the other branches and together they form a unity (it

---

2. Ibid., 208.

3. As with so many other instances where there is a problem about the background of Johannine thought, some scholars turn to gnostic and Mandean sources, while others stress the Old Testament and Jewish writings. On this issue see the analysis by Raymond Brown, who himself tends to see the most important background in the Old Testament and Jewish writings (Brown, *The Gospel According to John*, 669–71).

4. Værge, *Johannesevangeliet*, 173.*

is the same sap of life that flows through the tree and all the branches). The one who is in Christ is in the same way in intimate relation to all Christians; and it is the same sap of life (agapē) that flows through all of them. And the Father's divine essence (his glory) is revealed on earth through the fruit that the branches of the vine bear."[5]

It is worth asking how the metaphor relates to the subject in this explanation. Perhaps the point is merely that the imagery affects the subject, in that the sap of life image is transferred to the subject, with the additional explanation of *agapē* as the sap flowing through all of them. However, we may also go the opposite way and hazard a gnostic explanation, in which case the sap of life is the divine energy that flows out to humanity.[6] But is such a gnostic interpretation legitimate? Is the *content* of the message gnostic? Or is it merely something that the Greek and Hellenistic audience have *heard* in these words? See also the paragraph, "As a Gnostic to the Gnostics?" in chapter 12 of this study.

While we cannot fully reject the possibility that the first readers met Jesus' words in a gnostic context, it is hardly what John was aiming at, since the context points in another direction. The following section, vv. 9–17, shows that to remain in Christ means to remain in his love, just as he remains in the Father's love. And this love is shaped concretely. Under specific circumstances the implication might be a willingness to sacrifice oneself for the sake of others. "No one has greater love than this, to lay down one's life for one's friends" (15:13). The words refer in the first place to Jesus himself, but they might also be applicable to the disciples.

The metaphor of the vine and the branches in 15:1–17 strongly emphasizes the intimate relation between indicative and imperative. They are both comprehended in Christ, whose commands are inseparable from his person. In the discourse about the vine, believers *are* clean (15:3), but they must *remain* united with Christ the vine in order to bear fruit (15:4–5). Barren branches are cut away (15:2.6); to belong to Christ is to bear fruit.[7]

Rudolf Bultmann saw the fundamental issues of theology in terms of *being* (authentic existence) rather than *doing* (authentic action). In his view the indicative of God's act accepted in faith is always prior to and

---

5. Damm, *Johannesevangeliet*, 148.*

6. Cf. Steiner, who compares the blood with the plant sap in a reflection on the meaning of the Holy Communion. "And the sap that flows through the plants, which pulsates through the vine stalk, is like the blood pulsating through the human body" (Steiner, *The Gospel of St. John*, 114).

7. Nissen, "Community and Ethics," 204.

motivation for the imperative of ethical action, although the two remain dialectically united.[8] By contrast, José P. Miranda has pointed out that the question of being and doing must be seen as inseparable, so that authentic existence is neither apart from nor prior to authentic action, and divine being consists precisely in the ethical imperative.[9] The basic moral stance is not just a *consequence* of faith; it is a *constitutive* part of Christian existence. Faith and love are one. Our being shapes our doing.[10]

That faith and love are one is confirmed by the content of John 15:1–17, which has two parts, vv. 1–8 and vv. 9–17. The theme of the first is "abide in me" (v.4) and of the second "abide in my love" (v. 9), which is the same as "love one another." The two exhortations are two sides of the same coin. Both commands must be met if we wish to avoid being one-sided. The words "abide in me" can reflect a false Jesus-piety, an individualistic understanding of Christianity that is difficult to discern from a gnostic individualism. A Jesus-piety that focuses exclusively on the relation of the individual to Christ is a misunderstanding. It is fundamental to see this relation in a greater context. This explains the addition: "love one another."

To conclude, an individualistic interpretation of Jesus' words on the tree of life and the branches is wide of the mark. The aim of the image is not a specific focus on the individual. The tree is first and foremost a symbol of *coherence* and the human search for coherence in life. This is undoubtedly the reason why the tree is an important symbol not only in Christianity but also in many other religions. When Jesus says, "I am the (true) vine," he means "The tree of life—that is me." This is another way of saying that Jesus claims to be the fulfillment of the longing for wholeness and coherence in our existence.[11]

Contemporary Perspectives

The Tree of Enlightenment and the Tree of Crucifixion

Since Jesus is not the only tree of life in the world of religions, it is relevant to ask how he differs from other "trees." This difference may be summarized

---

8. Bultmann, *Theologie des Neuen Testaments*, 432–34.
9. Miranda, *Being and the Messiah*, 36–45; 73–86.
10. Nissen, "Community and Ethics," 204.
11. Cf. the remarks on John 6:35 in chapter 6 of this book.

in two points, the first being how Christians perceive the coherence of life. In other religions it is often related to the issue of vitality, about cultivating the force of life, a phenomenon which we also know from many therapy and health programs. In John 15 the point is *not* the vitality, but faith and love. The coherence of life and the meaning of life are not to be found in me or in my power of life, but outside myself. These things can only be perceived in faith and love—a love that if necessary lays down its life for the sake of others.

This links up with the second point: namely, that Christian love exists for others and gives itself as a sacrifice. Jesus' suffering and death is the decisive difference between Christianity and the other religions, as can be illustrated by the role of the tree in relation to Buddhism.[12] In Buddhism the focus is on the tree under which Buddha was sitting when he became enlightened.[13] The Bodhi-Tree or wisdom-tree is a sacred symbol in Buddhism primarily because it represents the site of Buddha's enlightenment.[14] The tree of enlightenment underlines knowledge and insight as the principal supports in life. By contrast, in Christianity the tree is seen as the cross on which Christ was crucified. For Christians, love is the most important thing (cf. also Phil 1:8), and in a conflict between knowledge and love, it is love that matters, for "knowledge puffs up, but love builds up" (1 Cor 8:1).

The Fourth Gospel maintains throughout the centrality of Jesus' suffering and death on the cross. John 3:14 is one of the first passages that hint at the tree of the cross, while it is mentioned more directly in the passion narrative itself.[15] It is worth noting that in contrast to the Synoptic Gospels John underlines that Jesus himself carries the cross (19:17). Readers are

---

12. Schelde, *Udenfor byporten*, 87.

13. It is sometimes argued that there is a resemblance to John 1:48 which describes Nathanael as sitting under the fig tree. (for references, see Thelle, *Buddha og Kristus*, 16). A number of commentators refer to a Jewish tradition according to which rabbis taught or studied under the fig tree. In the Johannine tradition Nathanael is corrected and invited to see far greater things!

14. Three other reasons are: (1) The Bodhi-Tree is ancient. Some would say it is a mythical World Tree. Thus, it is sacred temporally. (2) It represents growth towards liberation. Therefore, it is sacred developmentally. (3) It was said to rain blossoms, and is thus sacred aesthetically. See Wisdom-tree.com, The Bodhi Tree Meditation, www.wisdom-tree.com/.

15. In some biblical texts the symbol of the cross and the symbol of the tree of life are connected; e.g., Acts 5:30f., 10:30; 1 Pet 2:24. The story of a twig from the tree of life that becomes the tree of the cross appears in later Christian legends.

Part One: Images of a Greater Reality

probably reminded of the term the "only Son" in 3:16—with a possible allusion to the sacrifice of Isaac.

The Individual and the Community

Today's individualism has led one critic to speak of spiritual shoppers in the existential supermarket.[16] The divine is often seen as something that *resides in* man, and the focus in the spiritual work is directed towards the development of the self or the consciousness. The goal is to attain recognition of this divine core and allow it to unfold.[17] Such a focus on the salvation of the individual can easily lead to an egocentricity that is contrary to the Christian faith. Johannes Aagaard considers this approach to be both self-contradictory and unbiblical. Referring to a statement of the German theologian W. Löhe "Alone one cannot be saved, and alone I will not be saved," he claims that if we search for our own salvation our goal is wrong and misleading.[18]

The metaphor of the vine and the branches is a reminder that the individual is part of a greater community. We may have our own history but we are part of a fellowship that exists before and outside ourselves. Gudmund Rask Pedersen rightly says that Christian belief "is placed in a context where everything begins and ends in God. Through Jesus Christ we are bound to each other. At the same time we are also bound to the tree of life, from where God's love and God's forgiveness comes to us and gives us strength so that we can live with our responsibility and with our debt."[19] He further underlines that as branches on the vine we are already liberated from the power in the genealogical tree which binds us to death and hinders us from living in love and responsibility for each other. For we are grafted into a new bond. By virtue of the gospel we are bound to Christ as the tree of life; he is the power in all our responsibilities and engagement.[20]

The Fourth Gospel stresses that it is the community of Christ which unites the disciples—with its visible sign in foot-washing (13:14) and mutual love (15:10.12). In this way the divine life is embodied in the world.

---

16. Pedersen, *I lysets tjeneste*, 204f.; 227–28.
17. *Tro i tiden*, 21.
18. Aagaard, "Eksklusivitet og inklusivitet," 167.
19. Pedersen, *Forladthed og nærvær*, 251.*
20. Ibid., 252.

Part Two

The Gospel of John and the Religious Dialogue

12

The Fourth Gospel, Incarnation, and Inculturation

PART TWO OF THIS book sets the preceding analyses of selected texts from the Gospel into a wider context. To begin with there are some observations on the relation between incarnation and contextualization as reflected in the Gospel of John; then follow reflections on various models for dialogue with other religions, on images of Christ, on the truth, and the love as possible criteria for religious dialogue, and finally on the Johannine experience of faith and the interaction in the human search for God and God's search for man.

Incarnation, Inculturation, and Contextualization

The incarnation is crucial to an understanding of the Gospel of John.[1] It is also a concept that plays a significant role in recent theology of mission.[2] This can be illustrated by some of the conceptual tools or models that have been developed in modern times. What follows are a few comments on two of these models: inculturation and contextualization.[3]

---

1. Mission in John is characterized by Arias as "the Johannine Incarnational Model for Mission" (Arias and Johnson, *The Great Commission*, 78–97).
2. See Langmead, *The Word Made Flesh*.
3. Cf. Bosch, *Transforming Mission*, and Kirk, *What is Mission?* Two other models are "accommodation" and "indigenization"; for a description of these models, see, for instance, Kirk, *What is Mission?*, 89–90. In earlier time, people spoke of *accommodation* of the gospel to culture. By this was meant primarily people deciding on the essential

Part Two: The Gospel of John and the Religious Dialogue

Inculturation follows the model of incarnation. The gospel needs to be "enfleshed" or "em-bodied" in a people and its culture. Inculturation is a kind of *ongoing* incarnation. In this approach "it is not so much a case of the church being *expanded*, but of the church being *born anew* in each new context and culture."[4] Inculturation is a process by which the gospel becomes part of a particular culture through interaction with it. This can have two contrary effects: it can be enslaved by the culture, or it can liberate it. This in turn means that there are two opposite dangers in relating the church to a particular place. The first is that the church may not be truly local in that its language, worship, and style of life belong to another place and do not reverberate as the authentic call of God. The other danger is that the church may be so conformed to its "place" that it simply echoes and confirms the interests of its members, and does not communicate to them the sovereign judgement and mercy of God.[5]

Contextualization is the attempt to take the concrete human context in all its dimensions with the utmost seriousness. The *particularity* of each environment becomes the starting-point for both the questions and the answers which will shape the mission. What is the nature of the human condition for *these* people in *this* place? What *specific* problems do they face? What does the gospel say about *these* issues?

The theological roots of inculturation and contextualization are to be found in the incarnation. In Jesus Christ God has taken a *human* face, becoming Immanuel, "God with us." In a sense it is true that Jesus can only be met through the "dead" texts, but the fundamental reality for Christians is a living person. The word was embodied and God was revealed in a concrete historical context.

The African theologian John Pobee has described this by means of the term *skēnōsis* which is used in John 1:14.[6] The literal meaning of the Greek word *eskēnōsen* is "it tabernacled." The imagery of tabernacling un-

---

elements which distinguish the Christian faith from other systems of belief and adapting or adjusting these through the use of language, symbols, and illustrations to the recipients of another culture. The other model is *indigenization*. Gradually mission agencies and local churches came to recognize that indigenization as a model of cultural translation may have been too static. The danger inherent in all programs for the "indigenization" or "acculturation" of the gospel is that they involve the church with the conservative and backward-looking elements in society.

4. Bosch, *Transforming Mission*, 454.
5. Newbigin, "What Is 'A Local Church Truly United'?"
6. Pobee, "Skénósis."

derlines two crucial aspects of the operation: on the one hand an eternal, non-negotiable divine aspect which may be referred to as the Word of God, and on the other a temporary, contextual, contingent reality. Therefore, *skēnōsis* is and must be an on-going process of renewal.

The Swedish theologian Henry Cöster asks why the written word became crucial in later Christian tradition, while Christianity at its beginning in Jesus' proclamation was a non-scriptural religion. This is not to deny that Judaism, Christianity, and Islam have been conceived of as scriptural religions, and "the book" has a crucial and normative role in all three religions. On the other hand, it is significant that these three religions are often characterized as "historical religions"—unlike other religions that have revealed truths of eternal value as their normative basis.

The historical religions are not historical because they are ancient. On the contrary, they seem to be younger than most other religions. They are historical religions because they are formed by a historical truth that reveals itself as history, as changeable and material reality—and not because the proper intention of reality is to be found in eternity or in nature.[7] As a historical religion Christianity is a pointer that normativity might not be found in a truth which is communicated through literary (or scriptural) revelations, but rather in a history that is accessible to all who are living their concrete and changeable lives in history. The center of Christianity is the historical contingent Jesus. He did not leave any written documents. When he wrote, he wrote "in sand" (John 8: 8). His words and acts are bound to a reality that is changing. The fact that he wrote in sand is not to be deplored as showing a lack of historical understanding but rather indicates a specific understanding of what incarnation and historical reality mean.

Based on these observations we must ask: What is the significance of incarnation and historical reality when approaching other religions? What is the meaning of concepts like inculturation and contextualization for understanding the Gospel of John? When is "accommodation" indispensable, and how do we differentiate between a necessary accommodation and a problematic syncretism?

"As a Gnostic to the Gnostics"?

The question of necessary accommodation or unacceptable syncretism can be illustrated by some reflections on the relation of the Gospel of John

---

7. Cöster, *Skriften i verkligheten*, 11–13.

Part Two: The Gospel of John and the Religious Dialogue

to Gnosticism. This question has relevance for today when some groups (e.g., the Rudolf Steiner movement or even some Indian Christians)[8] offer a gnostic interpretation of this gospel. It is beyond dispute that Christian Gnostics in the second century were among the first to use the Fourth Gospel. But is the Gospel itself influenced by some sort of Gnosticism, or rather a kind of Pre-Gnosticism?[9]

For many years the discussion has been over whether the gospel has to be understood against the background of Palestinian Judaism or Gnosticizing Hellenism. The discoveries of the Qumran scrolls and the Nag Hammadi texts have strengthened the case for viewing the background not simply as one or the other, but as an extreme *syncretistic* milieu which had absorbed influences particularly from the Wisdom speculations of Hellenistic Judaism and the mythological soteriology typical of early proto-Gnosticism. There is indeed a growing consensus among New Testament scholars that influences from some kind of very syncretistic (or Gnosticising) Judaism have to be assumed if the character of the Fourth Gospel is to be explained and understood.[10]

This, however, raises the question: If a movement or tendency towards Gnosticism can be seen within and through the syncretistic "mix" of the period, is John part of that movement? And if an affirmative answer is at all appropriate, did the Gospel of John *increase* the Gnosticizing tendency of this trajectory, or did it *resist* that tendency?[11] The author seems to be very *reader*-oriented, but to what extent did he perceive his Gospel as fulfilling the longings and aspirations of his audience? How can we define what was the *original* meaning of the Gospel and differentiate between this original meaning of the text and its significance, i.e., how it was perceived?

In favor of the gnostic interpretation of the Gospel of John it is argued that the verb *ginōskein* (to know) occurs more frequently in the Johannine writings (John's Gospel 56; Johannine Epistles 26) than in the rest of the

---

8. Examples of Steiner's interpretation are given in chapter 3 of this book; examples of the interpretation of Indian Christian scholars are found in the chapter 4 and in chapter 9.

9. Whereas Gnosticism describes a religious movement of the second and third centuries, gnostic tendencies are found earlier including: cosmic dualism; valuing spirit over the flesh; a distinction between a transcendent God and a more immediate Creator; humanity being marked by possessing a divine spar, and salvation coming through divine knowledge (*gnōsis*), cf. Longmead, *The Word Made Flesh*, 252n72.

10. Dunn, *Unity and Diversity*, 298; Nissen, "Rebirth and Community," 122.

11. Dunn, *Unity and Diversity*, 298.

The Fourth Gospel, Incarnation, and Inculturation

New Testament. This observation does not help us very much, however, especially since the total avoidance of the noun *gnōsis* (knowledge) in the Johannine literature seems also to be deliberate.[12] Furthermore, a concrete statement must be interpreted in relation to its context. John's use of the concept of knowledge is to be seen within the major framework of knowledge—a concept that has a special importance in his Gospel. The relation between knowledge and love is in line with the view put forward in 1 Cor 8:1–3: knowledge "puffs up" while love "builds up." Then Paul continues by saying: "Anyone who claims to know something does not yet have the necessary knowledge, but anyone who loves God *is known by him*" (vv. 2–3). Finally, it is should be noted that the Fourth Gospel nowhere indicates that faith is reserved for the elite or for people who have experienced a special initiation or who are specially qualified. Faith is not just for those who have a higher consciousness as it usually is in the gnostic movements.

In 1 Cor 9:19–23 Paul says that for the Jews he became as a Jew and for the Greeks he became as a Greek (literally: "to those outside the law I became as one outside the law."). And all this he made for the sake of the gospel. Can we say that John in a similar way strives to become *as* a Gnostic for the Gnostics? Is that accommodation in order to preach the gospel? As mentioned previously John sometimes employs gnostic language and concepts, but this does not amount to a compelling argument that his theology is gnostic.

The clear doctrine of incarnation in John's Gospel is the central reason for rejecting the view that the Gospels' Christology is docetic or gnostic. That the Word "became flesh," that is, genuinely a human being, would have been offensive and unthinkable to Gnostically-oriented Hellenists, for whom the material world was inherently evil. A second reason is the importance of Jesus' death in John's Gospel.[13] Docetic theology sought to deny that Jesus really died a human death, but for John, paradoxically, the glory of Jesus was to be seen in his passion, death, and resurrection, to which the whole Gospel is directed. A third reason for seeing the Johannine Jesus as fully human is John's deliberate citing of Jesus' hunger, thirst, grief, anguish, and love for friends; cf. 4:6–7; 11:33.35; 12:27: 13:21; 19.26.28.[14]

---

12. Ibid., 299.
13. See Nielsen, "John's Understanding of the Death of Jesus."
14. Langmead, *The Word Made Flesh*, 28. Therefore I cannot agree with Ernst Käsemann's description of Jesus as the God who walks on the face of the earth, or his assessment of John's Christology as "naive docetism" (Käsemann, *Jesu letzter Wille*, 1966).

Part Two: The Gospel of John and the Religious Dialogue

The anti-docetism of the Fourth Gospel is based on two observations.[15] In the first place, the evangelist underlines that "The Word became flesh" (1:14). This statement is a clear assertion of the *historicity and reality of the incarnation*. It is affirmed simply and pointedly that the Word *became* flesh. This means that the Word did not appear as or "came down into", but it really "became" flesh; this is a confession which "can only be understood as a protest against all other religions of redemption in Hellenism and Gnosticism."[16] Furthermore, the noun is deliberately chosen too—that which the Word became was "*flesh*" and for John "flesh" signifies human nature in absolute contrast and antithesis to God (1:13; 3:6; 6:63; 8:15). A similar point is made in 1 John 1:1–4 with its reference to "what was from the beginning, what we have heard, what we have seen with our eyes, what we have looked at and touched with our hands." Davidsen rightly notes that "this identification is impossible from a Gnostic point of view, but it is crucial to the entire proclamation of John."[17]

The second point is *the central importance of Jesus' death* in John's theology. The incarnate Logos *dies*—something the Gnostics sought at all costs to deny. It forms the leitmotif of the John's Gospel that Jesus was glorified because of his death and resurrection, and not just because of his resurrection and ascension. Far from bringing the cross into view only at the very end, John *continually* points forward towards the climax of Jesus' death, resurrection, and ascension. This anti-docetic and anti-gnostic idea is expressed clearly in 19:34–35, where John goes out of his way to emphasize the historical veracity of the account of the blood and water coming from the side of the crucified Jesus after the spear thrust. The sufficiently close parallel with 1 John 5:6 tells us why John wishes to give convincing proof that the incarnate Logos really died, that his body was not simply a phantom. It seems difficult to avoid the conclusion that there is a deliberate anti-docetic polemic intended here. Finally, in 20:19–31 the evangelist demonstrates that it is the *wounded* that is resurrected (20:20). This aspect emphasizes the identity between the crucified and the glorified Christ.

Other aspects in a similar way point to John's anti-gnostic proclamation. Thus, there is a close link between faith in Christ and love of others. This is particularly clear in 1 John. So, for instance: 2:9: "Whoever says, 'I am in the light' while hating a brother or sister, is still in the darkness" and

---

15. Dunn, *Unity and Diversity*, 300–305.
16. Schnackenburg, quoted in Dunn, *Unity and Diversity*, 300.
17. Davidsen, *Johannesevangeliet*, 19.*

4:10–11: "In this is love, not that we loved God but that he loved us and sent his Son to be the atoning sacrifice for our sins. Beloved, since God loved us so much, we also ought to love one another." As Davidsen writes, "Redemption means that we are bound to the life of our fellow human beings. This is not the case in Gnosticism."[18]

Whether or not we conceive of John as one who for the sake of the gospel has become "as a Gnostic to the Gnostics," must depend on what we attach to the concepts. It cannot mean that John has given up the most crucial element in the Christian gospel. But perhaps we might say that John was deliberately attempting to portray Jesus in a manner as attractive as possible to would-be (Christian) Gnostics, while at the same time marking out the limits he himself imposed on such a presentation.[19]

The Holy Spirit and Creation

Another approach would be to focus on the role of the Holy Spirit in dialogue with religious traditions. This approach has recently been favored by many theologians. It had a decisive influence on the theme of the general assembly of the World Council of Churches in Canberra 1991: "Come, Holy Spirit—Renew the Whole Creation." The conference was an invitation to explore the presence and action of the Holy Spirit in all creation.[20]

We have many instances from both the Old and the New Testament that God or the Spirit is at work in all creation (Psalm 104), or among the pagans (e.g., Num 23–24 and Isa 45:1). In the New Testament we have the story of Jesus and the Syrophoenician woman in Mark 7:24–30 and the story of Peter and Cornelius in Acts 10:1—11:18, both of which reveal a discernment of God's presence and action in the lives of people regarded as pagans.

---

18. Ibid., 20.

19. Dunn underlines that the Fourth Gospel can be seen as a classic example of the challenge and danger of translating the good news of Jesus into the language and thought pattern of other cultures. John "used language and ideas which were meaningful to would-be Gnostics, he painted a portrait of the earthly Jesus in colours they would appreciate and respond to, he took over as much as possible of their sort of understanding Jesus, but *without going the whole way* with them" (Dunn, *Unity and Diversity*, 304; italics in the original).

20. As Stendahl notes: "When we call on the Holy Spirit to renew the whole creation, we become aware that God's Spirit permeates the whole cosmos and the whole oikoumene in ways which cannot be controlled or manipulated by us" (Stendahl, *Energy for Life*, 49).

Part Two: The Gospel of John and the Religious Dialogue

The Gospel of John similarly seems to affirm the concept of the Spirit at work in creation, blowing where it will (John 3:8). This is not an incidental spirit but the Word (Logos) known from the Prologue. The blowing of the Logos-Spirit is the precondition for an authentic dialogue that crosses all boundaries, cf. the story of the Samaritan woman in John 4. Yet the Gospel of John also demonstrates that the Spirit is the Spirit of truth that reveals the sin of the world (16:5–15).

At the last commission in John (20:19–23) the disciples receive the Spirit. At the same time they see the scars of Jesus in order to be sure of the identity between the crucified and the risen Lord. The point is that the Holy Spirit is not an incidental spirit, but the Holy Spirit of the crucified Christ.[21] The close link between Christ and the Spirit is also highlighted in 1 John 4:2: "By this you know the Spirit of God: every spirit that confesses that Jesus Christ *has come in the flesh* is from God." These words are a critique of the Gnostics who do not accept the doctrine of the incarnation of Jesus.

---

21. Aagaard, *Identifikation af kirken*, 261–62.

13

Models for Dialogue with Other Religions

Three Models for Dialogue

FOR SOME TIME NOW it has been customary to distinguish between three principal approaches to other religions: exclusivism, inclusivism, and pluralism.¹ However, it is more to the point to follow van Lin and speak of christocentric exclusivism, christocentric inclusivism and theocentric pluralism.²

(a) Christocentric exclusivism is the traditional approach of the Christian church. References are often made to Karl Barth, who declared religion to be unbelief. Religion is the opposite of revelation. There are no points of contact in humanity for the gospel. However, this statement is directed primarily not at the other religions, but at Christianity. Man is an "idol factory," and the idol thus manufactured is religion, Christian or otherwise.

---

1. In recent years many scholars have emphasized that this categorization into three approaches has to be refined. Thus Knitter in *Introducing Theologies of Religions* operates with four models: "replacement," "fulfilment," "mutuality," and "acceptance." While the first three categories are in line with the classic distinction into three models, the last model, "the acceptance model" refers to the diversity of religions, which the religious seeker has to accept. In D'Costa's *Christianity and World Religions*, 3–33, he differentiates between three forms of pluralism: unitary, pluriform, and ethical; two forms of inclusivism: structural and restrictivist inclusivism; and finally two forms of exclusivism: restrictive access exclusivism and universal access exclusivism (D'Costa's own position).

2. Cf. van Lin, "Models for a Theology of Religion."

Part Two: The Gospel of John and the Religious Dialogue

The biblical grounding for this is usually found in statements like John 14:6 and Acts 4:12. However, there are perspectives that are not taken seriously in this model. God has not left himself without witnesses—see Romans 1–2; Acts 14:15–17 and John 1:4. Some scholars therefore prefer a modified exclusivism, e.g., Paul Althaus, who refers to a "primeval" revelation ("Ur-Offenbarung"). But people are caught up in sin and so reject what they can know of God. Another representative is Emil Brunner who reckons with a natural theology, which, however, has been perverted by sin.

(b) Christocentric inclusivism is an approach which affirms the salvific presence of God in non-Christian religions. At the same time it maintains that Christ is the definitive and authoritative revelation of God. Jesus occupies a unique place in salvation history as Savior of all the world. Of all humanity he alone is of universal significance. But the claim to uniqueness and exclusivism, to the universality and absoluteness of the Christian faith, cannot mean that only Christians—to the exclusion of others—are recipients of God's saving grace and thus alone know him in the fullness of his truth. All of salvation history is directed toward Christ and is completely "christocentric" in nature. From creation on, humankind has been called by God to redemption in Jesus Christ. The scriptural basis for this approach is found particularly in Ephesians, Colossians and the Fourth Gospel; cf. the concept of the cosmic Christ. Another important background for inclusivism is the idea of the Holy Spirit working outside the church. Following the English mission theologian Max Warren we may speak of a "theology of attention."[3] This means that we walk humbly and honestly with people of other faiths and keep our eyes open for any evidence of the Spirit's work among them. The focus is on a dynamic understanding of the Holy Spirit, cf. John 3:8: The spirit moves among us like the wind, entirely free of human control.[4]

The paradigm of inclusivism is often linked to the *theory of fulfillment* put forward at the beginning of the twentieth century and related to the theory of evolution evolved in the nineteenth century. Other religions could prepare the way for Christianity. This can be compared to the relationship between Judaism and Christianity. Jesus did not come to abolish the religions, but to fulfill them, cf. Matt 5:17. The gospel fulfills the longings of the non-Christian religions and answers their questions. Christ is already present everywhere, including in other religions ("Christian presence"). This being so, it is presumptuous of Christian missionaries to talk of

---

3. Warren, *A Theology of Attention*.
4. For further details, see chapter 4 of this book.

Models for Dialogue with Other Religions

"bringing" Christ with them; for they "find" Christ already there and then help to "reveal" him.

Prominent theologians have developed the model of inclusivism in relation to the great world religions, e.g., Kenneth Cragg in relation to Islam, and Karl L. Reichelt in relation to Buddhism. In our context Reichelt's work is of special importance since the Prologue of the Fourth Gospel played a significant role in his thinking.[5]

(c) Theocentric pluralism argues that all religions provide ways of salvation which are equally valid, that is Christianity cannot claim to be either the only path (exclusivism) or the fulfillment of other paths (inclusivism). This position is taken by theologians with different backgrounds, for instance John Hick (Protestant), Wesley Ariarajah (Protestant) and Paul Knitter (Catholic). This model holds that Christianity should move from christocentrism to theocentrism. Both Knitter and Ariarajah argue that the original message of Jesus was theocentric. His mission and person were profoundly kingdom-centered, which means God-centered. In the Synoptic Gospels Jesus never called himself the Son of God, but the son of man. His own life was entirely God-centered, God-dependent, and God-ward oriented. In the New Testament there is a significant shift from the theocentric attitude that characterizes Jesus' own teaching to the Post-Easter confessions. Gradually, Jesus comes into the center and God is pushed to the periphery. The christocentrism of the New Testament does not mean that the original theocentrism of Jesus is abandoned. Even in the three New Testament texts John 1:1; 20:28 and Heb 1:8–9 where Jesus is proclaimed as God or divine, he is subordinate to God. Even though Paul is strongly christocentric, he also reminds his readers that they "belong to Christ, and Christ belongs to God" (1 Cor 3:23). Paul also states that in the end Christ will be subjected to God, so that "God may be all in all" (1 Cor 15:28).

According to this understanding the exclusive statements are not philosophical texts (universal statements) but texts of confession. They only have a meaning in their own context. Ariarajah illustrates this point by means of a metaphor: When his daughter tells him that he is the best daddy in the world, she is speaking the truth. For this comes out of her experience. But of course it is not true in another sense, because in the next house there is another little girl who also thinks that her daddy is the best father in the world. And she too is right. "It is impossible to compare the truth content

---

5. For further details, see chapter 3 of this book.

of the statement of the two girls. For here we are dealing not with absolute truths, but with the language of faith and love."[6]

The "pluralists" argue that Jesus is normative for Christians. To speak of Jesus as unique is to speak the language of faith. But exclusive uniqueness was not the intent of this language of faith.

The Uniqueness and Universality of Christ

This brief survey of different models for approaching other religions shows that we are dealing with a complex issue. There is no comprehensive solution available from the Bible, but it does offer certain leads.

The ambiguous character of religion is testified to by the Bible. On the one hand, religious experience has a *positive* value. Several New Testament texts show sympathy for the God-fearing pagans. The Magi have a vision of the star, a religious experience that draws them to Israel (Matt 2:1–12).[7] The centurion already has faith that puts God's people to shame (Matt 8:5–13). Even before baptism Cornelius was "a devout man who feared God with all his household" (Acts 10:2). Paul and other biblical writers acknowledged the possibility of "natural religion," whereby the true God could be detected in the order of his creation (cf. Rom 1). Luke describes Paul as acknowledging with respect the Athenian cult to the unknown God (Acts 17:22).

On the other hand, even though some biblical writers did recognize genuine religious experience in individual pagans, in no instance was a religious "system" other than Judaism and Christianity considered to have any validity. Explicit evaluations of other religions tended to be negative. Gentiles were said to suffer from "ignorance" and were considered to be caught in a life of idolatry and futility. There are also demonic expressions found in these religions, cf. the exorcism of demons conducted by Paul in Acts 16:18; 19:12. This too is part of the biblical approach to religions. In and of themselves they do not save, indeed, they may even enslave.[8] The attitude of

---

6. Ariarajah, *The Bible and People of other Faiths*, 26. According to Ariarajah, the exclusive statements of the New Testament are all statements of faith about Jesus Christ. They derive their meaning in the context of faith, and have no meaning outside the community of faith. They are confessions, but they are not definitive (ibid., 23).

7. For a more detailed analysis of this text, see Nissen, "Seeking God—Sought by God."

8. Hedund, "The Biblical Approach to Other Religions," 329. According to Hedlund religion is under the judgment of God: "That includes *Christian* religion as it was true

the Bible to people of other faiths is thus a complicated phenomenon. If we are to do them full justice, neither the pluralist nor the exclusivist position (at least in its radical form) are acceptable.

Evangelical particularity and catholic universality are both inherent in the biblical picture of the historical Jesus of Nazareth as the resurrected Christ of God. Carl Braaten rightly notes that the exclusive claim is not a footnote to the gospel; it is the gospel itself. Not part of the husk, but the very kernel. On the other hand, the uniqueness of Christ lies in his universality. Therefore, Braaten argues for a position between the Scylla of evangelicalism, without the universality of Jesus Christ, and the Charybdis of universalism without the uniqueness of Jesus Christ.[9]

The task, then, is to hold together the uniqueness of Christ and his universality. John's Gospel is one of the best examples in the Bible of the uniqueness *and* universality of Christ. The Gospel is important to the question of the religions in that "the Johannine Jesus takes words upon himself that were originally spoken in a context of many claims to divinity by foreign deities."[10] At the same time, the core of John's Christology is the affirmation that Jesus Christ is the unique revealer of the living God.

The Trinitarian God and the Cosmic Christ

The debate has been largely about which of the three approaches is correct, for each has its weaknesses. A narrow theo-centric approach to other religions will lead to pluralism or even syncretism. Conversely, a narrow christo-centric approach will lead to a radical exclusivism. Finally, an inclusive understanding of the Spirit makes it difficult to distinguish between the Spirit of God and the spirits of the world.

In recent years a growing number of scholars have been suggesting that we need look for a new approach that does not deny the strengths of the other three but goes beyond them. The most exciting development at the moment is the suggestion that it is through a deeper understanding of the Trinity itself that we will be led to a clearer theology of faiths. A Trinitarian Christology is an alternative to exclusivism, inclusivism, and pluralism.[11]

---

of the Hebrew religion of the Old Testament... Religion does not save. That was true of Yahwism, it is true of Christianity. It is Jesus Christ who saves" (ibid., 330).

9. Braaten, "The Uniqueness and Universality of Jesus Christ," 75–78 and 87.

10. Ball, "My Lord and my God," 53.

11. D'Costa has five concise theses for a Trinitarian approach. The first is that a

Part Two: The Gospel of John and the Religious Dialogue

We therefore have to ask: How is it possible to prevent creation from becoming sheer romanticism—and spirituality from becoming religious fanaticism? Only by insisting that the Spirit of the triune God is at work in creation. A proper starting-point for a theology of religion is the Trinitarian confession. *Missio Dei*—the mission of God—is the mission of the triune God. *Missio Dei* is the movement of God to man, in creation, in incarnation and redemption, a movement involving Father, Son, and Holy Spirit.[12] According to the orthodox theologian Mar Osthathios mission is the ontological nature of God which is love (*agapē*). Hence God is Himself Love or Mission. It is the outreach of this love that prompted God to create all things, visible and invisible and also prompted Him to send His only begotten Son for the salvation of the world and to send the Holy Spirit for the consummation of salvation.[13]

The strongest biblical support for understanding mission as Trinitarian is to be found in the Fourth Gospel, Colossians, and Ephesians. All three writings emphasize the concept of *the cosmic Christ*. In John's Gospel this concept is most clearly illustrated by the exalted Christ who draws all people to himself (12:32). The text is not a reference to the ascension, but rather to the uplifting of Christ on the cross, cf. the words about the wheat that falls into the earth in 12:24. Another example is the inscription on the cross: "Jesus of Nazareth, the King of the Jews." It is to be noted that this inscription was in Hebrew, Latin, and Greek, the three major languages of the Western World. In this way it is emphasized that Jesus as the King of the Jews is the Savior of the world (cf. 4:42).

Trinitarian Christology guards against exclusivism (Christomonism) and pluralism (theocentrism) by dialectically relating the universal and the particular; D'Costa, "Christ, the Trinity, and Religious Pluralism," 18.

12. Klaiber, *Call and Response*, 61.

13. Mar Osthathios, "Mission and the Uniqueness of Christ," 87. The author argues that the genuine motivation of mission is neither the fear of hell nor the hunger for heaven, but the love of Christ that constrains every Christian to manifest the sharing love of the Holy Trinity and always to do the will of God (ibid., 90).

14

Images of Christ

The Diversity of Interpretations of Jesus

For centuries the image of Christ has been portrayed in many different ways. The present time testifies to this both inside and outside the church. Sooner or later in any debate on the theology of religions, we must confront the blunt question from Jesus to his disciples: "Who do *people* say that I am?" (Mark 8:27). In its original context this question is followed by another: "Who do *you* say that I am?" (Mark 8:29). The two questions are closely related. The perception of Jesus among non-Christians should not be separated from that among Christians themselves. In both cases we must search for the criteria for the legitimate Christologies. What is authentic, and what is false or betrayed?[1]

The New Testament presents no single homogeneous image of Jesus, but offers a variety of christological formulations. More than fifty different titles or names of Jesus can be found within its pages: Messiah, *Kyrios*, Son of God, prophet, rabbi, King of the Jews, Logos, Immanuel (=God with us), Son of David, Shepherd, Lamb of God etc. The Gospel of John in particular has many christological titles as part of its christological confession. The following diagram indicates some characteristics of the New Testament Christology.[2]

---

1. On the criteria for legitimate Christologies see also my reflections in Nissen, "Christology Between the Local and the Global."

2. The scheme is adopted from Frankemölle, *Glaubensbekenntnisse*, 131—with minor changes.

Part Two: The Gospel of John and the Religious Dialogue

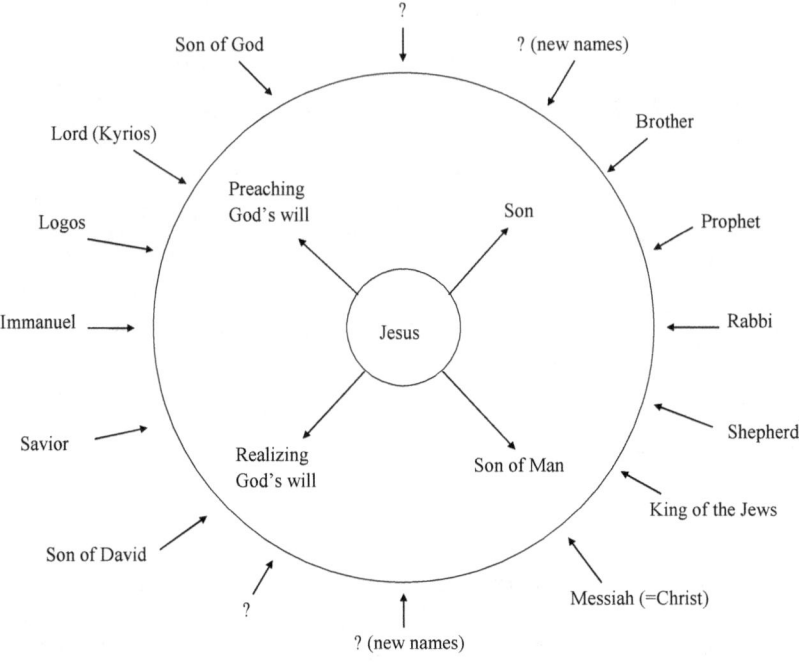

The variety of titles can be explained in various ways, three points in particular being worthy of note.

First, *Christology must be seen as functional and existential.* Each of the many titles reflects the way in which people perceive Jesus in a specific context. The title reveals something about the function of Jesus, and that Christology in the first place is functional and existential. The various titles help believers to express what Jesus means to them. The christological formulations correspond to the interpretations of Christ held by Palestinian Jewish Christians, Jewish Christians of the Diaspora, and Hellenistic Christians. They answered concrete questions of the day and within a specific cultural context.

Why is it that the titles are each important in their own context? The answer is straightforward. They were important because they were the most *relevant* and *meaningful* expressions of Christian faith in that situation. But this also means that the situation in which faith was confessed had a determinative say in the shaping of the confession. The situation called forth the confession. It helped provide the language content of the confessions and contributed something to its meaning.

Images of Christ

Second, there is *a need for new titles*. A christological formulation which was relevant and meaningful in one context often lost its meaning in another context. As Christianity moved outside Palestine the confession "Jesus is the Messiah" had little relevance to a Gentile in a Hellenistic environment. "Christ" became a proper name, and the confession had to be explained, supplemented, and so in effect superseded by other confessions, e.g., "Jesus is the Son of God," or "Jesus is the Lord (*Kyrios*)." In other words, if Jesus was to be understood by believers living in a new setting, the basic confession often had to be put differently.

This is an ongoing process. It can be illustrated by the conflicting views in the Johannine community testified to by 1 John. In confrontation with a docetic understanding the confession "Jesus is Christ" had to be further explained. Many Gnostics could make that confession too, but they conceived its content in another way (the divinity of Christ). Therefore the confession must be framed differently. "By this you know the Spirit of God: every spirit that confesses that Jesus Christ *has come in flesh* is from God . . ." (1 John 4:2). It seems that the opponents so stressed the divine principle in Jesus that his earthly career was neglected.[3] To clarify this point the author of the Epistle had to make the addition "has come in flesh." James D. G. Dunn rightly argues that the confessions framed in one context do not remain the same when the context changes.[4]

Third, we should notice the relation between *expectation and correction*. The understandings of Jesus reflected in the New Testament show a kind of interplay or two-way traffic between text and context, between the message and the recipients. When, for example, Jesus is called "Messiah," the term derives from a specific Jewish tradition which exerted a formative influence upon the way Jesus was seen and understood. On the other hand—and this is the new and giving side, so to speak, Jesus is the one who gives content and a new structure to the concept of Messiah.

Passages such as Mark 8:27–33 and Mark 14:61–62 indicate that Jesus was ambivalent about, or even *rejected*, the function ascribed to him by those around him—including his disciples. The confession of Peter in Mark

---

3. Brown, *The Community of the Beloved Disciple*, 111–12.

4. See also Dunn, *Unity and Diversity*, 58: "New situations call forth new confessions. A Christianity that ceases to develop new confessional language ceases to confess its faith to the contemporary world." Cf. Frankemölle, *Glaubensbekenntnisse*, 26: "Diese 'Übersetzung' christlicher Glaubens . . . ist heute sicherlich nicht leichter als im ersten Jahrhundert. Dennoch muss sie gewagt werden—im Interesse und für die Zukunft des Glaubens."

8:29 probably envisaged a Messiahship in nationalist and/or political terms, so he reacted strongly to the idea that the Messiah had to suffer and die. Yet Jesus rebuked him, "Get behind me, Satan" (8:33). And again, Jesus' response to the messianic charge of Caiaphas is best taken in the sense, "If you want to put it that way" (Mark 14:62); this is especially clear in the parallel in Matt 26:64: "You have said so. *But* I tell you . . ."

These are only a few examples of the interaction between the messenger (Jesus) and the recipients (the disciples, the people). On the one hand stand the expectations of the recipients, and on the other hand comes the correction of these expectations by Jesus. In the early church this correction became part of the confession. While Jesus had shown a marked ambivalence in his attitude to the title of "Messiah" because of its political connotations, the first Christians found it necessary to fight for the retention of the title, but suitably *redefined* in terms of his crucifixion (1 Cor 1:18–25).

In John's Gospel a similar correction takes place in the incident narrated in 6:14–15. This passage reflects the reaction of the crowds to Jesus' feeding of the five thousand (6:1–13). People consider him to be "the prophet who is to come into the world" and they try to take him by force in order to make him king, but Jesus withdraws again to the mountain to be alone.[5] This is not to say that Jesus refuses to be the king of the Jews—in fact this title plays a positive role in the passion narrative of the gospel. Those present probably considered Jesus to be a national, messianic figure who should fulfill their expectations to the coming kingdom of the Messiah. By contrast, John wants to demonstrate that Jesus is the kingdom of the Jews, but his kingdom is a different one; he is the king who dies on the cross, and he is the king for all people (the inscription is written in all three major languages of that time). Thus the title is *redefined* by virtue of his suffering and death.[6]

Portrayal or Betrayal?

The question of Jesus to his disciples: "Who do you say that I am?" provides the interpretive framework for Christian life. The various titles are the answers provided by the Christian tradition. They are taken further today

---

5. Some Greek texts even say that Jesus "flew" into the mountain.
6. See also chapter 6 of this book.

Images of Christ

with the development of contextual Christologies that describe Christ as ancestor, healer, guru, and so on. Yet we have to ask whether we are dealing with so many legitimate representations of Jesus Christ, or whether at times he is being misrepresented and even caricatured. To borrow a terminology from Anton Wesssels: when is it a portrayal, and when is it a betrayal of Jesus?[7] This is the knotty problem of syncretism. The issue is where to draw the line in using and applying local resources to fashion images of Jesus.[8]

In many cases it is difficult to say whether or not a particular title can aptly be used of Jesus. Three examples may illustrate this issue.

(a) First, it is relevant to ask if the title *guru* can be used of Jesus. Guru is a strictly Indian category, which is nevertheless not without precedents in the Jewish world with their scribes and rabbis. Indian theologians have often characterized Jesus as a guru. Is this a portrayal or a betrayal? The answer depends on what is meant by the term. If guru is defined in the same way as in the modern guru movements, it would be misleading to characterize Jesus thus (see also below).[9] If, however, guru is conceived of as a traditional wisdom teacher, such a description might be acceptable. Whatever the case, by using this title one should be ready to inculcate a strong correction of the expectations associated with it. For instance, we might ask in what sense can we speak of a "crucified" guru?[10] The Indian theologian Michael Amaladoss suggests that the popular concept of a guru as a teacher should be replaced by a concept of the guru as a guide. Used in a spiritual context, it refers to a person who has walked along the way and has experienced, or at least has had a glimpse of, the goal one is looking for. They are therefore able to guide the disciples in their own search. A guru is a guide who can initiate and lead the disciples to fulfillment, because the guru himself/herself has reached it and experienced it.[11]

Many Indian disciples of Jesus, whether Hindu or Christian, have considered him their guru. Christians will stress the uniqueness of Jesus

---

7. Wessels, *Images of Jesus*, 13–17.
8. Sugirtharajah, "Reconceiving Jesus," 260.
9. Aagaard, "Guruismens væsen," 187–89.
10. For an interesting discussion on how the concept of guru may be used creatively in Indian theology, see Thangaraj, *The Crucified Guru*.
11. Amaladoss, *The Asian Jesus*, 84–85. The author considers it to be a sad fact that in recent times a guru-cult seems to be developing in the East—and indeed in the world in general. "The guru from being a guide seems to become the goal. She/he is divinized and absolute obedience is demanded from the disciples to his/her directives" (ibid., 102).

by calling him *sadguru* or the true guru. It is a comparative term. But Amaladoss is not adopting a comparative approach in his analysis, only exploring various images that can lead us to a deeper understanding of Jesus in relation to ourselves. He thinks that "guru" is one such image and examines various passages from the gospels. His analysis demonstrates similarities with the Indian concept of the guru (in the sense of a guide), but also shows examples of where this category is transcended. For instance, as a guru, Jesus is not merely guiding people towards their personal fulfillment. He is launching and animating a global project that works for the fulfillment of all human beings and of the whole universe. Jesus' project is therefore personal, social, and cosmic. His movement does not take people away from the world, but is focused on life and community. In his encounter with the Samaritan woman we have an example of how a guru should handle a disciple respecting her or his freedom and guiding this person to make basic choices of life.[12]

(b) A second example is the understanding of *Jesus as the Enlightened One*. Within biblical scholarship it has often been argued that the historical Jesus came to a deeper self-awareness or changed his understanding of his mission and ministry as a result of historical circumstances. In this sense one might speak of him as the Enlightened One.[13] Moreover, it is argued that the exalted terms with which he is spoken of in the New Testament (Messiah, Son of God, Lord, Word of God, light of the world, bread of life etc.) are not literal doctrinal truths but are all metaphors pointing to what Jesus became in the experience and tradition of the early Christian movement.[14] Other scholars do not see any conflict between Jesus as the Enlightener of the world (Jesus as the light) and Jesus as the Enlightened One.[15]

---

12. Ibid., 103.

13. Phan, *Being Religious Interreligiously*, 133–35.

14. Borg, "Jesus and Buddhism," 94. According to Borg Jesus was a Jewish mystic or Spirit person who also became a healer, wisdom teacher, social prophet, and movement founder. Borg points to a number of similarities between Jesus and Buddha: "Both Jesus and the Buddha had transforming enlightenment experiences of a mystical kind at about age thirty. Both became teachers of a convention-subverting wisdom flowing out of their enlightenment experiences" (ibid., 94).

15. Phan, *Being Religious Interreligiously*. For further discussion, see previous chapters of this book: chapter 7 on the perception of light, and chapter 3, especially the paragraph: "Syncretism and accommodation."

Images of Christ

(c) A third example is the understanding of *Jesus in new religious movements.* Jesus is often seen as a yogi, a prophet, a healer, or a magician. A characteristic feature is the distinction between "Jesus" and "Christ," two concepts that have quite different connotations. The identification of Christ with Jesus is considered to be a disastrous failure. Jesus was a historical person of advanced ability within the limits of time, whereas "Christ" means a *state of consciousness,* the oneness with the eternal divine principle. This divine principle can be experienced within the soul of any human being who prepares for it. Jesus realized the "Christ within" as did Buddha, as do all great saints of all religions. We may call this inner enlightenment "Christhood" or "Buddhahood."[16]

In the modern guru movement with a Hindu background, Jesus is often seen as the perfect yogi free from suffering. According to this understanding Christ never suffered, not even on the cross. A Christian evaluation must give the same answer as Jesus gave to Peter when he wanted to escape the suffering on the cross. It is a satanic temptation, a stumbling block: "Get behind me, Satan!" Christ crucified is a stumbling block and foolish to the human way of religious thinking (1 Cor 1:23). A similar critique has to be raised against Muslims who think that Jesus did not die a real death on the cross.[17]

Transcending Categories— towards a "more than" Christology

There is an important interaction between Christ and all cultures: on the one hand Christ may change and transform all cultures; on the other hand all cultures may bring out features in the face of Christ that have not been revealed before. And therefore should we not add that aspects of Jesus may be discovered which *could* not have been known before? It is not only Christ who transforms the *nganga* (the native healer); it is also the *nganga* who transforms Christ.[18] Each title has its limitation—from New Testament times to the present day. In an analysis of African Christology, Francois Kabaséle points out that there are many parallels between Jesus and a

---

16. Romarheim, *The Aquarian Christ,* 20. See also the paragraph "Syncretism and accommodation" in chapter 3.

17. Romarheim, *The Aquarian Christ,* 101–2; see also Romarheim, "Testing the Spirits."

18. Wessels, *Images of Jesus,* 164.

Part Two: The Gospel of John and the Religious Dialogue

Bantu chief. One objection to a title such as "chief" is that it might occasion a triumphalist misunderstanding and imply the neglect of a *theologia crucis* in favor of a *theologia gloria*. In a similar way, Jesus can be called an "ancestor." Yet he is always more than that, and he is more than a healer.[19]

The Synoptic Gospels indicate in various ways that Jesus transcends traditional categories.[20] Thus he speaks of the prophet Jonah and states that "something greater than Jonah is here" (Matt 12:41). In a similar way he declares that here is more than Solomon (cf. Matt 12:42). The transcending of categories is a salient point in John's presentation of Jesus. In John 1:35–51 Jesus is successively presented as the Lamb of God, the rabbi, Messiah, the prophet announced by Moses, Son of God, King of Israel, and Son of Man. Jesus is the fulfillment of the expectations attached to each of these names. But he is also more than this. The intention of this characteristic of John is to incorporate deliberately into the understanding of John whatever christological labels are current in the church. In so doing the author seeks to express the universality of Jesus and to assert implicitly that the reality of Jesus transcends any such labeling.[21]

CHRIST AS GOD'S UNIVERSAL INVITATION

John's language has a distinctive and strong universalistic character. This is clearly seen from the Prologue which in the first part (vv.1–10) describes the divine-human encounter in general terms using designations like Logos, God, all things, life, light, shines, darkness, world etc. John's use of Logos is of particular interest. Scholars have sought the origin of Logos in many different places, e.g., Hermetic and gnostic literature, Stoicism, Philo, the creative Word of the Old Testament, the Wisdom literature.[22] The value

---

19. Kabaséle, "Jenseits der Modelle." On the problem of intercultural Christology, see also Küster, *The Many Faces of Jesus Christ*.

20. On this issue, see also Nissen, "Christology between the Local and the Global," 600–601.

21. MacRae, "The Fourth Gospel and *Religionsgeschichte*," 13–24. This is not to say that all titles have the same importance. The many titles in John 1:35–51 have their climax in v. 51. Nathanael will see the heaven opened and the angels ascending and descending upon the Son of Man. This is probably a reference to the dream of Jacob concerning a ladder to heaven. In Jewish tradition it is seen as the link between the world of man and the divine sphere. In John's Gospel the Son of Man is the ladder himself—the link—between the Father and the human world.

22. See the description in chapter 3 of this book.

of this research is that by way of comparison or contrast it brings out the manifold aspect of the Johannine thought. As mentioned in chapter 3, Jesus is seen as a fulfillment of all this but in a specific way. The thrust of the Prologue is that Logos for the Christian is not an abstract philosophical concept but a living, historical person.

The "I am" sayings in a similar way point to the universality of Christ. In these words the divine name is linked to such predicates as "bread," "truth," "life" or "way," each of them a symbol of the human quest for God. The hunger and longing signify the long search for the face of God, a search depicted in Wisdom literature precisely in such forms. Jesus implies by such declarations as "I am the bread of life" (6:35) and "I am the light of the world" (8:12) that in himself God's manifest presence and the human quest for God meet.[23]

The Johannine symbols stand on the border between various Jewish and Hellenistic modes of speech. They evoke associations from various quarters and transform them to convey a distinctive message. They are given a specifically christological referent, so that they point in their own way to Jesus, the Messiah and Son of God who came down from heaven to be crucified: he is *the* light, *the* bread, *the* wine. The various images direct attention to *the cross*, the distinctive lens through which all symbols should be viewed.[24] It should be noted that the "I am" sayings are not dogmatic demarcations, but *universal invitations* to discipleship. There are no limits to the range of the Christ-event—just as there are no limits to a light shining in the darkness.[25]

It has been argued that the tendency to move from the local to the global, from the particular to the universal is itself a phenomenon that can be seen in many religious systems of the first century. But for John's community this is not simply due to the impact of a more cosmopolitan culture. The universalism of the message flows from the universal significance of Christ himself. Jesus reveals God, and only faith in this Jesus is adequate. John intends us to see that Jesus Christ is the fulfillment of the expectation of mankind. But "he wishes to imply as long as one tries to grasp Jesus as

---

23. Cf. the paragraph "'I am the bread of life'—the human quest and the revelation of God" in chapter 6 of this book.

24. Images with strong roots in Judaism are expanded and universalized, enabling them to evoke a broad range of associations: manna becomes bread for the world, and the light of the temple becomes the light of the world. Koester, *Symbolism in the Fourth Gospel*, 234.

25. Arendt, *Er det den samme Gud?*, 91.

a Jew or a Greek, as a Gnostic or a traditional Christian would, he both succeeds and fails, for Jesus is the fulfillment of these expectations, but he is caught up in none of them. Only the act of self-giving love which engenders love within the Christian community can reach him."[26]

John's Christology is marked by a peculiar combination of inclusive and exclusive aspects. Uniqueness and universality need to be combined if we would wish to propound an open theology of religions. As Jacques Dupuis says: "Without universality, uniqueness is exclusivism. Without uniqueness universality would lead us down the pluralist path. In combination, however, the notes of uniqueness and universality accord with inclusive Christology."[27]

The Open Door and the Spacious House

Other symbols and metaphors in the Fourth Gospel reveal a similar combination of exclusive and inclusive aspects. This applies to the two metaphors of "the way" and "the house" in John 14. Usually the metaphor of "the way" is connected to the open space, whereas the metaphor of the house is seen as something closed and demarcated. In this passage, however, these elements are inverted. Jesus is the *only* way whereas the Father's house is spacious with "many dwelling-places."

There is a debate about the meaning of the last two words. According to some scholars they reveal a pluralist way of thinking, while others think they support an inclusivist position. Probably, the imagery reflects the concept of God's universal salvific intention, almost in the same manner as 1 Tim 2:4–6: God our Savior desires everyone to be saved and to come to knowledge of the truth; simultaneously it is pointed out that there is only one mediator between God and humankind. This is Jesus Christ, who gave himself as ransom for all. Does this combination of the "way" and "house" perhaps imply that any dialogue between religions should include two things—a christological exclusivism and an inclusive or even pluralist concept of God? At any rate, this paradoxical position has gained a certain consensus: it is the task of Christians to proclaim the salvation in Jesus Christ; on the other hand they cannot set any limits to the acts of God. He has the freedom to save whom he will.[28]

26. MacRae, "The Fourth Gospel and *Religionsgeschichte*," 23.
27. Dupuis, *Toward a Christian Theology*, 297.
28. Mortensen, "Mission, kirkens hjerte og åndedræt," 23.

Images of Christ

Two other metaphors are presented in John 10. Jesus is depicted as the "Good Shepherd" and as "the door." Even at this point inclusive and exclusive traits are combined. Lene Højholt argues that the parable of the Good Shepherd has an aspect which reminds us of the house in John 14. The metaphor of the many dwelling-places reflects the spaciousness of the heavens; at the same time it reflects that life on earth also has "many dwellings" in my Father's house. There are many ways in which we can live with God; there are many ways of living as human beings.[29] In John 10 the Good Shepherd says: "I have other sheep that do not belong to this fold. I must bring them also, and they will listen to my voice. So there will be one flock, one shepherd" (10:16).

The words "do not belong to this fold" are open to interpretation. Højholt points to three levels of meaning. In the first place they could be a reference to all those people to whom the disciples are sent. Second, they could be a reference to the message of Jesus that is not for the Jews ("this fold") alone, but for all mankind. Third, they could be a statement about Jesus acting in an invisible way in other religions, in "other folds." According to most scholars the passage should be interpreted in the first or the second way, but according to Højholt all three meanings must be considered: when the final goal is that "there will be one flock, one shepherd," this somehow includes all people and all world religions.[30]

If we combine the metaphors of the door in John 10 and the house in John 14, we may say that Jesus is *the* life, because he has opened the door to the Father's house with "many dwelling-places," and this door is still kept open for humankind. The core of Christianity is not dogmatic statement, but a person who cannot be demarcated by a circle enclosing the saved while the rejected remain outside. Instead, Christians must point clearly and unambiguously to Christ as God's image and the center of life. By virtue of his self-giving love, all people have been granted the possibility of having their "home" at God. Thanks to Christ the door to God's house has been opened wide forever, so that people can enter and take the place which has been prepared for them. It is suggestive that the Johannine Jesus not only provides this place, but is also himself the *entrance* to that place or even *the place* itself. In the Fourth Gospel we can speak of a "hospitality Christology."[31] In such an all-encompassing Christology Jesus is the temple

---

29. Højholt, *Vejen*, 208.
30. Ibid., 131.
31. Koenig, *Jews and Christians in Dialogue*, 133.

for the true worship of the Father (John 4). He is the new holy place. Yet at the same time the exclusiveness and uniqueness of Christ are maintained. He is the exclusive revealer: no one has ever seen God except the one and only Son (1:18), who is the only way to the Father (14:6).

15

The Truth and the Love— on Criteria for Religious Dialogue

The Truth and the Way

THE ISSUE OF TRUTH is crucial to any religious dialogue. Proponents of the different paradigms answer the question of truth claims differently. Those who favor the exclusive model argue that the ultimate truth has already been revealed in Christ, while those who favor the pluralist model argue that the different religions should be seen as different ways to the truth.[1] According to the pluralist model the truth is something we have before us—something we have yet to discover.

In the New Testament Christ as the truth is both behind us and before us. The truth is behind us in the sense that it has been revealed definitively in Christ, and is therefore not the goal of the dialogue but rather its pre-supposed starting-point.[2] Yet in another sense the truth is before us. Christ went before us; he transcended the borders to the unknown, and he called people to follow him. In the light of this double character it is not

---

1. According to Koyama, there are, within pluralism, two different approaches to the same truth: (1) there are not one but many truths from the beginning ("hard pluralism"), (2) truth is one but is appears in many forms ("soft pluralism"). The difference between the two forms is unclear because we cannot grasp what "the truth" itself is. The important thing is that our grasp of the truth is not identical with the ultimate truth itself. (Koyama, "A Theological Reflection on Pluralism," 161–62).

2. Berentsen, "Den umulige dialog," 17.

Part Two: The Gospel of John and the Religious Dialogue

possible to give a final answer to the relationship between Christianity and other religions.

Often truth is conceived of as dogmatic sentences, as something closed and definitive. We tend to use the truth as a wall of protection so that we need not face strange and unknown things from outside. In these cases the truth has become a hindrance for any genuine encounter between persons of different faiths.

The Gospel of John uses the concept of truth more often than any other New Testament book. It has a number of characteristics which are significant for the religious dialogue.[3]

First, in the Fourth Gospel "truth" is not to be understood as a concept which can be acquired and possessed once for all. Truth cannot be achieved through philosophical and religious speculations. It is *related to a person, not a dogma*: "The truth will make you free" (8:32); "The Son makes you free" (8:36); "I am the way, and the truth, and the life" (14:6). "Spirit and truth" (4:23) means that God is a living person who has revealed himself in Jesus Christ.

Second, knowing the truth is also closely related to *doing the truth*: "But those who do what is true come to the light so that it may be clearly seen that their deeds have been done in God" (3:21). The truth is "done" or "practiced" by disciples, who thus become the gift of the word. Gutierrez speaks of a liberating *praxis*, which is, in the final analysis, a praxis of love. This praxis is based on the gratuitousness of God's love.[4]

Third, in the Prologue John says that "grace and truth came through Jesus Christ" (1:17), "from his fullness we have all received, grace upon grace" (1:16). The concept of "fullness" should be noticed. As Koyama says, "'Fullness (*plērōma*) of grace and truth' does not mean 'absoluteness of grace and truth'. 'Fullness' is a hot biblical concept while 'absoluteness' is a cold philosophical concept."[5] Moreover, truth grasps us, not the other way around. "You did not choose me but I chose you" (John 15:16).

Fourth, the disciples also have "to be of the truth" (18:37, cf. 1 John 3:19), meaning they must gradually acquire an interior disposition that conditions the practice of Christian life. We might say that John insists on

---

3. The following points are mainly a summary of what has been presented previously in this book, especially in chapter 8, but with the addition of some new aspects.

4. Gutiérrez, *The Truth Shall Make You Free*, 97–100.

5. Koyama, "A Theological Reflection on Pluralism," 163.

experiential knowledge. It is an understanding of truth in which there can be no separation between theory and practice.[6]

Finally, the Holy Spirit is characterized as the Spirit of Truth: "When the Spirit of truth comes, he will guide you into all the truth" (John 16:13). The function of the Holy Spirit is to lead the community to *all* the truth. There is the prospect here of coming into a new understanding beyond what the community has already acquired, and the community will be given guidance on the meaning of Scripture for new historical situations. The Spirit enables the community to perceive senses of the biblical text that had previously remained hidden.[7]

This personal and dynamic understanding of the truth must be seen together with John's *peculiar combination of truth and way*, cf. 14:6.[8] Craig R. Koester rightly notes that the image of "the way" can best be understood as Jesus *going the way* himself before *being the way* for others. Jesus' own journey is mentioned repeatedly in John 13–14 and in typically Johannine fashion his statements encompass multiple dimensions of meaning. Accordingly, when Jesus speaks of "where I am going" (13:33.36), his words can be taken on two levels: his destination and his route.[9] John's use of the image of "the way" in John 14:6 is an indication that there is no distinction between means and end. The opening up of the way and the coming of Jesus Christ are one and the same. Cracknell comments: "So be it. We will follow that Way, that Truth, that Life now, in the midst of our religious plural world. We will ourselves assuredly see the marks of the nails, for dialogue is an element of the cross, we are called to bear."[10]

So the only way to know Jesus as the truth is to follow his footsteps. The truth is discovered, encountered, or revealed by following his way. In this sense we can speak of a "discipleship-Christology." Such a Christology

---

6. According to Ucko, the Bible portrays truth in more than one way. The Hebrew word for truth is *emeth*, which denotes a reality, which is firm, solid, valid and binding. The emphasis is not so much on truth as being as on truth as truthfulness, trustworthiness and dependability. God is truthful. One can rely on God. The Greek word *alētheia* says Christ is the answer to the question of true being in an absolute sense. Traditional Christian theology oscillates at best between these two understandings. It would be important to keep this in mind when seeking to come to terms with the question of truth in a religious plural world (Ucko, "Truth or Truths," 34).

7. Hays, *The Moral Vision of the New Testament*, 252.

8. On John's understanding of the way, see also chapter 10 of this book.

9. Koester, "Jesus as the Way," 5.

10. Cracknell, *Towards a New Relationship*, 152.

does not express itself primarily in concepts but in stories of discipleship.[11] Christian life is, above all else, a *following* of Christ. The proper *doing* of theology (the method, the way) has its place within this movement (itself a way) toward the Father. Jesus calls himself the truth, but he also describes himself as the way and the life (14:6). His actions and words, his practice, show us the course to follow. Jesus proclaims a truth that must be put into practice.[12]

If truth is understood primarily not as doctrine or theory, but as a concrete person and an event, this will inevitably have consequences for the proclamation of the Christian gospel. Christian proclamation must always take place with respect for the audience. Those who receive it must be exempted from pressure and manipulation.[13] Christians should be seen as witnesses to Christ rather than people who "possess" the truth. "Hence, the truth must be understood as something that has 'hit' us and has put us in our place."[14] A truth that is not owned by human beings but can only be found in God will have to be granted again and again. That is an additional reason why Christians need to take up the challenge from other religions. "The ultimate truth which for the Christian is revealed in Jesus of Nazareth, is not setting one group of people above another group of people, but setting all people on the very same level."[15]

THE LOVE AND THE TRUTH

The encounter between Christianity and other religions is facing the crucial issue of setting up criteria for true and false religion. The concepts of truth and love play a significant role in this discussion. They are frequently seen as opposites; truth is interpreted as fanaticism, while love is connected with indulgence and boundless tolerance. However, this contrast is not an apt description of Christianity and it certainly misses the point when it comes to the Gospel of John.

---

11. Wessels, "Images of Jesus," 189; Nissen, "Christology between the Local and the Global," 607.

12. Gutiérrez, *The Truth Shall Make You Free*, 97.

13. Arendt, *Er det den samme Gud?*, 125. See also the paragraph "Truth as a person" in chapter 8 of this book.

14. Ibid., 129–30.*

15. Arendt, *Gud er stor!*, 17.*

The Truth and the Love—on Criteria for Religious Dialogue

In the Fourth Gospel love and truth are fused into each other, forming a unity which is expressive of God's nature. This means that we are not dealing with two separate aspects of reality: love as affect and truth as theoretical acknowledgment of a fact. Rather, the two form a unity in their reflection of the same divine reality in two different ways.[16]

Richard Burridge has suggested that the relation between truth and love in John's Gospel may be seen under the headline: "Teaching the truth in love."[17] The author observes that truth and love, being so central to this evangelist's thought and theology, also come close to the way in which words and deeds, the teaching of Jesus and his life, are combined. While his words are often highly demanding, his deeds are all-embracing. "In John's gospel in general as well as 3:16–21 in particular, Jesus brings the 'truth' from God, even if people do not hear it, but he also comes as the expression of the divine love to help us 'love' one another. To borrow one of the later Pauline letters, Eph 4:15, in the fourth gospel Jesus comes 'teaching the truth in love.'"[18]

It is beyond dispute that love is the nerve in the understanding of God in the New Testament. The New Testament texts speak unambiguously of the love of God. God is love (1 John 4:8) and his love is boundless and forgiving (Luke 15). But it also proclaims that Jesus Christ is the image of God and that communicates the authentic image both of God and of man. Hence, the claim of Christianity is that it cannot be reduced to a religion of love; it is a religion of truth as well. It is the simultaneous assertion of Christianity that it represents belief in the true God and respect for the dignity of each person.

It has been proposed that the Christian criterion for discerning truth and revelation in other religions can be summed up in one word, love (*agapē*). As Peggy Starkey states "God's central revelation, which is given through Jesus Christ, is *agapē*. An examination of Christian scripture shows that *agapē* is active and involve justice, risk, compassion, charity, respect, service, and forgiveness towards others without expecting love in return. This *agapē* is selfless love and constitutes a way of life."[19] The New Testament makes it clear that *agapē*, though made up of two dimensions, is one, and that indeed the love of God necessarily passes through the love

---

16. Jervell, *Større kærlighed har ingen*, 38.
17. Burridge, *Imitating Jesus*, 285–346.
18. Ibid., 286.
19. Starkey, "Agapē," 433–34.

of humankind (cf. 1 John 4:20). In Christ God has united with humankind in an irrevocable bond of love. This is why saving *agapē* finds in Christ its decisive theological foundation.[20] *Agapē* is the overflow in us of the love by which God loved us first. The practice of agapē is the reality of salvation, present and operative in human beings in response to God's self-disclosure and revelation.[21]

In a sermon entitled "The Power of Love," Paul Tillich has reflected on the meaning of certain biblical texts, including 1 John 4:16 and John 13:34–35. He asks first what it means to say that God *is* love. His answer is that God and love are not two realities: they are one. Tillich further underlines that God's being is the being of love and that Gods infinite power of being is the infinite power of love. He continues: "Therefore, he who professes devotion to God, *may* abide in God, if he abides in love, or he may not abide in God, if he does not abide in love. And he who does not speak about God, may abide in him, if he is abiding in love. And since the manifestation of God as love is His manifestation in Jesus Christ, Jesus can say that many of those who do not know Him belong to Him, and that many of those who confess their allegiance to him do not belong to Him. The criterion, the only ultimate criterion, is love. For God is love, and divine love is triumphantly manifest in Christ the crucified."[22]

Love as the Only Absolute

It is often argued that there are two types of religion: the mystical and the kerygmatic.[23] Both distinguish between two kinds of reality: concrete reality and absolute reality. Kerygmatic religion confronts us with a message from outside. In the mystical religions divine reality is met within each person.

---

20. Dupuis, *Toward a Christian Theology*, 325. In his fifth thesis on a Trinitarian approach to other religions D'Costa claims that the normativity of Christ implies the normativity of crucified self-giving love, and this prescribes the *mode* of relationship with those of other traditions; in addition, the pattern of self-giving love is a standard that can validate witness to Christians from other traditions; D'Costa, "Christ, the Trinity, and Religious Plurality," 20.

21. Dupuis, *Toward a Christian Theology*, 323. See also Dupuis, "The Practice of Agapē is the Reality of Salvation," 473. This article is a response to the thesis of Starkey. Other responses are given in the same issue of *International Review of Mission*.

22. Tillich, *The New Being*, chapter 3; Danish version, Tillich, *En ny skabelse*, 29.

23. Theissen, *Lichtspuren*, 159.

The Truth and the Love—on Criteria for Religious Dialogue

We might say that through the experience of the Spirit Christianity has genuine access to the mystical religions: these are dominant in the East, and encountered as backwaters in the prophetic religions of the West, in Judaism, Islam, and Christianity. The experience of the Spirit is a mystical experience of unity with God. Christians are united with him not by nature, but by grace. This aspect of the Christian faith is anthropocentric: here the transformation of the human being by the Spirit is central.

Christianity is at the same time a kerygmatic religion, sharing with all Western religions the faith in God as creator. This God is transcendent, and nothing finite is able to embrace him. All prophetic religions underline the difference between God and human beings—it is the other side of mystic unity with God. This aspect of the Christian religion is theocentric, with the sovereignty and transcendence of God being central.

How then does the Gospel of John fit into these two types of religion? In its basic structure the Gospel is kerygmatic. God reveals himself to human beings by means of a call from outside. Between God and humankind is a deep gulf, as between light and darkness, between truth and falsehood, between life and death etc. As God's messenger Jesus has bridged the gulf, but at the same time he has voiced a claim for absoluteness: "I am the way, and the truth, and the life" (John 14:6). It is as if any dialogue is excluded. Nevertheless, as we have seen several times in previous chapters, there is also a mystical dimension in the gospel.[24] It would therefore be more to the point to say that in the Fourth Gospel the kerygmatic and the mystical are related to each other in a peculiar way. People are not just receiving the message as something that is radical and otherworldly. Rather, they are transformed by this message. They themselves are embodying the message (e.g., the Samaritan woman). In this way, the will that comes from outside is connected to our own will.

It is interesting to note that the Fourth Gospel combines the claim for absoluteness with boundless love, which is the core of the mystical tradition. Gerd Theissen argues persuasively that on the basis of this Gospel love must be seen as the only thing which is absolute in the religious dialogue.[25] John has two passages on the commandment to love one another: 13:34 and 15:12–15. I will comment on them in reverse order.

---

24. See, for instance, the paragraph, "Worship in 'spirit and truth'—the concrete reality and the Johannine mysticism" in chapter 5 of this book.

25. Theissen, *Lichtspuren*, 161.

Part Two: The Gospel of John and the Religious Dialogue

There is a clear indication in John 15:12-15 that the most important thing in the Gospel is now being said:

> This is my commandment, that you love one another as I have loved you. No one has greater love than this, to lay down one's life for one's friends. You are my friends if you do what I command you. I do not call you servants any longer, because the servant does not know what the master is doing, but I have called you friends, because I have made known to you everything that I have heard from my Father.

Theissen underlines that "previously Jesus had often stated that he has to proclaim the decisive message from God, that he says what he has heard from the Father. But we never hear what he has heard there, in the heavenly world. Only once in the Gospel is it expressly emphasized that Jesus has now said *everything* he has heard from the Father, namely, the second formulation of the commandment to love."[26] If Jesus has said everything in the commandment to love, he has indicated that *agapē* is the only way to the Father, the only truth, and the only entrance to life. Jesus is the manifestation of this love. The implication of this for a theology of religion is that love must be the critical yardstick for everything, even our own religion.

The first passage on the love commandment, John 13:34-35, is also worth noting: that the disciples give witness to the world in so far as they love each other. As Jesus has loved them until the last second of his life, so must they love one another. In and through this mutual love they are called to give public witness to the life-giving power of God's love in Jesus. By this *praxis of agapē* all people will know that they are Jesus' disciples.[27]

John's hermeneutic has aptly been described as a "hermeneutic of the Spirit of Love."[28] The love of the disciples among themselves and their unity let the world recognize that the Father has sent Jesus into the world as bearer of his love (13:34; 17:23). Thus, love in the Gospel of John is first and foremost the hallmark of Christ himself. If—as has been argued above—the way of Christ is the way of the cross (cf. the chapters 13-14), this way is the

---

26. Theissen, *A Theory of Primitive Christian Religion*, 196. Theissen continues: "Not only is it explicitly said here that everything—really everything—that Jesus has to communicate on the basis of his familiarity with the Father has been said; in addition it is made clear that here all previous revelation has been surpassed. For hitherto the disciples were servants in their relationship to God and Jesus; now they have become friends" (ibid., 197).

27. Nissen, *New Testament and Mission*, 81.

28. Klaiber, *Call and Response*, 72-74.

way of divine love. "The absolute quality of the statement 'I am the way' expresses the absolute quality of God's love for the world."[29]

---

29. Koester, "Jesus as the Way."

16

The Johannine Experience of Faith

The Witness

In recent years there has been much debate about the relation between mission and dialogue. For some Christians, mission and dialogue are opposed to each other. However, this need not be the case. A positive understanding of dialogue means that mission first and foremost should have the character of witness. This point is supported by the document *Tro i lære* (2008) based on interviews with representatives of the Danish Lutheran Church. These Christians are engaged in dialogue with religious seekers who have been inspired by Eastern spirituality and religiosity. The Christian representatives see themselves as witnesses who share their faith in dialogue with others. One of them says that the missionary task is to be witnesses.[1] Another says that the missionary task is "to share with generosity the communion that I have with God" and "to be a witness; however it is the Holy Spirit that gives the growth to the seed we are spreading," and then adds: "The language of mission in the encounter with people marked by Eastern spirituality is primarily the witness which is based on personal experience. The task is to share our own faith with others rather than have an interchange of theological viewpoints."[2]

---

1. *Tro i lære*, 11.
2. Ibid., 31.*

The Johannine Experience of Faith

The category of witness plays a significant role in recent missiological thinking. By way of example we can point to the San Antonio Conference (Texas, 1989) which underlined that "our ministry of witness among people of other faiths presupposes our *presence* with them, *sensitivity* to their deepest faith commitments and experiences, *willingness* to be their servants for Christ's sake, *affirmation* of what God has done and is doing among them, and *love* for them . . . We are called to be *witnesses* to others, not judges of them."[3]

Likewise mission as bearing witness is important to the New Testament, especially in Acts and the Fourth Gospel. John points to various aspects of this witnessing. One aspect is community as witness, e.g., John 13:34–35; another is the relation between the Holy Spirit and witness, e.g., 15:26–27; a third aspect is witnessing as sharing faith, particularly evidenced in John 4 (Jesus and the Samaritan woman) and John 1:35–51 (the calling of the first disciples, cf. also the next paragraph, "Come and see!").

1 John 1:1–4 is another text which emphasizes witness as sharing faith:[4] "What was from the beginning, what we have heard, what we have seen with our eyes . . . concerning the word of life—this life was revealed, and we have seen it and testify to it and declare to you the eternal life. . . . so that you also may have fellowship. . . ." In this text we have four elements: 1) the *apostolic experience* ("heard," "seen," "looked," "touched," 2) the *Christ event* ("what was from the beginning," "the word of life" etc). 3) *sharing* ("we testify," "and declare"), 4) *purpose* ("so that you also may have fellowship . . .").[5]

So the concepts of sending and witness are closely related in the Gospel of John. In fact, the entire Gospel is about being sent. One of the most important designations of Jesus is the "one sent." Christ's identity is defined as the envoy of God, sent into the world on a specific mission. The identity of the church is closely linked to sending (4:38; 17:3; 20:21). The disciples are commissioned to carry on the work of Jesus who is to be sent by the Father. But apart from this the disciples are not told *what* to do. The key to

---

3. "Mission and Evangelism in Unity," 122.

4. See also the paragraph "Experience and theological reflection" in chapter 1 of this book.

5. Vellanickal, "The Gospel of John in the Indian Context," 145–46. The author points to the clear parallel statement in John 20:30–31. "The content of the Gospel, namely, the words and deeds of Jesus recorded in the Gospel are signs inviting us to recognise and experience God's life revealed in Jesus and thus to believe in Jesus as the Word of Life (Christ and Son of God) and consequently to share in the same life" (ibid., 146).

this is the incarnation. The disciples are called to follow the foundational pattern of the incarnation: "The Word became flesh and lived among us." (1:14). This means that the sending should be shaped according to the context in which the disciples are living.

There are four types of sending that occur in the Fourth Gospel: (1) John the Baptist is sent by God to testify about Jesus (1:6–8; 3:28). (2) Jesus himself is sent by the Father to testify about the Father and do his work (4:34; 17:4 etc.). (3) The Spirit is sent by both the Father and Son to give testimonies about Jesus. (4) Finally, the disciples are sent by Jesus to do as he did (20:21; 17:18).

These missions are interrelated.[6] All revolve around Jesus. John announces his coming, the Paraclete confirms his presence, the disciples proclaim his Word to the world. In this sense all mission is *witness to Christ*. But the endpoint of this Gospels' missiology is not Jesus but the Father. The Father alone is *not* sent. He is the origin and the goal of all the testimony of the Gospel, cf. John 1:1–18 and 17:20–23.

The Gospel is about Jesus, but Jesus is about God: "John was concerned to confront his readers through Jesus with God."[7] Johannine Christology is perfectly transparent in the sense that Jesus does not attract attention to himself but points to the Father whom he constantly reveals. The Father is the center of the Gospel. Jesus is "only" the medium; in other words "the way." As revealed of God, he lets all light pass through him to the Father.

"Come and see!"

"What are you searching for" (John 1:38).[8] These are the first words of Jesus in the Fourth Gospel. They indicate a theme of great importance for the author. Throughout the gospel people are searching for something. It seems as if they are searching for fellowship with God and other persons, for the meaning of life, for a place to belong. What is the answer to this search?

In 1:35–51 we have essential notes of the call of discipleship[9]: "seeking" (v. 38a), "finding" (v. 38b), "coming and seeing" (v. 39), "remaining

---

6. Nissen, *New Testament and Mission*, 76.
7. Barrett, *The Gospel According to John*, 97.
8. This is a direct translation of the Greek *zēteite*. NRSV has "What are you looking for?"
9. See the observations by Vellanickal, "Discipleship According to the Gospel of John," 134–35; cf. Kavunkal, "Mission in the Fourth Gospel,"131–32. In a very stimulating article D'Sa ("Sehen—Glauben—Innewohnen") argues that John 1 should be seen

The Johannine Experience of Faith

with Jesus" (v. 39b), "missionary sharing" (v. 40–42) are among them.[10] Each of these characteristics is worth considering:

Seeking. This term is often used to designate the deep desire that characterizes religiously significant attitudes and actions. Throughout the Gospel such themes as "seeking glory," "seeking to kill," "seeking the will of the one who sent me," and "seeking the truth" emphasize the theological importance of the term by making the ultimate motivations of various character.

Finding: John refers several times to "where Jesus is and remains." The ultimate purpose of the work of Jesus is to reveal to the disciples this "where" of his living and to take the disciples there with him: "…where I am, there will my servant be also" (12:26; cf. 14:2–3).[11]

Coming and seeing: Both are terms indicating faith. "Coming to Jesus" is the same as "believing in Jesus" (6:35). Both terms indicate the experiential dimension of faith.

Remaining: At the invitation of Jesus the disciples came and saw where he was staying, and they remained with him (v. 39). The term "remain" is often used by John. Its theological importance is particularly evident in 15:1–17. This term designates the intimate union that expresses itself in a way of life lived in love (15:9 and 15:17).

Missionary sharing: In the Fourth Gospel discipleship implies missionary sharing of the experience of Jesus. Already John the Baptist witnesses to his experience of Jesus (1:34) leading his disciples to the same experience (1:35–42). Later the Samaritan woman shares her experience of the prophet with the people of the town (4:29). In a similar way, Mary Magdalene is asked to share her experience of the risen Lord with others (20:17).

The invitation of Jesus to "come and see" seems therefore to mean. "Here is the fulfillment of your dreams and longings." This is not to say that all the disciples had great experiences. Nathanael for one was skeptical. Nevertheless

---

as a hermeneutical model for reading the entire Gospel. According to Klaiber (*Call and Response*, 62), the long session of 1:19—2:11 ought to become a model of how to lead someone to Jesus.

10. Gutiérrez, in a similar way, emphasizes that John 1:35–42 can be seen as a sketch of an encounter with the Lord that becomes a paradigm for the many others that would take place in the lives of Christians of every age; Gutiérrez, *We Drink from Our Own Wells*, 39.

11. See also chapter 10 of this study.

Part Two: The Gospel of John and the Religious Dialogue

Philip said: "Come and see!" (1:46). Nathanael follows the invitation and does indeed see greater things: heaven is opened to him (1:51).

The Fourth Gospel is centripetal in its call to "come and see," a call made not only to the initial disciples (1:39.46), to the Samaritan (4:29) and to Jesus' contemporary addressees (5:40; 6:35.37), but to all the potential readers and hearers as well. This centripetal emphasis of the evangelistic invitation is intimately related to an incarnational revelation that is located and is "to be seen." This revelation is a center of universal attraction, cf. 12:32: "And I, when I am lifted up from the earth, will draw all people to myself."[12]

Seeking God—Sought by God

The previous chapters have demonstrated that the religious quest is of great importance for the Gospel of John. When Jesus meets people, they see greater things, and "heaven is opened" (cf. 1:50–51); a new perspective on life is revealed to them. This new insight is often communicated by means of metaphors and symbols. It is particularly clear in Jesus' conversation with Nicodemus and the Samaritan woman. In these stories we see Jesus inviting people to an attentiveness towards a greater reality (rebirth, the living water): "It is not man's mind or heart that creates the object of attention. There is a hidden reality so deeply immanent in the totality of existing things, that only someone who knows can draw other people's attention to it. This is exactly what Christ did."[13]

Unlike many other masters of contemplation Jesus never invites people to a kind of "ecstatic attention." He does not teach methods of contemplation that cut people off from involvement in their existential human situation. Instead, what Jesus proposes is deeply rooted in concrete being and existence. In essence, it is attention to the beyond, the afterwards, the deeper, the higher, the more intimate. We are to see "the depths of God," or more precisely, discover "the depth of God in the depth of man." It is in this self-discovery that we find God.[14] John's is the Gospel of deep human encounters, where relationships pass beyond appearances and plunge into

12. Arias, *The Great Commission*, 96–97.
13. Raguin, *The Depth of God*, 143.
14. Cf. Raguin, *The Depth of God*, vi–vii. "Jesus leads each person he questions, or who questions him to the point of self-revelation. Then and only then, can dialogue start and the truth penetrate" (ibid., 93).

The Johannine Experience of Faith

authentic intimacy.[15] A greater reality is revealed. As the Samaritan woman talks to this stranger, she sees herself in a new light. She realizes who she is, and at the same time she sees things greater than this; a divine reality is revealed. She recognizes that Jesus is Messiah (4:26).[16]

The religious search of humankind for truth or a divine reality is crucial to the encounter between the different religions. Some also emphasize that God is searching for us too, most obviously the three that underline the personal character of God: Judaism, Christianity, and Islam.

But of these three there is a special focus in Christianity on the interactive search by both God and human beings. This point is underlined by all four gospels. Again and again the Synoptic Gospels tell how Jesus is searching for those who are poor, sick, marginalized, and sinful. Most characteristically in the parable of the Prodigal Son (Luke 15:11–32). Similarly, John's Gospel describes God as searching for human beings, as when Jesus tells the Samaritan woman: "the true worshipers will worship the Father in spirit and truth, for the Father *seeks* such as these to worship him" (John 4:23). And he seeks such worshipers by sending his Son.

It is sometimes said that there is nothing unique in Christianity. All the important things can also be found in other religions. And of course there are parallels between the religions, but not always carrying the same weight in the spirituality of everyday life. Thus in the Buddhist "equivalent" to the Prodigal Son it is not the concept of the merciful father that dominates Buddhist belief and everyday life.[17] It is only Christianity that in an unambiguous way speaks of God *searching* for human beings. It is only here that we find a God who "runs" to meet human beings (Luke 15:11–32).

It is in the "excess" of his humanity that Christ shows us his divinity. He is not more God by being less man, but rather, in being human to the utmost degree he shows that he is God. John wishes to make this clear by saying: "Having loved his own who were in the world, he loved them to the end" (13:1).[18] The ultimate theological foundation of mission is this movement of the triune God toward human beings. Mission is first and foremost

---

15. Ibid., 93.

16. For a more detailed analysis, see chapter 5 of this book.

17. Henningsson, *Tro möter tro*, 89. On the similarities and differences between the two versions of the Prodigal Son; see also Thelle, *Buddha og Kristus*, 46–50.

18. As Raguin says: "This is the Christian way that transcends the way of other religions at which the Incarnation is not the complete key to life" (Raguin, *The Depths of God*, 95).

the God who comes.[19] Moreover, God's mission is the invasion of love in history. It is of vital importance that God finds us in Jesus Christ, who is himself God's incarnated search for humankind. It is this image of the searching God—the Word which became flesh and lived among us—that is the decisive difference between Christianity and other religions.

---

19. Legrand, *Unity and Plurality*.

Bibliography

Aagaard, Anna Marie. *Identifikation af kirken*. Copenhagen: Anis, 1991.
———. *Ånd har krop*. Teologiske essays. Copenhagen: Anis, 2005.
Aagaard, Johannes. "Guruismens væsen og dens verdensmission." In *Mødet mellem hinduisme og kristendom*, edited by Lars Thunberg, 182–206. Aarhus: TF-tryk, 1982.
———. "Den religiøse dimension i kirkens mission." *Mission and Evangelism* 1–2 (1983) 3–21.
———. "Eksklusivitet og inklusivitet missionsteologisk belyst." *Nordisk Missionstidsskrift* 96 (1985) 146–70.
———. "Findes der en elementær kosmologi?" In *Teologi og kirke*, edited by Johannes Nissen and Heine Simonsen, 169–180. Copenhagen: Unitas, 1986.
———. "Tao." *Østen og vi* 1 (1987) 3.
Albrecht, Mark. *Reincarnation: A Christian Critique of a New Age Doctrine*. Downers Grove, IL: InterVarsity, 1982.
Amaladoss, Michael. *The Asian Jesus*. Delhi: ISPCK, 2005.
Amalorpavadass, D. S. "Foreword." In *Waters of Fire* by Sister Vandana. Madras: CLS, 1981.
Appasamy, A. J. *Christianity as Bhakti Marga: A Study of the Johannine Doctrine of Love*. Madras: CLS, 1926.
Arendt, Niels Henrik. *Gud er stor! Om Islam og kristendom*. Copenhagen: Anis 1994.
———. *Er det den samme Gud? Gud i kristendommen og andre religioner*. Copenhagen: Unitas, 2009.
Ariarajah, Wesley. "The Water of Life." *Ecumenical Review* 34 (1982) 271–79.
———. *The Bible and People of Other Faiths*. Geneva: World Council of Churches, 1985.
Arias, Mortimer, and Alan Johnson. *The Great Commission: Biblical Models for Evangelism*. Nashville: Abingdon, 1992.
Ball, David. "'My Lord and my God': The Implications of the 'I Am' Sayings for the Religious Pluralism." In *One God, One Lord in a World of Religious Pluralism*, edited by A. D. Clarke and B. C. Winter, 53–71. Cambridge: Tyndale House, 1991.
Barrett, Charles K. *The Gospel According to John*. 2nd ed. London: SPCK 1978.
Berentsen, Jan-Martin. "Den umulige dialog—og den nødvendige." *Nordisk Missionstidsskrift* 105/3 (1994) 15–18.
Berger, Klaus. *Exegese des Neuen Testaments*. Heidelberg: Quelle & Meyer, 1977.
Biehl, Peter. *Symbole geben zu lernen. Einführung in die Symboldidaktik anhand der Symbole Hand, Haus und Weg*. Vluyn: Neukirchener, 1989.
Bjerg, Svend. *Øjnenes faste. Homiletisk læsning af teksterne til faste- og påsketid*. Copenhagen: Anis, 1997.

Bibliography

Boff, Leonardo. *The Lord's Prayer: The Prayer of Integral Liberation*. New York: Orbis, 1983.
Bollmann, Kaj. *Kirke til tiden: Visioner for en folkekirke i forandring*. Copenhagen: Unitas, 2009.
Borg, Marcus J. "Jesus and Buddhism: A Christian view." *Buddhist-Christian Studies* 19/1 (1999) 93–97.
Borup, Jørn. *Dansk Dharma. Buddhisme og buddhister i Danmark*. Aarhus: Univers, 2005.
Bosch, David J. *Transforming Mission: Paradigm Shifts in Theology of Mission*. Maryknoll NY: Orbis, 1991.
Braaten, Carl. "The Uniqueness and Universality of Jesus Christ." In *Faith Meets Faith*, edited by Gerald H. Andersen & Thomas F. Stransky, 69–89. Mission Trends 5. New York: Paulist, 1981.
Brown, Raymond E. *The Gospel According to John*. 2 vols. Anchor Bible 29–29A. Garden City, NY: Doubleday, 1966–1970.
———. *The Community of the Beloved Disciple: The Life, Loves and Hates of an Individual Church in New Testament Times*. London: Chapman, 1979.
Bultmann, Rudolf. *Das Evangelium des Johannes*. 19th ed. Göttingen: Vandenhoek & Ruprecht, 1968.
———. *Theologie des Neuen Testaments*. Tübingen: Mohr/Siebeck, 1977.
Burridge, Richard A. *Imitating Jesus: An Inclusive Approach to New Testament Ethics*. Grand Rapids: Eerdmans, 2007.
Cahill, P. Joseph. "The Johannine *Logos* as Center." *Catholic Biblical Quarterly* 38 (1976) 54–72.
Camps, Arnulf. *Partners in Dialogue: Christianity and Other World Religions*. Maryknoll, NY: Orbis, 1983.
Cardenal, Ernesto. *Evangeliet fra Latinamerika. Bønder fra Solentiname maler og fortæller*. Translated by Karl-Erik Schøllhammer. Aarhus: Anis, 1984.
Chappuis, Jean-Marc. "Jesus and the Samaritan Woman: The Variable Geometry of Communication." *Ecumenical Review* 34 (1982) 8–34.
Cracknell, Kenneth. *Towards a New Relationship: Christians and People of Other Faith*. London: Epworth, 1986.
Critical Theology Group (Aarhus). "Truth Will Set You Free: Biblical Study of John 8." In *Before the Cock Crows—Biblical and Theological Reflections in the Student Christian Movements in Europe Today*, 36–49. Madras: CLS, 1983.
Culpepper, R. Alan. *Anatomy of the Fourth Gospel: A Study in Literary Design*. Philadelphia: Fortress, 1983.
Cöster, Henry. *Skriften i verkligheten*. Stockholm: Verbum, 1987.
Damm, Richard. *Johannesevangeliet. En kommentar*. Copenhagen: Gjellerup, 1973.
———. *Kristendommen i antroposofiens lys*. Odense: Jupiter, 1983.
———. *Paulus mellem øst og vest*. Odense: Jupiter, 1987.
Davidsen, Andreas. *Komponenter til kristendomsundervisningen 2: Johannesevangeliet*. Copenhagen: Gjellerups, 1979.
D'Costa, Gavin. "Christ, the Trinity, and Religious Plurality." In *Christian Uniqueness Reconsidered: The Myth of a Pluralistic Theology of Religions*, edited by G. D'Costa, 16–29. Maryknoll, NY: Orbis, 1990.
———. *Christianity and World Religions: Disputed Questions in the Theology of Religions*. Oxford: Wiley-Blackwell, 2009.
Dodd, Charles H. *The Interpretation of the Fourth Gospel*. Cambridge: Cambridge University Press, 1953.

Bibliography

D'Sa, F. X. "Sehen—Glauben—Innewohnen: Joh 1 als hermeneutischer Modell." In *Wir werden bei ihm wohnen: Das Johannesevangelium in indischer Deutung*, edited by George M. Soares-Prabhu, 99–121. Freiburg: Herder, 1984.
Dunn, James D.G. *Unity and Diversity in the New Testament: An Inquiry into the Character of Earliest Christianity*. London: SCM, 1977.
———. *Christology in the Making: An Inquiry into the Origins of Incarnation*. London: SCM, 1980.
Dupuis, Jacques. "The Practice of Agape is the Reality of Salvation." *International Review of Mission* 74 (1985) 472–77.
———. *Toward a Christian Theology of Religious Pluralism*. Maryknoll, NY: Orbis, 1997.
Duraisingh, C. "The Gospel of John and the World of India Today." In *India's Search for Reality and the Relevance of the Gospel of John*, edited by C. Duraisingh and C. Hargreaves, 41–55. Delhi: ISPCK, 1975.
Eliade, Mircea. *The Sacred and the Profane: The Nature of Religion*. Translated by W. R. Trask. New York: Harcourt, Brace & World, 1957.
Erling, Bernhard. *A Reader's Guide to Dag Hammarskjöld's Waymarks*. St. Peter, MN: privately printed, 2009.
Falk, Bent. *Kærlighedens pris*. Copenhagen: Anis, 1998.
Frankemölle, Hubert. *Glaubensbekenntnisse. Zur neutestamentlichen Begründung unseres Credos*. Düsseldorf: Patmos, 1974.
Gadamer, Hans-Georg. *Truth and Method*. 2nd ed. New York: Crossroad, 1990.
Gjesing, Lars Ole. "Tekstvejledning (til Joh 14,1–11)." *Præsteforeningens Blad* 82 (1992) 371–373.
Green, Joel B. "The Practice of Reading the New Testament." In *Hearing the New Testament: Strategies for Interpretation*, edited by Joel B. Green, 411–27. Grand Rapids: Eerdmans, 1995.
Gregersen, Niels Henrik. "Kirkens grænsegængere og kristendommens grænser". In *Tro i Lære*, edited by Berit Schelde Christensen et al., 37–42. Aarhus: Folkekirke og Religionsmøde, 2008.
Gutiérrez, Gustavo. *We Drink from Our Own Wells: The Spiritual Journey of a People*. Maryknoll NY: Orbis, 1984.
———. *The Truth Shall Make You Free*. Maryknoll NY: Orbis, 1990.
Hammar, Karl Gustav. *Det som hörs—et predikoteoretiskt perspektiv*. Stockholm: Verbum, 1985.
———. *Vägen valde dig. Ärkebiskop KG Hammars meditationer över Dag Hammarskjölds "Vägmärken."* Uppsala, Svenska Kyrkan 2005.
Hammarskjöld, Dag. *Markings*. Translated by W. H. Auden and Leif Sjöberg. London, Faber & Faber, 1964. Originally published as *Vägmärken*, Stockholm: Bonnier, 1963.
Hays, Richard H. *The Moral Vision of the New Testament: Community, Cross, New Creation—A Contemporary Introduction to New Testament Ethics*. Edinburgh: T. & T. Clark, 1997.
Hedlund, Roger E. "The Biblical Approach to Other Religions." In *Bible and Mission in India Today*, edited by Jacob Kavunkal and F. Hrangkhuma, 308–35. Bombay: St. Paul's, 1993.
Henningsson, Jan. *Tro möter tro: Ett kristet perspektiv på andra religioner*. Stockholm: Verbum, 1992.
Hick, John. *Death and Eternal Life*. London: Collins, 1976.

Bibliography

Højholt, Lene. *Vejen: Meditativ fordybelse i Johannesevangeliet.* Copenhagen: Borgen, 2006.
Images of Life: an invitation to bible study. Edited by World Council of Churches. Geneva: World Council of Churches, 1982.
Jervell, Jacob. *Større kærlighed har ingen... Om Johannesevangeliets Jesusbillede.* Translated by Preben Holm. Copenhagen: Unitas, 1995.
Kabaséle, Francois. "Jenseits der Modelle." In *Der schwarze Christus. Wege afrikanischer Christologie*, edited by Y. Atlé et al., 138-61. Freiburg: Herder, 1989.
Kavunkal, Jacob. "Mission in the Fourth Gospel." In *Bible and Mission in India Today*, edited by Jacob Kavunkal & F. Hrangkhuma, 117-46. Bombay: St. Paul's, 1993.
Kieffer, René. *Johannesevangeliet I-II.* Uppsala: EFS, 1987-1988.
Kim, Kirsteen. *Mission in the Spirit: The Holy Spirit in Indian Christian Theologies.* New Delhi: ISPCK, 2003.
Kirk, J. Andrew. *What is Mission? Theological Exploration.* London: Darton, Longman & Todd, 1999.
Kirkegaard, Karl Aage. *Reinkarnation er forenelig med kristendom. En dokumentation.* Copenhagen: Sankt Ansgars,1999.
Klaiber, Walter. *Call and Response: Biblical Foundations of a Theology of Evangelism.* Nashville: Abingdon, 1997.
Knitter, Paul. *Introducing Theologies of Religions.* Maryknoll, NY: Orbis, 2007.
Koenig, John. *Jews and Christians in Dialogue: The New Testament Foundations.* Philadelphia: Fortress, 1979.
Koester, Craig K. *Symbolism in the Fourth Gospel: Meaning, Ministry, Community.* Minneapolis: Fortress, 1995.
———. "Jesus as the Way and the Mission of the Church According to the Gospel of John." Paper presented at The SNTS Conference, Bonn, 2003. 10 pages. Online: www.vanderbilt.edu/AnS/religious_studies/SNTS2002/Koester.htm.
Koyama, Kosuke. *Theology in Contact.* Madras: CLS, 1975.
———. "A Theological Reflection on Pluralism." *Ecumenical Review* 51 (1999) 160-71.
Kysar, Robert. *John the Maverick Gospel.* Atlanta: Knox, 1976.
Küster, Volker. *The Many Faces of Jesus Christ: Intercultural Christology.* London: SCM, 2001.
Käsemann, Ernst. *Jesu letzter Wille nach Johannes 17.* Tübingen: Mohr/Siebeck, 1966.
Langmead, Ross. *The Word Made Flesh: Towards an Incarnational Missiology.* Lanham, MD: University Press of America, 2004.
Larsen, Daniel Ettrup. *Jesus i Koranen.* Aarhus: Teoltryk, 2004.
Legrand, Lucien. *Unity and Plurality: Mission in the Bible.* Maryknoll NY: Orbis, 1990.
Lincoln. A. T. "Pilgrimage and the New Testament." In *Explorations in a Christian Pilgrimage*, edited by C. Bartholomew and F. Hughes, 29-49. Hants: Ashgate, 2004.
Link, Hans-Georg. "The Bread of Life: Comments on a Fundamental Biblical Experience," *Ecumenical Review* 34 (1982) 249-59.
Lundegaard, Ole. "At være menighed i håbets lys". *Baptist* 146/53.1 (1999) 5-8.
Lönnebo, Martin. *Religionens fem språk. Om religionens mening och förnyelse.* Stockholm: Verbum, 1975.
———. "Trons språk." In *Vägen hem och resan vidare* by H. Månsus, 9-15. Örebro: Brommadialogen, 2003.
MacGregor, Geddes. *Reincarnation as a Christian Hope.* London: Macmillan, 1982.

MacRae, G. W. "The Fourth Gospel and *Religionsgeschichte*." *Catholic Biblical Quarterly* 32 (1970) 13–24.
Madsen, Ole Skjerbæk. "Theology in Dialogue with New Age or the Neospiritual Milieu." In *Theology and the Religions: A Dialogue*, edited by Viggo Mortensen, 257–86. Grand Rapids: Eerdmans, 2003.
Månsus, Harry. *Shalom jord. Om fred, helhetssyn och jordens framtid*. Örebro: Libris, 1983.
———. *Vägen hem och resan vidare*. Örebro: Brommadialogen, 2003.
Mar Osthathios, Geevarghese. "Mission and the Uniqueness of Jesus Christ." *Mission Studies* 12/1 (1995) 79–94.
Mar Osthathios, Geevarghese. *Sharing God and a Sharing World*. Thiruvalla: Christhava Sahithya Samithy, 1995.
Martensen, Hans. *Dåb og Gudstro*. Copenhagen: Steensens, 1982.
———. *Kirke og reinkarnation? Har kirken fordømt læren om reinkarnation?* Aarhus: Dialogcentret, 1991.
Meeks, Wayne A. "The Man from Heaven in Johannine Sectarianism." *Journal of Biblical Literature* 91 (1972) 44–72.
Miranda, José P. *Being and the Messiah: The Meaning of St. John*. Maryknoll NY: Orbis, 1977.
"Mission and Evangelism in Unity Today." *International Review of Mission* 88 (1999) 109–127.
Mogensen, Kaj. *Tro, håb og kærlighed. Konfirmationsforberedelse*. Undervisningsvejledning 2. Copenhagen: Nyt Nordisk, 1991.
———. *Således elskede Gud verden: Temaer fra Johannesevangeliet*. Copenhagen: Unitas, 1993.
———. "Symboler og symboldidaktik. Hvordan bliver bibelundervisningen livsoplysning?" In *Bibel, formidling og dialog*, edited by Ole Davidsen and Aage Pilgaard, 233–270. Copenhagen: Anis, 2006.
———. *Frelse og fortabelse*. Copenhagen: Aros, 2012.
Mogensen, Mogens, S. *Kristendom, sekularisering, multireligiøsitet og nyåndelighed. En oversigt over religiøse åndsstrømninger i Danmark i starten af det 21. århundrede*. Aarhus: Folkekirke og Religionsmøde, 2009.
Mortensen, Viggo. "For All God's People: Being Church in Multireligious Societies." In *Theology and the Religions: A Dialogue*, edited by Viggo Mortensen, 465–79. Grand Rapids: Eerdmans 2003.
———. "Mission, kirkens hjerte og åndedræt." In *Mission og forkyndelse*, edited by Selskabet til Støtte for Pakistans Kirke, 15–24. N.p.: Selskabet til Støtte for Pakistans Kirke, 2003.
Moucarry, Chawkat. *Faith to Faith: Christianity and Islam in Dialogue*. Leicester: InterVarsity, 2001.
Moxnes, Halvor. "Jesu galilæiske kontekst. Den historiske Jesus i forhold til hus, landsby og by." In *Den historiske Jesus og hans betydning*, edited by Troels Engberg-Pedersen, 103–36. Copenhagen: Gyldendal, 1998.
———. *Putting Jesus in His Place: A Radical Vision of Household and Kingdom*. Louisville: Westminster John Knox, 2003.
Møllehave, Johannes. *Den livsild som forbrænder. 24 prædikener*. Copenhagen: Lindhardt & Ringhof, 1979.
Nereparampil, Lucius. *Destroy this Temple: An Exegetico-Theological Study on the Meaning of Jesus's Temple-Logion in Jn 2:19*. Bangalore: Dharmaram College, 1978.

Bibliography

Newbigin, Lesslie. *The Good Shepherd: Meditations on Christian Ministry in Today's World.* Madras: CLS, 1974.

———. "What is 'a local church truly united'?" *Ecumenical Review* 29 (1977) 115–28.

———. *The Open Secret: Sketches for a Missionary Theology.* London: SPCK, 1978.

———. *The Light Has Come: An Exposition of the Fourth Gospel.* Edinburgh: Handsel, 1982.

Nielsen, Helge Kjær. "John's Understanding of the Death of Jesus." In *New Readings in John: Literary and Theological Perspectives,* edited by Johannes Nissen and Sigfred Pedersen, 232–54. Sheffield: Sheffield Academic, 1999.

———. *Johannesevangeliet.* Aarhus: Aarhus Universitetsforlag, 2007.

Nilsson, Kjell Ove. *At giva de förtryckta frihet.* Stockholm: Verbum, 1974.

Nissen, Johannes. "Kongemagt og discipelmenighed i Johannesevangeliet. Om forholdet mellem kristologi, ekklesiologi og etik." In *Nytestamentlige studier,* edited by Sigfred Pedersen, 147–80. Aarhus: Aros, 1976.

———. *Poverty and Mission: New Testament Perspectives on a Contemporary Theme.* Leiden-Utrecht: Interuniversitair Instituut voor Missiologie en Oecumenica, 1984.

———. "Rebirth and Community—A Spiritual and Social Reading of John 3:1–21." In *Apocryphon Severini: Presented to Søren Giversen,* edited by Per Bilde, Helge Kjær Nielsen and Jørgen Podemann Sørensen, 121–39. Aarhus: Aarhus University Press, 1993.

———. "Helligånden sprænger grænser og sætter skel—om Helligåndsforståelsen i Canberra og i Ny Testamente." In *Du som går ud fra den levende Gud. Bibelteologiske og teologihistoriske overvejelser over Helligånden,* edited by Henning Thomsen, 13–54. Copenhagen: Anis, 1993.

———. "The Distinctive Character of the New Testament Love Command in Relation to Hellenistic Judaism." In *The New Testament and Hellenistic Judaism,* edited by Peder Borgen and Søren Giversen, 123–50. Aarhus: Aarhus University Press, 1995.

———. "Mødet mellem Bibelen og nutidens mennesker". In *Bibelbrug og livsoplysning: Bibeldidaktiske overvejelser,* edited by Birgitte Thyssen, 41–97. Frederiksberg: Religionspædagogisk Center, 1997.

———. *New Testament and Mission: Historical and Hermeneutical Perspectives.* Frankfurt: Lang, 1999.

———. "Community and ethics in the Gospel of John." In *New Readings in John: Literary and Theological Perspectives,* edited by Johannes Nissen and Sigfred Pedersen, 194–212. Sheffield: Sheffield Academic, 1999.

———. "Scripture and Experience as the Double Source of Mission: Hermeneutical Reflections." In *To Cast Fire Upon the Earth: Bible and Mission Collaborating in Today's Multicultural Global Context,* edited by Teresa Okure, 178–93. Pietermaritzburg: Cluster, 2000.

———. "Christology between the Local and the Global." *Swedish Missiological Themes* 88 (2000) 593–609.

———. "Sted og rum i Johannesevangeliet." In *Collegium Biblicum Årsskrift,* edited by Ole Davidson, 21–32. N.p.: Danish Society of Biblical Studies, 2001.

———. "Mission and Globalization in a New Testament Perspective." In *For All People: Global Theologies in Context,* edited by Else Marie Wiberg Pedersen, Holger Lam, and Peter Lodberg, 32–51. Grand Rapids: Eerdmans, 2002.

———. "Matthew, Mission and Method." *International Review of Mission* 91 (2002) 73–86.

---. "Seeking God—Sought by God: New Testament Perspectives on the Gospel in a Multifaith Context." In *Theology and the Religions: A Dialogue*, edited by Viggo Mortensen, 321-35. Grand Rapids: Eerdmans, 2003.

---. "Bible and Ethics: Moral Formation and Analogical Imagination." In *Theology and Literature: Rethinking Reader Responsibility*, edited by Gaye W. Ortiz and Clara A.B. Joseph, 81-100. New York: Palgrave MacMillan, 2006.

Nørgaard-Højen, Peder. "Reinkarnation og historie. Overvejelser til et omstridt tema i mødet mellem religionerne." In *Kristendommen og de andre religioner*, edited by Peder Nørgaard-Højen, 299-332. Aarhus: Anis, 1988.

---. "Kristendommens absoluthedskrav i dogmatisk belysning." In *Kristendommen og de andre religioner*, edited by Peder Nørgaard-Højen, 232-62. Aarhus: Anis, 1988.

Okure, Teresa. *The Johannine Approach to Mission: A Contextual Study of John 4:1-42*. Tübingen: Mohr/Siebeck, 1988.

Olofson, Peter. *Så I bliver som Gud. Nyreligiøsitet og kirkens mission*. Copenhagen: Credo, 1988.

Olsson, Birger. "*Deus semper major?* On God in the Johannine Writings." In *New Readings in John*, edited by Johannes Nissen and Sigfred Pedersen, 143-71. Sheffield: Sheffield Academic, 1999.

Padilla, René. "Bible Studies." *Missiology* 10/3 (1982) 319-38.

Pedersen, Gudmund Rask. *Forladthed og nærvær. Litteratur og kristendom*. Copenhagen: Anis, 2000.

Pedersen, René Dybdal. *I lysets tjeneste. Nye religiøse og spirituelle grupper i Danmark*. Aarhus: Univers, 2005.

Phan, Peter C. *Being Religious Interreligiously*. Maryknoll NY: Orbis, 2004.

Pieris, Aloysius. *Love Meets Wisdom: A Christian Experience of Buddhism*. Maryknoll, NY: Orbis, 1988.

Pobee, John. "Skénósis. The Tabernacling of the Word." *Mission Studies* 3/2 (1986) 4-13.

The Qur'an. Translated by M. A. S. Abdel Haleem. Oxford World's Classics. Oxford: Oxford University Press 2004.

Raguin, Yves. *The Depth of God*. Wheathampstead, UK: Clarke, 1979.

Rayan, Samuel. "Jesus and the Poor in the Fourth Gospel." *Biblebhashyam* 4/3 (1978) 213-28.

Rebell, Walter. *Gemeinde als Gegenwelt. Zur soziologischen und didaktischen Funktion des Johannesevangeliums*. Frankfurt: Lang, 1987.

Reichelt, Karl Ludvig. *Fra Kristuslivets helligdom. Foredrag og meditasjoner*. Copenhagen: Gad, 1931.

---. "The Johannine Approach." In *Authority of the Faith: International Missionary Council meeting at Tambaram, December 12th to 29th 1938*, 90-101. Tambaram 1. Oxford: Oxford University Press, 1939.

Rensberger, David. *Overcoming the World: Politics and Community in the Gospel of John*. London: SPCK, 1989.

Riisager, Filip. *Lotusblomsten og korset: En studie i Karl Ludvig Reichelts missionsforståelse med særligt henblik på buddhistmissionens første periode som en selvstændig organisation 1926-1929*. Copenhagen: Gad, 1998.

Romarheim, Arild. "Various views of Jesus Christ in new religious movements: A typological outline." *Norsk Tidsskrift for Misjon* 4 (1987) 91-113.

---. "Testing the Spirits (Part I)". *Areopagos* 3/3 (1990) 8-9.

Bibliography

———. *The Aquarian Christ: Jesus Christ as Portrayed by New Religious Movements.* Hong Kong: Tao Fong Shan Christian Centre, 1992.
Russell, Letty M. *Becoming Human.* Philadelphia: Westminster, 1982.
Samartha, Stanley. *Courage for Dialogue: Ecumenical Issues on Inter-Religious Movements.* Geneva: World Council of Churches, 1981.
———. "The Holy Spirit and People of Other Faiths." *Ecumenical Review* 42 (1990) 250–63.
Samtalen er nødvendig—mellem kristne og muslimer. Edited by Bjarne Jørgensen and Lissi Rasmussen. Translated by Anker Gjerding. Copenhagen: DMS, 1996.
Samuel, Simon. "The Kairos of the Galilaioi: An Indian Liberationist Reading of John 1–7." *Jeevadhara* 25/146 (1995) 149–60.
Sauter, Gerhard. "Wie kann Theologie aus Erfahrung entstehen?" In *Theologie im Entstehen. Beiträge zum ökumenischen Gespräch im Spannungsfeld kirchlicher Situationen,* edited by L. Vischer, 99–119. Munich: Kaiser, 1976.
Schelde, Michael. *Udenfor byporten. Udviklingslinier i asiatisk teologi.* Copenhagen: Anis, 1989.
Schillebeeckx, Eduard. "Erfahrung und Glaube." In *Christlicher Glaube in moderner Gesellschaft 25,* edited by F. Böckle et al., 25:72–116. Freiburg: Herder, 1980.
Schneiders, Sandra M. *The Revelatory Text: Interpreting the New Testament as Sacred Scripture.* San Francisco: HarperSanFrancisco, 1991.
Schüssler-Fiorenza, Elisabeth. *In Memory of Her: A Feminist Theological Reconstruction of Christian Origins.* London: SCM, 1983.
Senior, Donald, and Caroll Stuehlmueller. *The Biblical Foundations for Mission.* London: SCM, 1983.
Signs of the Spirit: Official Report. Seventh Assembly. Edited by M. Kinnamon. Geneva: World Council of Churches, 1991.
Soares-Prabhu, George. "The Man Born Blind: Understanding a Johannine Sign in India Today." In *India's Search for Reality and the Relevance of the Gospel of John,* edited by C. Duraisingh and C. Hargreaves, 65–77. Delhi: ISPCK, 1975.
———. "From Alienation to Inculturation: Some Reflections on Doing Theology in India Today." In *Bread and Breath. Essays in Honour of Samuel Rayan,* edited by T. K. John, 55–99, Anand Gujarat: Gujarat Sahytya Prakash, 1991.
Spindler, Marc. "Recent Indian Studies of the Gospel of John: Puzzling Contextualizations." *Exchange* 4 (1980) 1–55.
Spohn, William C. *What Are They Saying about Scripture and Ethics?* Rev. ed. New York: Paulist, 1995.
Stambaugh, John and David Balch. *The Social World of the First Christians.* London: SPCK, 1986.
Starkey, Peggy. "Agapé: A Christian Criterion for Truth in Other World Religions." *International Review of Mission* 74 (1985) 425–63.
Steiner, Rudolf. *The Gospel of St. John.* Translated by Maud B. Monges. 2nd ed. New York: Anthroposophic, 1940.
———. *The Gospel of St. John and Its Relation to the Other Gospels.* Translated by Samuel and Loni Lockwood and revised by Maria St. Goar. 2nd ed. Spring Valley, NY: Anthroposophic, 1982.
Stendahl, Krister. *Energy of Life: Reflections on the Theme: "Come Holy Spirit—Renew the Whole Creation."* Geneva: World Council of Churches, 1990.

Bibliography

Sugirtharajah, R. S. "Reconceiving Jesus: Some Continuing Concerns." In *Asian Faces of Jesus*, edited by R. S. Sugirtharajah, 258–63. Maryknoll, NY: Orbis, 1993.
Tamez, Elsa. "The Bread of Life." *International Review of Mission* 71 (1982) 505–9.
Thangaraj, Thomas. "What Are the Implications of My Experience of Interfaith Dialogue for the Understanding of Christology?" In *Who is Jesus Christ in a World of Many Faiths*, edited by Churches Commission on Inter-Faith Relations, 8–16. London: Churches Commission on Inter-Faith Relations, 1999.
———. *The Crucified Guru: An Experiment in Cross-Cultural Christology*. Nashville: Abingdon, 1994.
Theissen, Gerd. *Lichtspuren. Predigten und Bibelarbeiten*. Gütersloh: Kaiser, 1994.
———. *A Theory of Primitive Christian Religion*. London: SCM, 1999.
Thelle, Notto. *Buddhismen—en søken mot den fullkomne frihet*. Oslo: Thronsen, 1974.
———. *Hvem kan standse vinden? Vandringer i grænselandet mellem Øst og Vest*, Translated by Eleonora Faber. Copenhagen: Ecumenical Council, 1998.
———. *Buddha og Kristus. Refleksioner og spiritualitet i grænselandet mellem øst og vest*. Translated by Asger Sørensen. Copenhagen: Alfa, 2007.
Thompson, Ross. *Christian Spirituality: A SCM Studyguide*. London: SCM, 2008.
Tillich, Paul. *Grundvoldene vakler*. Translated by Ejgil Stok. Copenhagen: Jespersen, 1965. Originally published as *The Shaking of the Foundations* (New York: Scribner's Sons, 1948). Quotations from the online version: www.religion-online.org/showbook.asp?title=378.
———. *En ny skabelse*. Translated by Ejgil Stok. Copenhagen: Jespersen, 1966. Originally published as *The New Being* (New York: Scribner, 1955). Quotations from the online version: www.religion-online.org/showbook.asp?title=375.
Tro i lære. Lytterunde. Folkekirkens møde med åndelige strømninger. Edited by Berit Schelde Christensen et al. Aarhus: Folkekirke og religionsmøde, 2008.
Tro i tiden. Lytterunde blandt mennesker inspireret af østlig religiøsitet og spiritualitet. Edited by Lars Mollerup-Degn, Mogens S. Mogensen, and Leif Vestergaard. Aarhus: Folkekirke og religionsmøde, 2008.
Ucko, Hans. "Truth or Truths." *Current Dialogue* 37 (2001) 30–37.
Uppsala Report, The. Edited by N. Godall. Geneva: World Council of Churches, 1969.
Valkenberg, Pim. *Sharing Lights. On the Way to God: Muslim-Christian Dialogue and Theology in the Context of Abrahamic Partnership*. Amsterdam: Rodopi, 2006.
Van Lin, Jan. "Models for a Theology of Religion." In *Missiology: An Ecumenical Introduction*, edited by A. Camps et al., 177–93. Grand Rapids: Eerdmans, 1995.
Vandana, Sister. *Waters of Fire*. Madras: CLS, 1981.
Vellanickal, Matthew. "Drink from the Source of the Living Water." *Biblebhashyam* 5 (1979) 309–18.
———. "Discipleship according to the Gospel of John." *Jeevadhara* 56 (1980) 131–47.
———. "The Gospel of John in the Indian Context." *Jeevadhara* 68 (1982) 140–55.
Verhey, Allen. *The Great Reversal: Ethics and the New Testament*. Grand Rapids: Eerdmans, 1984.
Vivekananda, Swami. *The Yogas and Other Works*. Edited by Swami Nikhilananda. New York: Ramakrishna-Vivekananda Center, 1953.
Vogel, Hans-Jochen. "Nicodemus—Bible Study of John 3:1–21." In *Before the Cock Crows: Biblical and Theological Reflections in the Student Christian Movements in Europe Today*, edited by G. Köberlin, 74–86. Madras: CLS, 1983.

Bibliography

Volf, Miroslav. *Exclusion and Embrace: A Theological Exploration of Identity, Otherness, and Reconciliation*. Nashville: Abingdon, 1996.
Værge, Johannes. *Johannesevangeliet*. Copenhagen: Danske Bibelselskab, 1996.
Ward, Keith. *Concepts of God: Images of the divine in five religious traditions*. Oxford: Oneworld, 1998.
Warren, Max. *A Theology of Attention*. Madras: CLS, 1971.
Weber, Hans-Ruedi. *Experiments with Bible Study*. Geneva: World Council of Churches, 1981.
Wessels, Anton. *Images of Jesus: How Jesus is Perceived and Portrayed in Non-European Cultures*. London: SCM, 1990.
West, Gerald. *Contextual Bible Study*. Pietermaritzburg: Cluster, 1999.
Wieser, Thomas. "The Way of Life." *Ecumenical Review* 34 (1982) 221–27.
Wikström, Ove. *Det blændende mørke*. Translated by Lage Jennervall and Elizabeth Knox-Seith. Copenhagen: Anis, 2003.

www.ingramcontent.com/pod-product-compliance
Lightning Source LLC
Chambersburg PA
CBHW070323230426
43663CB00011B/2201